AF766728

VETERAN INCARCERATION

Through qualitative interviews with formerly incarcerated veterans, this book focuses on the lived experiences, and behaviors associated with the incarceration of veterans. Guided by the life-course perspective, the authors have identified novel turning point behaviors linked with incarceration. They provide an in-depth and nuanced understanding of veteran incarceration, blend veteran-centric behaviors with known incarceration factors (i.e., substance use and mental health disorders), and provide a glimpse into how these behaviors interact with other known factors (i.e., homelessness and unemployment). Understanding veterans' lived experiences with incarceration can provide policymakers and practitioners with the foundation for disrupting the incarceration cycle and positively impacting mental health and substance use problems, homelessness, and unemployment. The authors discuss social and health policy implications and provide recommendations on future research on veteran populations. This volume is enlightening and inspiring for researchers and scholars in public health, social work, and sociology/criminal justice programs, as well as all policymakers and practitioners concerned with veterans' adjustment to civilian life.

Jason D. Flake is a veteran of the armed forces and retired law enforcement officer. He is a research scientist at the VA North Texas Health Care System conducting research that focuses on identifying mental health and substance use treatment barriers among justice-involved veterans.

Steven L. Arxer is Professor of Sociology in the Department of Sociology & Anthropology at the University of Texas at Arlington. He also serves as co-investigator and lead qualitative researcher on a study that explores intervention strategies to help veteran's better transition from prison back to society.

James P. LePage is the Associate Chief of Staff for Research and Development for the VA North Texas Health Care and a professor in the Department of Psychiatry at the University of Texas Southwestern Medical Center. He also serves as a principal investigator on the Veterans Affairs' Office of Research and Development funded research consortium "Supporting Employment and Resources for Veterans' Economic Security."

VETERAN INCARCERATION

Lived Experience and Pathways to Rehabilitation

Jason D. Flake, Steven L. Arxer and James P. LePage

Routledge
Taylor & Francis Group
NEW YORK AND LONDON

Designed cover image: Getty Images

First published 2026
by Routledge
605 Third Avenue, New York, NY 10158

and by Routledge
4 Park Square, Milton Park, Abingdon, Oxon, OX14 4RN

Routledge is an imprint of the Taylor & Francis Group, an informa business

ISBN: 978-1-032-86307-8 (hbk)
ISBN: 978-1-032-86304-7 (pbk)
ISBN: 978-1-003-52230-0 (ebk)

DOI: 10.4324/9781003522300

Typeset in Times New Roman
by Newgen Publishing UK

CONTENTS

ACKNOWLEDGMENTS

This work was supported, in part, by Merit Review Award # I01 RX003225 from the United States (U.S.) Department of Veterans Affairs Rehabilitation Research and Development Service, James P. LePage, principal investigator. We would like to thank all the veterans who participated in our study, without their cooperation and insight into their lived experiences this book would not be possible.

1

THE PERSONAL IMPACT OF INCARCERATION

Introduction

Imagine a disease, a virus, that infects over six million Americans; a virus that will have over 400,000 new infections this year. Veterans are at a 70% greater risk of contracting the disease. This disease affects racial and ethnic minority members at a high rate and is particularly aggressive in Black males in their early 30s where as many as 6.4% will contract the disease. The likelihood of dying within two weeks of contracting the disease is 12 times that of those without the disease. The increase in mortality continues for more than a year with death rates of 3.5 times higher than expected almost two years after infection. Of significant concern, those with the disease are 3.4 times more likely to commit suicide. The disease will interfere with employment resulting in 10–23% less work over a lifetime. Those with the disease are more likely to become homeless and divorced. Additionally, those with the virus have a 30% chance of ending up arrested within three years of contracting the virus. If such a virus existed what would our response be? What should our response be?

The disease described is not a medical condition but the real consequences and realities facing those released from prison. The most recent numbers from the Bureau of Justice Statistics (Carson & Kluckow, 2023) report there were 1,230,000 being held in US state and federal prisons, 663,000 held in local jails, and over 3.6 million under community supervision, that is, parole and probation (Buehler & Kluckow, 2024). Most of these prisoners will return to the community. Annually, the number released from prison is high with 448,000 prisoners released from state and federal prisons in 2022 (Carson & Kluckow, 2023).

The overall imprisonment rate in the US is 449 per 100,000 adults; however, incarcerations are disproportionately from ethnic and racial minority

DOI: 10.4324/9781003522300-1

populations with 69% of male inmates coming from these groups. White males have an incarceration rate population of 181 per 100,000, while 434 per 100,000 Hispanics and 901 per 100,000 African American are currently incarcerated. The highest rate is among African American males, age 30–34, where 6.2% are incarcerated (Carson, 2022). Data from the early 2000s found that 4.9% of all males were or had been incarcerated in prison, with 7.7% of Latino males and 16.6% of all African American males (Bonzcar, 2003).

US veterans are at high risk for involvement with the criminal justice system. Snowden and colleagues (2017) evaluated nationally representative data of over 450,000 US civilians and former military including whether the person had been arrested and jailed, from the National Study on Drug Use and Health. Veterans in the evaluation (n = 20,508) were over 70% more likely than non-veterans to be arrested and booked. Even after statistically controlling for gender, race, employment, and family income, veterans were still 36% more likely to be arrested and 21% more likely to be on probation in the past 12 months. It is important to note that other studies have found lower rates (e.g., Tsai et al., 2022), but the Snowden work is the most comprehensive evaluation that makes a direct comparison between veterans and non-veterans.

The make-up of incarcerated veterans in prison are different from incarcerated non-veterans on a number of key factors. In the most recent Department of Justice reports on veteran incarceration (Maruschak et al., 2021c), veterans incarcerated were significantly more likely to be male, 98% vs 92%, and older, 52 years vs 38 years compared to non-veterans. Half were White, non-Hispanic, compared to non-veterans where only 29% were White non-Hispanic. There was a higher rate of marriage or previous marriage in veterans, 76% vs 44%, and a higher percentage that had at least graduated high school, 72% vs 39% (Bronson et al., 2015). Veterans were less likely to be in prison for drug and property crimes but more likely to be incarcerated for violent sexual crimes; they were also slightly less likely to have been incarcerated previously. Overall, the differences between incarcerated veterans and non-veterans reflect the differences between the veteran and the non-veteran populations outside of prison.

What to Expect after Incarceration

Those released from prison have unique challenges after release that will affect their overall success and well-being. We present here evidence related to the most significant negative events associated with incarceration.

Rearrests

Re-incarceration rates in the US are catastrophically high. The US Department of Justice performed perhaps the most comprehensive reviews of reincarceration to date (Alper & Durose, 2018; Antenangeli & Durose, 2021; Durose & Antenangeli, 2021). In a nine-year follow-up of prisoners released in 2005 (Alper & Durose, 2018), data was collected on 70,878 individuals released from prison from 30 US states in 2005; this sample was drawn from a total number of 412,731 prisoners released who had been sentenced for more than one year. Women prisoners were oversampled to improve the precision of the estimates. After the number of prisoner deaths during the follow-up period and those with insufficient records were removed, the final sample was 67,966. Rearrests excluded parole or probation violations, focusing the evaluation on new crimes.

The findings were disheartening and highlight the significant struggles to avoid contact with the legal system after release from prison. The released individuals had a combined total of an estimated 1,994,000 arrests over the nine-year follow-up. There was a subset of high-arrest individuals, approximately 23% of the sample, accounting for half of the total arrests. However, these high-arrest individuals do not account for the catastrophically high rearrest rates over the entire sample.

Among all released prisoners, the first year after release showed the highest rate of rearrest with 44% having their first arrest that year. By the third year after release, 68% of all released prisoners had been rearrested. By the end of the nine-year follow-up, 83% had been arrested at least once for a new crime.

There were a number of noted patterns in the rearrest data. Those most likely to be arrested in the first year after release tended to be male, younger (age 24 or below), and Black or Hispanic. Overall, male prisoners were more likely to be arrested in the first year than female prisoners; however after year one, the rates were similar. Black and Hispanic prisoners were more likely to be arrested during the first year than White prisoners. By the ninth year, 87% of Black, 81% of Hispanic, and 81% of White prisoners had been rearrested. Property crimes (e.g., theft, burglary, robbery) and drug-related crimes were the most common reasons for rearrests throughout the follow-up years. Those who were initially convicted of a violent crime were more likely to be rearrested for a subsequent violent crime than those initially convicted of a property or drug crime.

A companion report (Antenangeli & Durose, 2021) followed 73,600 individuals released from prison from 24 states in 2008 for 10 years. The results were generally consistent with the nine-year follow-up with 66% of prisoners being rearrested within the first three years, and 82% being rearrested within 10 years. This companion report does expand on the earlier findings in a number of key ways. The first is the finding that 61% of those released returned to prison within the 10-year period for either a new crime or a parole/probation violation and almost half returned to prison within three years. Overall, those released from serving violent crime sentences were less likely to be rearrested compared to those convicted of a property or drug-related crime; though consistent with previous findings, they were more likely to be arrested for a subsequent violent crime. Not surprisingly, those convicted of violent crimes served longer sentences than other types of crimes. Those who served shorter sentences had a higher rearrest rate than those who served longer sentences; however, the impact of longer sentences on the age at release was not accounted for in the model.

Although the various Department of Justice studies have followed individuals released from different states, one important and encouraging fact is the rates of rearrests within the first five years after release appear to be declining. Rearrest rates within five years were 77% of those released in 2005 (Alper & Durose, 2018), 75% in 2008 (Antenangeli & Durose, 2021), and 71% in 2012 (Durose & Antenangeli, 2021). Though methodological and sampling differences exist creating cautious interpretations, this change is also reflected in return-to-prison rates where the five-year rate of those released in 2005 was estimated at 55% (Durose et al., 2014) compared to 46% of those released in 2012 (Durose & Antenangeli, 2021).

Veterans are not immune to the high rate of reincarceration. Statistics from the Department of Justice found 73% of male veteran prisoners had been incarcerated in the past, jail or prison. Veterans were more likely to have been arrested 1–3 times but less likely to be arrested 4 or more times compared to non-veterans.

Death

Those released from prison demonstrate a significantly higher than expected likelihood of premature death. This phenomenon initially received widespread documentation by Binswanger (Binswanger et al., 2007) where statewide data of over 30,000 prisoners found the risk of death within two weeks of release was 12.7 times that of those not incarcerated, adjusted for age, sex, and race. Higher death rates continue for more than a year where, at 1.9 years post-release, death rates of released offenders were 3.4 times that of nonreleased individuals.

More recently, in one of the largest studies of its kind, Khatri and colleagues (Khatri et al., 2025) collected data from the American Community Survey from 2008, the Vera Institute of Justice Incarceration Trends Dataset, and the National Death Index to evaluate death rates between those who had recently been incarcerated and those that had not. This combination, after exclusion of missing data, resulted in the evaluation of 3,255,000 individuals, of which approximately 45,000 were incarcerated in 2008. Results found formerly incarcerated individuals had a 39% higher rate of all-cause mortality and over three times the risk for death by overdose than rates of nonincarcerated individuals

Other studies have had similar findings with mortality ratios ranging from 1.0 to 9.4 (Merrall et al., 2010). The premature death rates are not found solely in the US with similar findings in the Netherlands (Dirkzwager et al., 2012), England (Farrell & Marsden, 2008), Russia (Pridemore, 2014), and France (Verger et al., 2003). Death rates may be more pronounced in Black populations (Bovell-Ammon et al., 2021).

There are a number of potential causes, contributors, and predictors of the premature mortality observed which are associated with incarceration. Substance overdose has been identified as the primary cause of death (Binswanger et al., 2013; Forsyth et al., 2014; Jama-Alol et al., 2015), but other factors include suicide (Binswanger, Redmond, et al., 2012; Binswanger, Stern et al., 2007; Jones & Maynard, 2013; Pratt et al., 2010; Verger et al., 2003; Wortzel et al., 2009) and violence (Binswanger et al., 2007; Lize et al., 2015). Time incarcerated has also been shown to be associated with premature death after release (Patterson, 2013).

A large-scale study from the US state of Minnesota (Hill et al., 2024) examined the one-year risk of death based on the US Census American Community Survey, the Minnesota Department of Health's Office of Vital Records, and the Minnesota Department of Corrections. Using a sample from March 1, 2020, to December 31, 2021, 6261 individuals were identified who had been released back to the community from prison. These were compared to a general population sample of more than four million.

Results found all-cause mortality to be higher for those released from prison compared to the general population. Those released from incarceration were twice as likely to die as those not incarcerated even after controlling for age, gender, and the timeframe evaluated. The risk for overdose death was especially striking with a rate in the incarcerated group being more than 25 times that of the general population.

Medical and mental health conditions may also contribute to premature death (Binswanger et al., 2007; Spaulding et al., 2015; Verger et al., 2003). Data from the Bureau of Justice Statistics (Maruschak et al., 2025) found 40% of jail and prison inmates had a chronic medical condition, 1.5 times the rate of a standardized general population sample, and 24% reported more than one chronic disease. The large-scale evaluations of mental illness in prison by the US Department of Justice (Bronson et al., 2015; James & Glaze, 2006; Maruschak et al., 2021a) found between 26% and 40% of prisoners were receiving treatment for mental health problems and more than half had a substance use disorder.

The increased risk of death was also present in the veteran population. In a large sample, five million veterans' records were evaluated and found that those with histories of incarceration seen by the VA's Veterans Justice Program services were 150% more likely to die by suicide (Palframan et al., 2020). Of note, LePage and colleagues found death rates of veterans in the first year after prison were 60% higher than nonincarcerated veterans, even after controlling for medical conditions (LePage et al., 2016). Death rates were also collected in an evaluation of 30,000 prisoners released from state prison (Wortzel et al., 2012). Overall, veterans had a higher unadjusted all-cause death rate and higher rates of overdose. However, after statistically controlling for age, race, sex, and length of incarceration, veterans were found to have similar death rates to non-veterans. The findings suggest that veterans share an equal risk as non-veterans in premature death associated with release from incarceration.

Family Relationships

Incarceration has been shown to have a deleterious effect on family and family relationships. Divorce is a common consequence of incarceration. Among married men, those incarcerated were twice as likely to become divorced or separated compared to those not incarcerated, 59% vs 32% respectively (Lopoo & Western, 2005). The divorce rate is similar to another study (Massoglia et al., 2011) that found 55% of prisoners who were married at the time of incarceration were divorced after incarceration with approximately 40% occurring after release. If married in the year before incarceration, there is an additional 20% chance of divorce within five years of release.

There are several apparent contributors to the high divorce rate. These include time incarcerated (Massoglia et al., 2011), negative financial situations (Kincaid & Lawrence, 2011; Schwartz-Soicher et al., 2011), interpersonal styles developed in prison (Haney, 1997; Holzer et al., 2003; Ruiz et al., 2014), time separated (Massoglia et al., 2011), and general mental health consequences of incarceration (Schnittker et al., 2012). This risk to relationships may be more pronounced in populations that are more vulnerable; for example, 55% of men with HIV lost their relationships while incarcerated (Khan et al., 2011).

In a large study evaluating the associations between incarceration and divorce over a six-year period, 1919 young married couples were interviewed as part of the National Longitudinal Study of Adolescent Health (Siennick et al., 2014). Though the overall sample was large, only 5.4% of couples experienced an incarceration during the follow-up period. Though a relatively small group, there were a number of important findings. Incarceration during the marriage was associated with shorter marriages. Risk for divorce was higher in those incarcerated even when factors such as substance use and age were statistically controlled, with almost twice the chance of divorce compared to couples without incarceration. Even relatively short periods of incarceration predicted divorce. The increased likelihood of divorce was relatively steady at about 15% per year, i.e. 15% in year one and almost 60% by year six. Some of the apparent collateral impacts of incarceration on the marriage included increased likelihood of economic strain, marital violence, and extramarital sex.

The children of those incarcerated also are impacted. It has been estimated by the US Department of Justice that half of those incarcerated are parents of at least one minor child (Maruschak et al., 2021b). This translates into approximately

1.5 million people aged 17 or younger having a parent incarcerated in a US state or federal prison. The average age of a child with an incarcerated parent was 9 to 10, with approximately 19% of the children of parents in state prison aged 4 or below. Black and Hispanic prisoners were more likely to have a minor child than White prisoners.

Children with a parent who has been incarcerated are at high risk for a number of negative events and experiences. The most comprehensive evaluation of parental incarceration's impact on children was conducted in the 2010s, using the National Survey of Children's Health (NSCH). The NSCH was a survey conducted on 95,000 children, aged 0–17, and designed to assess children's physical and mental health, as well as other factors which may impact physical and mental health. Turney and her contributors (Turney, 2017) compared children's health between those with a parent incarcerated and those without. No information was available on the parent (sentence length, time out of house, specific crime, etc.), other than a binary incarcerated/not-incarcerated descriptor. What made this study stand out is the survey allowed the author to statistically control for known socio-relevant variables associated with incarceration, factors such as race, income, employment, education, access to care, household mental illness, etc. This assured that, to the extent allowed by the data, findings focused only on the unique contribution of parental incarceration. The findings were illuminating. Initially before controlling for any variables, children with parents incarcerated demonstrated a wide range of difficulties from poor overall health, to obesity, to depression, to bone problems. After controlling demographic and socio-relevant variables, a number of significant differences remained. These were learning disabilities, ADD/ADHD, behavior and conduct problems, developmental delays, and speech limitations. Taken together, this study highlights the overall potential impact of parental incarceration on academic and development progress, relative to similar children without parental incarceration.

Other more recent studies have added to this information. For example, children of incarcerated parents in rural settings, compared to urban settings, are more likely to be sent into foster care. These children may have difficulties with caregiver attachment (Poehlmann-Tynan et al., 2017), pre-age-15 sexual activity (Turney & Goldberg, 2019), and earlier drug and alcohol use (Forster et al., 2025). Also, in Dallaire's review, evidence is presented that children of incarcerated parents experience increased stigma, inhibited peer relationships, and aggressive behavior (Dallaire et al., 2025). Finally, recent data finds that incarceration, when combined with housing instability and family violence, is a strong predictor of non-violent 'delinquent' behavior (Talaugon & Turanovic, 2025).

There has been little focus on the specific impact of incarceration on families and relationships of veterans. However, it is expected that similar family consequences of incarceration would be experienced in veteran families.

Employment

As a population, those with felony histories have demonstrated significant difficulties obtaining employment (Carson et al., 2021; Decker et al., 2015; Garin et al., 2025; Western et al., 2015). For example, Western found that six months after release, only 52.6% of individuals had found employment (Western et al., 2015).

Gordon and colleagues (Gordon et al., 2023) conducted one of the most comprehensive evaluations using data from the National Longitudinal Survey of Youth 1979. Using a nationally representative sample, Gordon evaluated the data from 9600 participants for the convergence of education, employment, and incarceration. Rates of incarceration (defined by this study as jail and/or prison) revealed Black males with less than high school education had experienced incarceration at the highest rate 27.5%, as compared to 13.2% for White less than high school education participants. Related to earnings, Gordon found first time incarceration was associated with 32% lower lifetime earnings and six fewer years of employment for Black participants and 51% lower earnings and 10 fewer years of employment for White participants compared to their non-incarcerated counterparts.

The impact of incarceration is also present in the veteran population. For example, Kelton and colleagues (Kelton et al., 2023) evaluated factors associated with incarceration in 2900 US veterans. Those reporting employment were significantly less likely to report a history of incarceration, 20%, than those who were unemployed, 30%.

Housing

Homelessness is a significant possible outcome for those being released from prison. An evaluation from the Prison Policy Institute found individuals who are incarcerated one time are 7 times more likely to become homeless, and those who were incarcerated more than one time are 13 times more likely to experience homelessness than those without a history of incarceration (Couloute, 2018).

There is a strong reciprocal association between homelessness and incarceration (Moschion & Johnson, 2019). In a large meta-analysis of 79 studies which included over 1.2 million veterans who had a history of incarceration, 40% had a history of homelessness (Edwards et al., 2025). In a survey of 1600 incarcerated Veterans, 27% identified being homeless at some time in the 12 months prior to incarceration (Elbogen et al., 2023). In an evaluation of 7260 veterans, those with a history of incarceration, the largest predictor of homelessness were 5 times as likely to be experiencing homelessness or housing instability (Umucu et al., 2024).

Overall, a there is strong evidence of incarcerations association with homelessness (Tsai et al., 2016; Tsai & Rosenheck, 2015). Depending on the setting and population, the incarceration history percentage of those in homeless programs or living in homeless shelters generally range from approximately 25% to over 70%. (Kushel et al., 2005; Levitt et al., 2009; Petrovich et al., 2014; Tejani et al., 2014). For those homeless and with severe mental illnesses, incarceration history rates were between 48% and 67% (Roy et al., 2014). Time incarcerated may also be a predictor of homelessness as veterans with incarceration of greater than six months have been found to spend more days homeless after release than those with less than six months of incarceration (McGuire & Rosenheck, 2004). The concern about the high prevalence of histories of incarceration and homeless service use is compounded as homelessness is a risk factor for reincarceration (Metraux & Culhane, 2004; Roy et al., 2014).

A number of factors have been shown to predict homelessness after incarceration including age, race, and substance use disorders (Remster, 2021). Adding to the difficulties after incarceration, there are frequently barriers imposed by communities or landlords related to where ex-offenders can live, though efforts from the US Department of Housing and Urban Development have been made to change this pattern (McCain, 2022).

Summary

As can be seen, the impact of prison on the lives of those released from incarceration can be catastrophic. However, though much is known about formerly incarcerated veterans through the evaluation of various data sources, there is still limited focus on understanding the lived experience of those released from prison. Both researchers and practitioners now generally agree that engaging veterans in this way helps research and services to be more relevant and tailored to the experiences and needs of the veteran population.

Organization of the Book

This book centers on the voices of justice-involved veterans to understand incarceration pathways from a veteran standpoint. From this vantage point, this book offers an understanding of what veterans want to see happen in justice research and outreach.

Chapters 2 and 3 provide the contextual and conceptual foundation for the book. Chapter 2 surveys current knowledge about veteran incarceration in the US, identifying both established contributing factors and critical gaps in understanding. Chapter 3 builds on this by focusing on the importance of veterans' lived experiences as a central lens for research, reviewing prior studies and demonstrating why an experiential focus is essential for understanding incarceration pathways. These chapters establish the rationale for the study and frame the unique contribution of a veteran-centered approach.

Chapters 4 and 5 explore the primary theoretical frameworks that inform our analysis. Chapter 4 examines *veteran identity*. We discuss how it is formed, sustained after service, and how it shapes treatment-seeking behaviors and interactions with healthcare and social service providers. Chapter 5 applies a *life course perspective* to highlight key turning points and transitions in veterans' lives, linking these moments to pathways toward or away from incarceration. Read together, these chapters provide the conceptual bridge between the study's broader focus on identity and the concrete life events that structure incarceration trajectories.

Chapter 6 details our study's methodology, including participant recruitment, trust-building strategies, data collection, and analysis. Special attention is paid to the relational and ethical considerations needed when conducting qualitative research with veterans who have experienced incarceration.

Chapters 7 through 11 represents our empirical findings, each focusing on a different dimension of veterans' experiences: service history, reintegration challenges, coping strategies, negative life events, and institutional interactions. These chapters integrate veterans' narratives with analysis, identifying patterns that link personal experiences, identity, and critical life events to incarceration risk. Some chapters also include preliminary practice and policy considerations tied to their thematic findings.

Finally, Chapter 12 concludes the book by synthesizing the study's findings and emphasizing the significance of veteran identity in understanding incarceration pathways. It draws out the broader implications for research, policy, and practice, offering concrete recommendations for program development, evaluation, and systemic reform. We hope that by the end of this book, readers will have a greater understanding of the lives of those leaving prison and appreciation for their barriers and experiences.

References

Alper, M., & Durose, M. R. (2018). *2018 update on prisoner recidivism: A 9-year follow-up period (2005–2014)* (NCJ 250975). U.S. Department of Justice, Office of Justice Programs, Bureau of Justice Statistics. https://bjs.ojp.gov/library/publications/2018-update-prisoner-recidivism-9-year-follow-period-2005-2014

Antenangeli, L., & Durose, M. R. (2021). *Recidivism of prisoners released in 24 States in 2008: A 10-year follow-up period (2008–2018)* (NCJ 256094). U.S. Department of Justice, Office of Justice Programs, Bureau of Justice Statistics. https://bjs.ojp.gov/BJS_PUB/rpr24s0810yfup0818/Web%20content/508%20compliant%20PDFs

Binswanger, I. A., Blatchford, P. J., Mueller, S. R., & Stern, M. F. (2013). Mortality after prison release: Opioid overdose and other causes of death, risk factors, and time trends from 1999 to 2009. *Annals of Internal Medicine, 159*(9), 592–600. https://doi.org/10.7326/0003-4819-159-9-201311050-00005

Binswanger, I. A., Redmond, N., Steiner, J. F., & Hicks, L. S. (2012). Health disparities and the criminal justice system: An agenda for further research and action. *Journal of*

Urban Health: Bulletin of the New York Academy of Medicine, 89(1), 98–107. https://doi.org/10.1007/s11524-011-9614-1

Binswanger, I. A., Stern, M. F., Deyo, R. A., Heagerty, P. J., Cheadle, A., Elmore, J. G., & Koepsell, T. D. (2007). Release from prison—A high risk of death for former inmates. *The New England Journal of Medicine, 356*(2), 157–165. https://doi.org/10.1056/NEJMsa064115

Bonzcar, T. P. (2003). *Prevalence of imprisonment in the U.S. population, 1974–2001* (NCJ 197976). U.S. Department of Justice, Office of Justice Programs, Bureau of Justice Statistics. www.bjs.gov/index.cfm?ty=pbdetail&iid=1042

Bovell-Ammon, B. J., Xuan, Z., Paasche-Orlow, M. K., & LaRochelle, M. R. (2021). Association of incarceration with mortality by race from a national longitudinal cohort study. *JAMA Network Open, 4*(12), e2133083. https://doi.org/10.1001/jamanetworkopen.2021.33083

Bronson, J., Carson, E. A., Noonan, M., & Berzofsky, M. (2015). *Veterans in prison and jail, 2011–12* (NCJ 249144). U.S. Department of Justice, Office of Justice Programs, Bureau of Justice Statistics. https://bjs.ojp.gov/content/pub/pdf/vpj1112.pdf

Buehler, E. D., & Kluckow, R. (2024). *Correctional populations in the United States, 2022 – Statistical tables* (NCJ 308699). https://bjs.ojp.gov/document/cpus22st.pdf

Carson, E. A. (2022). *Prisoners in 2021* (NCJ 305125). U.S. Department of Justice, Office of Justice Programs, Bureau of Justice Statistics. https://bjs.ojp.gov/sites/g/files/xyckuh236/files/media/document/p21st.pdf

Carson, E. A., Bhaskar, R., & Porter, S. R. (2021). *Employment of persons released from federal prison in 2010* (NCJ 303147). U.S. Department of Justice, Office of Justice Programs, Bureau of Justice Statistics. https://bjs.ojp.gov/content/pub/pdf/eprfp10.pdf

Carson, E. A., & Kluckow, R. (2023). *Prisoners in 2022 – Statistical tables* (NCJ 307149). U.S. Department of Justice, Office of Justice Programs, Bureau of Justice Statistics. https://bjs.ojp.gov/document/p22st.pdf

Couloute, L. (2018). *Nowhere to go: Homelessness among formerly incarcerated people.* Prison Policy Initiative. www.prisonpolicy.org/reports/housing.html

Dallaire, D. H., Traver, J. M., & Forester, S. L. (2025). Parental incarceration and pediatric health. In M. H. Bornstein & P. E. Shah (Eds.), *APA handbook of pediatric psychology, developmental-behavioral pediatrics, and developmental science: Developmental science and developmental origins of risk and resilience in childhood and adolescence* (pp. 583–606). American Psychological Association. https://doi.org/10.1037/0000413-027

Decker, S. H., Ortiz, N., Spohn, C., & Hedberg, E. (2015). Criminal stigma, race, and ethnicity: The consequences of imprisonment for employment. *Journal of Criminal Justice, 43*(2), 108–121. https://doi.org/10.1016/j.jcrimjus.2015.02.002

Dirkzwager, A., Nieuwbeerta, P., & Blokland, A. (2012). Effects of first-time imprisonment on postprison mortality: A 25-year follow-up study with a matched control group. *Journal of Research in Crime and Delinquency, 49*(3), 383–419. https://doi.org/10.1177/0022427811415534

Durose, M. R., & Antenangeli, L. (2021). *Recidivism of prisoners released in 34 States in 2012: A 5-year follow-up period (2012–2017)* (NCJ 255947). U.S. Department of Justice, Office of Justice Programs, Bureau of Justice Statistics. https://bjs.ojp.gov/sites/g/files/xyckuh236/files/media/document/rpr34s125yfup1217.pdf

Durose, M. R., Cooper, A. D., & Snyder, H. N. (2014). *Recidivism of prisoners released in 30 states in 2005: Patterns from 2005 to 2010* (NCJ 244205). U.S. Department of Justice, Office of Justice Programs, Bureau of Justice Statistics. https://bjs.ojp.gov/content/pub/pdf/rprts05p0510.pdf

Edwards, E. R., Fortuna, A., Holliday, R., Addison, H., & Tsai, J. (2025). Prevalence of mental health conditions, substance use disorders, suicidal ideation and attempts, and experiences of homelessness among veterans with criminal-legal involvement: A meta-analysis. *Clinical Psychology Review, 115,* 102533. https://doi.org/10.1016/j.cpr.2024.102533

Elbogen, E. B., DuBois, C. M., Finlay, A. K., Clark, S., Kois, L. E., Wagner, H. R., & Tsai, J. (2023). How often does homelessness precede criminal arrest in veterans? Results from the US survey of prison inmates. *American Journal of Orthopsychiatry, 93*(6), 486–493. https://doi.org/10.1037/ort0000693

Farrell, M., & Marsden, J. (2008). Acute risk of drug-related death among newly released prisoners in England and Wales. *Addiction, 103*(2), 251–255. https://doi.org/10.1111/j.1360-0443.2007.02081.x

Forster, M., Shaverdi, A., Zhang, X., Toledo-Corral, C. M., & Grigsby, T. J. (2025). Family incarceration and adolescent nicotine, alcohol, and cannabis use: A coarsened exact matching approach. *Addictive Behaviors, 164*, 108270. https://doi.org/10.1016/j.addbeh.2025.108270

Forsyth, S. J., Alati, R., Ober, C., Williams, G. M., & Kinner, S. A. (2014). Striking subgroup differences in substance-related mortality after release from prison. *Addiction, 109*(10), 1676–1683. https://doi.org/10.1111/add.12646

Garin, A., Koustas, D., McPherson, C., Norris, S., Pecenco, M., Rose, E. K., Shem-Tov, Y., & Weaver, J. (2025). The impact of incarceration on employment, earnings, and tax filing. *Econometrica, 93*(2), 503–538. https://doi.org/10.3982/ECTA22028

Gordon, G., Jones, J. B., Neelakantan, U., & Athreya, K. (2023). Incarceration, employment, and earnings: Dynamics and differences. *Review of Economic Dynamics, 51*, 677–697. https://doi.org/10.1016/j.red.2023.06.007

Haney, C. (1997). Psychology and the limits to prison pain: Confronting the coming crisis in Eighth Amendment law. *Psychology, Public Policy, and Law, 3*(4), 499–588. https://doi.org/10.1037/1076-8971.3.4.499

Hill, K., Bodurtha, P. J., Winkelman, T. N. A., & Howell, B. A. (2024). Postrelease risk of overdose and all-cause death among persons released from jail or prison: Minnesota, March 2020–December 2021. *American Journal of Public Health, 114*(9), 913–922. https://doi.org/10.2105/AJPH.2024.307723

Holzer, H. J., Raphael, S., & Stroll, M. A. (2003). *Employment barriers facing ex-offenders*. Urban Institute. www.urban.org/sites/default/files/alfresco/publication-pdfs/410855-Employment-Barriers-Facing-Ex-Offenders.PDF

Jama-Alol, K. A., Malacova, E., Ferrante, A., Alan, J., Stewart, L., & Preen, D. (2015). Influence of offence type and prior imprisonment on risk of death following release from prison: A whole-population linked data study. *International Journal of Prisoner Health, 11*(2), 108–118. https://doi.org/10.1108/IJPH-10-2013-0046

James, D. J., & Glaze, L. E. (2006). *Mental health problems of prison and jail inmates* (NCJ 213600). U.S. Department of Justice, Office of Justice Programs, Bureau of Justice Statistics. http://bjs.gov/content/pub/pdf/mhppji.pdf

Jones, D., & Maynard, A. (2013). Suicide in recently released prisoners: A systematic review. *Mental Health Practice, 17*(3), 20–27.

Kelton, K., Van Voorhees, E. E., Elbogen, E. B., Workgroup, V. A. M.-A. M., & Dillon, K. H. (2023). Correlates of incarceration history among military veterans. *Military Psychology, 35*(6), 577–589. https://doi.org/10.1080/08995605.2022.2141049

Khan, M. R., Behrend, L., Adimora, A. A., Weir, S. S., White, B. L., & Wohl, D. A. (2011). Dissolution of primary intimate relationships during incarceration and implications for post-release HIV transmission. *Journal of Urban Health: Bulletin of the New York Academy of Medicine, 88*(2), 365–375. https://doi.org/10.1007/s11524-010-9538-1

Khatri, U. G., Hakes, J. K., Buckler, D., Zebrowski, A., & Winkelman, T. (2025). Individual- and area-level incarceration and mortality. *JAMA Network Open, 8*(6), e2513537–e2513537. https://doi.org/10.1001/jamanetworkopen.2025.13537

Kincaid, E., & Lawrence, A. (2011). *Ex-offender employment opportunities*. National Conference of State Legislatures. www.ncsl.org/documents/cj/pew/ex-offenderreport.pdf

Kushel, M. B., Hahn, J. A., Evans, J. L., Bangsberg, D. R., & Moss, A. R. (2005). Revolving doors: Imprisonment among the homeless and marginally housed population. *American Journal of Public Health, 95*(10), 1747–1752. https://doi.org/10.2105/AJPH.2005.065094

LePage, J. P., Bradshaw, L. D., Cipher, D. J., Crawford, A. M., & Parish-Johnson, J. A. (2016). The association between recent incarceration and inpatient resource use and death rates: Evaluation of a US veteran sample. *Public Health, 134*, 109–113. https://doi.org/10.1016/j.puhe.2016.01.009

Levitt, A. J., Culhane, D. P., DeGenova, J., O'Quinn, P., & Bainbridge, J. (2009). Health and social characteristics of homeless adults in Manhattan who were chronically or not chronically unsheltered. *Psychiatric Services, 60*(7), 978–981. https://doi.org/10.1176/appi.ps.60.7.978

Lize, S. E., Scheyett, A. M., Morgan, C. R., Proescholdbell, S. K., Norwood, T., & Edwards, D. (2015). Violent death rates and risk for released prisoners in North Carolina. *Violence and Victims, 30*(6), 1019–1036. https://doi.org/10.1891/0886-6708.VV-D-13-00137

Lopoo, L. M., & Western, B. (2005). Incarceration and the formation and stability of marital unions. *Journal of Marriage and Family, 67*(3), 721–734. https://doi.org/10.1111/j.1741-3737.2005.00165.x

Maruschak, L. M., Berzofsky, M., & Unangst, J. (2025). *Medical problems of state and federal prisoners and jail inmates, 2011–12* (NCJ 248491). U.S. Department of Justice, Office of Justice Programs, Bureau of Justice Statistics. https://bjs.ojp.gov/content/pub/pdf/mpsfpji1112.pdf

Maruschak, L. M., Bronson, J., & Alper, M. (2021a). *Indicators of mental health problems reported by prisoners* (NCJ 252643). U.S. Department of Justice, Office of Justice Programs, Bureau of Justice Statistics. https://bjs.ojp.gov/media/document/44841

Maruschak, L. M., Bronson, J., & Alper, M. (2021b). *Parents in prison and their minor children* (NCJ 252645). U.S. Department of Justice, Office of Justice Programs, Bureau of Justice Statistics. https://bjs.ojp.gov/content/pub/pdf/pptmcspi16st.pdf

Maruschak, L. M., Bronson, J., & Alper, M. (2021c). *Veterans in prison: Survey of prison inmates, 2016* (NCJ 252646). U.S. Department of Justice, Office of Justice Programs, Bureau of Justice Statistics. https://bjs.ojp.gov/content/pub/pdf/vpspi16st.pdf

Massoglia, M., Remster, B., & King, R. D. (2011). Stigma or separation? Understanding the incarceration-divorce relationship. *Social Forces, 90*(1), 133–155. https://doi.org/10.1093/sf/90.1.133

McCain, D. L. (2022). Implementation of the office of general counsel's guidance on application of fair housing act standards to the use of criminal records by providers of housing and real estate-related transactions. https://nlihc.org/sites/default/files/Sign-On_HUD-PIH_Final.pdf

McGuire, J. F., & Rosenheck, R. A. (2004). Criminal history as a prognostic indicator in the treatment of homeless people with severe mental illness. *Psychiatric Services, 55*(1), 42–48. https://doi.org/10.1176/appi.ps.55.1.42

Merrall, E. L. C., Kariminia, A., Binswanger, I. A., Hobbs, M. S., Farrell, M., Marsden, J., Hutchinson, S. J., & Bird, S. M. (2010). Meta-analysis of drug-related deaths soon after release from prison. *Addiction, 105*(9), 1545–1554. https://doi.org/10.1111/j.1360-0443.2010.02990.x

Metraux, S., & Culhane, D. P. (2004). Homeless shelter use and reincarcertation following prison release. *Criminology and Public Policy, 3*(2), 139–160. https://doi.org/10.1111/j.1745-9133.2004.tb00031.x

Moschion, J., & Johnson, G. (2019). Homelessness and incarceration: A reciprocal relationship? *Journal of Quantitative Criminology, 35*(4), 855–887. https://doi.org/10.1007/s10940-019-09407-y

Palframan, K. M., Blue-Howells, J., Clark, S. C., & McCarthy, J. F. (2020). Veterans justice programs: Assessing population risks for suicide deaths and attempts. *Suicide and Life—Threatening Behavior, 50*(4), 792–804. https://doi.org/10.1111/sltb.12631

Patterson, E. J. (2013). The dose-response of time served in prison on mortality: New York State, 1989-2003. *American Journal of Public Health, 103*(3), 523–528. https://doi.org/10.2105/AJPH.2012.301148

Petrovich, J. C., Pollio, D. E., & North, C. S. (2014). Characteristics and service use of homeless veterans and nonveterans residing in a low-demand emergency shelter. *Psychiatric Services, 65*(6), 751–757. https://doi.org/10.1176/appi.ps.201300104

Poehlmann-Tynan, J., Burnson, C., Runion, H., & Weymouth, L. A. (2017). Attachment in young children with incarcerated fathers. *Development and Psychopathology, 29*(2), 389–404. https://doi.org/10.1017/S0954579417000062

Pratt, D., Appleby, L., Piper, M., Webb, R., & Shaw, J. (2010). Suicide in recently released prisoners: A case-control study. *Psychological Medicine, 40*(5), 827–835. https://doi.org/10.1017/S0033291709991048

Pridemore, W. A. (2014). The mortality penalty of incarceration: Evidence from a population-based case-control study of working-age males. *Journal of Health and Social Behavior, 55*(2), 215–233. https://doi.org/10.1177/0022146514533119

Remster, B. (2021). Homelessness among formerly incarcerated men: Patterns and predictors. *Annals of the American Academy of Political and Social Science, 693*(1), 141–157. https://doi.org/10.1177/0002716221993447

Roy, L., Crocker, A. G., Nicholls, T. L., Latimer, E. A., & Ayllon, A. R. (2014). Criminal behavior and victimization among homeless individuals with severe mental illness: A systematic review. *Psychiatric Services, 65*(6), 739–750. https://doi.org/10.1176/appi.ps.201200515

Ruiz, M. A., Cox, J., Magyar, M. S., & Edens, J. F. (2014). Predictive validity of the Personality Assessment Inventory (PAI) for identifying criminal reoffending following completion of an in-jail addiction treatment program. *Psychological Assessment, 26*(2), 673–678. https://doi.org/10.1037/a0035282

Schnittker, J., Massoglia, M., & Uggen, C. (2012). Out and down: Incarceration and psychiatric disorders. *Journal of Health and Social Behavior, 53*(4), 448–464. https://doi.org/10.1177/0022146512453928

Schwartz-Soicher, O., Geller, A., & Garfinkel, I. (2011). The effect of paternal incarceration on material hardship. *Social Service Review, 85*(3), 447–473. https://doi.org/10.1086/661925

Siennick, S. E., Stewart, E. A., & Staff, J. (2014). Explaining the association between incarceration and divorce. *Criminology: An Interdisciplinary Journal, 52*(3), 371–398. https://doi.org/10.1111/1745-9125.12040

Snowden, D. L., Oh, S., Salas-Wright, C. P., Vaughn, M. G., & King, E. (2017). Military service and crime: New evidence. *Social Psychiatry and Psychiatric Epidemiology, 52*(5), 605–615. https://doi.org/10.1007/s00127-017-1342-8

Spaulding, A. C., Sharma, A., Messina, L. C., Zlotorynska, M., Miller, L., & Binswanger, I. (2015). A comparison of liver disease mortality with HIV and overdose mortality among Georgia prisoners and releasees: A 2-decade cohort study of prisoners incarcerated in 1991. *American Journal of Public Health, 105*(5), e51–e57. https://doi.org/10.2105/AJPH.2014.302546

Talaugon, A. R., & Turanovic, J. J. (2025). Childhood exposure to family violence, residential instability, and parental incarceration: Compounding household adversities and adolescent delinquency. *Journal of Research in Crime & Delinquency, 62*(3), 387–428. https://doi.org/10.1177/00224278241280903

Tejani, N., Rosenheck, R., Tsai, J., Kasprow, W., & McGuire, J. F. (2014). Incarceration histories of homeless veterans and progression through a national supported housing program. *Community Mental Health Journal, 50*(5), 514–519. https://doi.org/10.1007/s10597-013-9611-9

Tsai, J., Edwards, E., Cao, X., & Finlay, A. K. (2022). Disentangling associations between military service, race, and incarceration in the US population. *Psychological Services, 19*(3), 431–442. https://doi.org/10.1037/ser0000537

Tsai, J., Link, B., Rosenheck, R. A., & Pietrzak, R. H. (2016). Homelessness among a nationally representative sample of US veterans: Prevalence, service utilization, and correlates. *Social Psychiatry and Psychiatric Epidemiology, 51*(6), 907–916. https://doi.org/10.1007/s00127-016-1210-y

Tsai, J., & Rosenheck, R. A. (2015). Risk factors for homelessness among US veterans. *Epidemiologic Reviews, 37*(1), 177–195. https://doi.org/10.1093/epirev/mxu004

Turney, K. (2017). Unmet health care needs among children exposed to parental incarceration. *Maternal and Child Health Journal, 21*(5), 1194–1202. https://doi.org/10.1007/s10995-016-2219-2

Turney, K., & Goldberg, R. E. (2019). Paternal incarceration and early sexual onset among adolescents. *Population Research & Policy Review, 38*(1), 95–123. https://doi.org/10.1007/s11113-018-9502-4

Umucu, E., Lee, B., Chang, C., Szymkowiak, D., & Tsai, J. (2024). Geographic and psychosocial correlates of homelessness or unstable housing among US veterans in the midwest. *American Journal of Community Psychology, 74*, 142–151. https://doi.org/10.1002/ajcp.12751

Verger, P., Rotily, M., Prudhomme, J., & Bird, S. (2003). High mortality rates among inmates during the year following their discharge from a French prison. *Journal of Forensic Sciences, 48*(3), 614–616.

Western, B., Braga, A. A., Davis, J., & Sirois, C. (2015). Stress and hardship after prison. *American Journal of Sociology, 120*(5), 1512–1547. https://doi.org/10.1086/681301

Wortzel, H. S., Binswanger, I. A., Anderson, A., & Adler, L. E. (2009). Suicide among incarcerated veterans. *Journal of the American Academy of Psychiatry & the Law, 37*(1), 82–91.

Wortzel, H. S., Blatchford, P., Conner, L., Adler, L. E., & Binswanger, I. A. (2012). Risk of death for veterans on release from prison. *Journal of the American Academy of Psychiatry and the Law, 40*(3), 348–354.

2

CONTRIBUTORS TO VETERAN INCARCERATION

Introduction

As described in Chapter 1, veterans are at a 70% greater risk of incarceration sometime during their lifetime (Snowden et al., 2017). The higher rates of incarceration of US military veterans are potentially influenced by several factors, which, for our purposes, are classified into three categories (1) those existing prior to military enlistment; (2) those primarily associated with military experience; and (3) those that present themselves after leaving the military. The factors associated with the primary timeframes are often interrelated and create a complex web of direct, indirect, and potential contributors to veteran incarceration. In this chapter, we will describe these factors and evaluate them as likely contributors to the increased rate of veteran incarceration.

There are several factors that make veterans unique to non-veterans when evaluating predictors of incarceration. For example, though prior incarceration is a strong predicator of future incarceration, typically, a history of incarceration precludes an individual from entering the military. Additionally, though the lack of high school diploma or equivalent has been associated with incarceration, especially in Black men, at this time, the military predominantly requires a minimum of a high school graduation or a General Education Development (GED) certification prior to enlistment. These are examples of risk factors that are less present in veterans, lowering the overall rate of incarceration in veterans.

For the purposes of our evaluation, we are evaluating factors associated with incarceration to determine if they are a contributor to the higher rate of incarceration of veterans compared to non-veterans. For a risk factor to be a likely contributor to the higher rates of incarceration, it must meet two criteria.

DOI: 10.4324/9781003522300-2

The first is there must be strong evidence that the risk factor is associated with higher rates of incarceration. The second is the risk factor must be present at a higher rate in veterans than the general population. Obviously, if a risk factor is not associated with incarceration, then it cannot be a contributor to veteran incarceration. If the risk factor is associated with incarceration but not present in veterans at a higher rate, it may predict incarceration within the veteran population, but it is not likely contributing to increased rates of incarceration for veterans compared to non-veterans.

Factors Existing Prior to Enlistment

Social science has a long history of attempting to predict or at least describe those factors that are most associated with future incarceration. These studies have focused on broad societal factors which, though potentially not directly causative, are associated with a higher probability of becoming incarcerated.

Race

Race as a predictor of incarceration: One of the strongest predictors of incarceration in the US is race. Those incarcerated in the US are disproportionately from racial and ethnic minorities when compared to those who are White, non-Hispanic. Though Whites comprised 57.8% of the national population (Jensen et al., 2021), they only comprised 46% of those under correctional supervision (incarceration, probation, or parole). In fact, Black individuals represent the highest percentage of those in prison while Whites made up the largest percentage on probation, parole, or in jail (Buehler & Kuckow, 2024). Evaluating federal and state prisons demonstrates the striking association between race and incarceration. Statistics from the Bureau of Justice Statistics (BJS) Prisoners in 2022 (Buehler & Kuckow, 2024) found that 911 per 100,000 Black individuals, 801 native American or Alaskans per 100,000, and 429 Hispanic per 100,000 were incarcerated, compared to 188 Whites. The racial disparity is further highlighted by the fact that between 2021 and 2022 as the population of White persons in the correctional system, that is, incarcerating, prison, and parole, decreased by 4%, the number of Hispanics incarcerated increased by 4% and that of African Americans increased by 1%.

Within the veteran population, there is evidence this disparity exists, though perhaps not as strong as with the non-veteran population. For example, Kelton and colleagues (2023) evaluated a sample of 2904 Iraq and Afghanistan veterans, 700 of who had been incarcerated. Race was found to be a significant predictor of whether the veteran had been incarcerated with veterans from marginalized groups having a 44% increased chance of a history of incarceration. Additional information from the Bureau of Justice Statistics (Maruschak et al., 2021b) finds

50% of male veterans in state prison were White compared to 23% of veterans in prison being Black, again at odds with census data showing nationally 57% of adults are White and 12% are Black.

Race as a predictor of military service: Though the classifications of race have changed over time, minority groups are more likely to join the military. For example, Black service members comprise the second largest group of active military service members at 17.6% (US Department of Defense, 2023) and 16.2% of veterans leaving the military in 2017 (US Department of Veterans Affairs, 2020). This contrasts US census data which finds only 12.1% of the US population is African American (Jensen et al., 2021).

Findings: There is strong evidence that race is a significant risk factor for incarceration and that racial minorities have greater representation in the veteran population. As such, race is a potential contributor to the differences in incarceration rates between veterans and non-veterans.

Education

Education as a predictor of incarceration: Education has also been shown to have a strong association with incarceration (e.g., Jung et al., 2015. In federal prison more than a quarter of federal prisoners, 28%, did not graduate high school (Kyckelhahn & Kerbel, 2023), substantially less than the national rate of 9% (US Census Bureau, 2023). State prisoners had an even lower average education, with Department of Justice surveys of over 1.4 million prisoners finding 62% had less than a high school education (Beatty & Snell, 2021). Education also is highly tied to race with approximately 81% of Black students and 83% of Hispanic students graduating high school compared to 90% of Whites (Irwin et al., 2024). Though only 15% of White males without a high school or equivalent diploma will experience incarceration, 69% of Black males without a high school diploma or equivalent will be incarcerated (Pew Research Center, 2024,).

When comparing veterans and non-veterans, there are noticeable differences in educational achievements. At lower levels of educational attainment, those that are most highly associated with incarceration, less than 0.1% of *active* military, have less than a high school degree compared to 9% of the general US population; rates of veterans with less than a high school equivalent has been estimated at 2.1% compared to 11.7% in the general population (Ward et al., 2024). Veterans have higher percentages of "some college" but overall lower levels of attaining a bachelors; however, gender differences exist with women veterans achieving a bachelor's at higher rates than their non-veteran counterparts (US Census Bureau, 2023; US Department of Veterans Affairs, 2011; Ward et al., 2024).

Education as a predictor of military service: As indicated earlier, enlistment in the US military requires a minimum of a high school diploma or GED, likely truncating the predictability of education as a factor in incarceration. However, though studies are limited, there are several that have included education in their analysis. For example, Greenberg and Rosenheck (2009) evaluated data from local jails and compared incarcerated and nonincarcerated veterans. They found similar rates between groups of those with high school diplomas or GEDs; however, a significantly lower percentage of those incarcerated (31%) had more than a high school education compared to veterans not incarcerated (58%), suggesting higher education may be associated with decreased risk. This finding was mirrored by Kelton and colleagues (Kelton et al., 2023) who found a very small yet significant difference in years of education between veterans with and without a history of incarceration, 13.5 years vs 13.7 years or about a one-month difference; however, after more advanced statistics were employed, education was no longer a significant predictor.

Findings: Though poor education is a predictor of incarceration, there is no evidence this risk is more prevalent in veterans. In fact, the higher education standards may suggest education serves to decrease the risk for broad veteran incarceration. As such, education is not seen as a likely contributor to the differences in incarceration rates between veterans and non-veterans.

Adverse Childhood Factors

Adverse childhood events and incarceration: Adverse childhood events (ACEs), for example, childhood neglect, physical abuse, sexual abuse, family member incarceration, and so on, have been shown to be strong predictors of incarceration (Chassay & Kremer, 2025; Farrington, 2011; Herrenkohl et al., 2017; Lee et al., 2015; Lee & Luo, 2024). These childhood events appear to increase the risk of coming in contact with law enforcement with a greater total of ACEs being associated with a history of arrests (Ashekun et al., 2023; Roos et al., 2016).

Children whose parent has been incarcerated have been shown to be at risk for aggression and violence (Geller et al., 2012; Horton, 2021; Lee & Luo, 2024), so-called delinquent behaviors (Farrington et al., 2025; Talaugon & Turanovic, 2025; Woodard & Copp, 2016), and substance use (Khan et al., 2018; Muentner et al., 2024; Zhao, 2025). This connection extends to veterans. In an evaluation of over 2900 US veterans (Kelton et al., 2023), 37% of veterans with a history of incarceration reported a family history of incarceration compared to only 23% of those veterans without a history of incarceration.

ACEs and veterans: One important study, conducted by Blosnich and colleagues (Blosnich et al., 2014), examined childhood factors associated with joining the military in a sample of over 23,000 US citizens from the Centers for Disease Control and Prevention's Behavioral Risk Factor Surveillance System (BRFSS) surveys. The BRFSS evaluated 11 ACEs, including abuse, divorce, domestic violence, and substance use. The advantage of this study is that it breaks down childhood experiences by the military draft era and the volunteer military era.

The findings from this study are very revealing. In the draft era no ACEs were present at a higher rate in military veterans compared to non-veterans. However, the comparison with the volunteer era is dramatic. Those with military histories from the volunteer era have significantly higher rates on all areas of childhood adverse events including emotional, sexual, and physical abuse, family drug use, and incarcerated household members.

Findings: There is strong evidence that ACEs are a significant risk factor for incarceration and that ACEs are greater in the veteran population. As such, childhood adverse events are a potential contributor to the differences in incarceration rates between veterans and non-veterans.

Factors Associated with Active Military Service

Posttraumatic Stress Disorder (PTSD)

Posttraumatic Stress Disorder and incarceration: There is a logical connection between incarceration and the symptoms of posttraumatic stress disorder (PTSD), which can include aggression or destructive behavior. Estimates suggest that approximately 6% of people in the US, 4% of males and 8% of women, will reach the diagnostic threshold for PTSD during their lifetime, with about 5% experiencing PTSD in a given year (National Center for PTSD, 2025a).

The rates in the general population are lower than the rates of those incarcerated. In a meta-analysis performed by Baranyi and colleagues (2018), publications from 1980 to 2017 were reviewed for data regarding PTSD in incarcerated populations. Prevalence rates ranged from 0.1% to 27% with rates across studies estimated at 6.2% for males and 21% for females. In a large study conducted by the Department of Justice (Maruschak et al., 2021a) of state and federal prisoners, estimates for PTSD based on face-to-face interviews were 14% for state prisoners and 7% of federal prisoners.

PTSD and veterans: Veterans are at a higher risk for developing PTSD, largely due to the high rate of combat and witnessing violence (Pew Research Center, 2019). Rates of PTSD observed for veterans serving in the Operation Iraqi Freedom and Operation Enduring Freedom (OEF/OIF) era starting in 2001 are approximately 15% in the last year, and 29% experiencing PTSD at some point in life (National Center for PTSD, 2025b). Veterans with PTSD also are at high risk for a number of stressors, including substance use (41%), financial difficulties (61%), and access to care difficulties (42%) (Pew Research Center, 2019).

The higher incident rate of PTSD in veterans would suggest a strong contribution of PTSD and veteran incarceration. However, the results are mixed. LePage and colleagues (2016) compared a group of 665 veterans released from state prison to a matched group of nonincarcerated veterans. Though many psychiatric diagnoses were higher in the recently incarcerated population, including bipolar disorder and substance use disorders, the rates of PTSD diagnoses showed no significant difference between those incarcerated and those not incarcerated, 13.4% vs 13.2%, respectively. As another example, in an evaluation of 2900 veterans (Kelton et al., 2023), approximately half with histories of incarceration, basic evaluations of trauma scores on psychological tests found significant differences between those who had been incarcerated and those who had not. However, this study additionally employed more sophisticated evaluation techniques which accounted for a number of other clinical and demographic variables which were associated with incarceration, including age, race, substance use, unemployment, and family history of incarceration. After these variables were accounted for, the level of trauma symptoms was similar between the two groups. Finally, Department of Justice data from 2011 (Bronson et al., 2015) found that veterans surveyed were twice as likely to report having been told they had PTSD than their non-veteran counterparts.

Taylor and colleagues (Taylor et al., 2020) conducted a review and meta-analysis of published reports of veterans, PTSD, and criminal justice involvement. Data from the ten studies evaluated found an overall trend toward PTSD's association and increased criminal justice involvement with 6 of the 10 studies demonstrating a significant positive association but 4 demonstrating no significant association; overall the likelihood of having an arrest for violence was estimated at 60% higher for those with PTSD. One caveat was it was unknown why PTSD was associated with incarceration leaving room for other factors such as substance use, aggression, or other cooccurring mental illnesses to contribute.

Findings: Overall, though there is a logical and easy-to-perceive connection between PTSD and combat, and prison; support for this in the literature is mixed. However, as there is evidence of PTSD being associated with incarceration and PTSD is more prevalent in veterans, PTSD should be considered contributor to the differences in incarceration rates between veterans and non-veterans. It is important to note that other factors such as substance use, childhood trauma, race, and unemployment may better explain the association

Combat Exposure

Veterans and combat exposure: Combat exposure, an event almost exclusively experienced in veterans, is closely associated with PTSD. In a Pew Research Institute (Pew Research Center, 2019) study, the combat and deployment experiences of 1284 veterans were collected. Among veterans who served the military post 2001, 49% reported combat experience, significantly higher than those that served before 2001, 24%. Sixty-two percent of combat veterans know someone who was killed while in the military. The high percentage of recent service members experiencing combat contributes to the high rates of PTSD, estimated at a lifetime prevalence rate of 29% for OEF/OIF veterans (National Center for PTSD, 2025b).

Combat and incarceration: One prevailing theory has been that those exposed to combat may be more likely to commit violence and potentially other crimes; however, the literature on this is somewhat mixed. Approximately 28% of state and 21% of federal prisoners reported combat experience (Maruschak et al., 2021b). Cesur et al. (2020) evaluated data from two large national databases and found combat exposure was associated with increased probability of violent and drug crimes. However, in the meta-analysis by Taylor (Taylor et al., 2020), no association between combat exposure and criminal justice involvement in veterans with PTSD was found. Additionally, in a US Department of Justice survey of 41,000 state and federal prisoners, there was no difference between combat and noncombat veterans in the types of crimes convicted, that is, sexual crimes, other violent crimes, and crimes related to drug or property(Bronson et al., 2015), though those with combat experience had a higher percentage of mental health problems, a factor also associated with incarceration and reviewed later in this chapter.

Findings: The data here finds limited support that combat exposure alone is a significant contributor to the differences in incarceration rates between veterans and non-veterans.

Traumatic Brain Injury (TBI)

TBI as a predictor of incarceration: Traumatic brain injury (TBI) is a significant injury to the brain by an external force that results in temporary or permanent difficulties in cognitive or motor functioning (National Institutes of Neurological Disorders and Stroke, 2025). These difficulties can include light sensitivity, pain, difficulty with concentration and memory, headaches, and confusion. Compared to other factors in this chapter, TBI is a more recent area of evaluation with widely varying diagnostic methodology.

A number of behaviors associated with TBI would logically increase the risk of criminal justice involvement. For example, depending on the location and severity of the injury, TBI can be associated with intolerance to frustration, variable mood, sexual disinhibition, aggression, and other socially disruptive behaviors (Torregrossa et al., 2023). Those with criminal justice involvement have a high incident rate of TBI. In a systematic review of TBI and incarceration in Australia, Europe, and the US, Durand and colleagues (2017) found 46% experienced some level of TBI. This prevalence rate is remarkably similar to a meta-analysis reviewing studies primarily from 2009 to 2018 (Hunter et al., 2023). The Hunter et al. meta-analysis estimated the lifetime history of TBI at 46% for all involved in the criminal justice system, with 32% experiencing a moderate to severe TBI. The highest prevalence rate for lifetime TBI were those in jail with an estimated rate of 52%. The authors are careful to state that there were differences in classification of TBI in the evaluated studies.

TBI and veterans: Military experience, especially combat exposure, is associated with a high prevalence of TBIs, or similar terms such as Acquired Brain Injury or Post Concussive Syndrome. TBI demonstrated a dramatic increases in prevalence in the early days of the most recent OEF/OIF conflicts (Moore et al., 2010). Estimates from studies conducted on military service members returning from deployment to combat areas find between 9% (Schwab et al., 2017) and 24% (Karr et al., 2025) screened positive for mild TBI though not all endorsed behavior symptoms. Approximately 14% of TBIs experienced in the OEF/OIF conflict were due to explosive armaments which can result in poor psychological health and greater disability levels (Miller et al., 2024). One study from the state of Minnesota of approximately 1000 prisoners found TBI rates of incarcerated veterans in state prisons to be approximately 60% higher than non-veterans (Logan et al., 2021).

Not surprisingly, TBI has been found at higher rates in studies directly comparing veterans to non-veterans (Akhanemhe et al., 2024). Additionally, TBIs suffered by service members compared to civilians tend to be more severe (Nakase-Richardson et al., 2017) and more likely to result in death (Wittine et al., 2025). A review of the TBI literature conducted by Greer and colleagues (Greer et al., 2020), found TBI was associated with higher rates of depression, substance use, PTSD, and anxiety disorders. There is at least one study that finds civilians reported higher rates of TBI and veterans reported more non-TBI neck and head injuries, but this data was collected with self-report surveys (Kornblith et al., 2020) and may reflect data found that military service members may underreport TBIs (Escolas et al., 2020).

Findings: Currently, though the number of large-scale studies is limited, there is compelling evidence that TBI is associated with incarceration and is more prevalent and more severe in the veteran population. As such, TBI should be considered a likely contributor to the differences in incarceration rates between veterans and non-veterans.

Factors Associated with Postmilitary Experiences

A number of factors which are associated with increased risk of incarceration can be classified as "postmilitary risk factors," including homelessness, substance use, mental illness, and unemployment. Though many of these factors may have manifested themselves before or during military service, they are classified as postmilitary here for both simplicity's sake and because they are not necessarily directly caused by military service.

Substance Use

SUD and incarceration: Nationally, government estimates are that 16.5% of the population meets criteria for a substance use disorder (Substance Abuse and Mental Health Services Administration, 2022). Rates of use over the past 30 days vary in adults over the age of 26, with 51% using alcohol, 12% using marijuana, 1.6% using cocaine, and 0.5% using heroin.

There is a strong connection between prison incarceration and substance use disorders. Behaviors associated with substances (e.g., using, committing crimes under the influence, distribution) are highly associated with criminal justice involvement with drug crimes accounting for about 15% (Federal Bureau of Investigations, 2019) of all arrested and 13% of those in state and federal prisons (Carson, 2022). Findings from the US Department of Justice's Bureau of Justice Statistics (Maruschak & Bronson, 2021) found in an analysis of 1.4 million state and federal prisoners that almost 40% reported using illegal drugs at the time of their crime and 30% reported being under the influence of alcohol; overall rates of substance use disorders were estimated at 47% in the year prior to incarceration

Veterans and substance use: Substance misuse is highly prevalent in active duty military, primarily alcohol (Bray et al., 2010). However, after leaving the military, veterans appear to have only a slightly higher risk of nontobacco-related use disorders. In a large study comparing 3119 veterans to 33,182 non-veterans, Boden and Hoggatt (Boden & Hoggatt, 2018) found no differences in "past year" rates of use of any nontobacco substances or alcohol compared to non-veterans, 17% vs 16%; veterans only demonstrated higher lifetime use of alcohol, not other substances. The findings by the Bureau of Justice Statistics further minimize the association between substance use and incarceration in veterans. Data comparing incarcerated veterans and non-veterans finds the percentage of those in state prisons for drug use is lower in veterans, 8.6%, than non-veterans, 14.8% (Maruschak & Bronson, 2021).

Other studies have found different results only when focusing on a specific sub-population. For example, in an evaluation of 37 million Black males (Bennett et al., 2023), veteran status did not predict illegal substance use; however, there was a significant interaction between veteran status and medical and psychiatric comorbidities with veterans experiencing medical or psychiatric comorbidities being at higher risk for substance use. This is supported by a study of 4.4 million veterans seen at Veteran Affairs clinics where 8.3% had a substance use diagnosis; however, in those patients with a mental illness, rates of comorbid substance use was almost three times higher for those with PTSD, depression, and anxiety disorders, 22%, 23%, and 22%, respectively (Trivedi et al., 2015).

Findings: Though there is substantial evidence to support the association between substance use and incarceration, there is no compelling evidence to suggest that substance use is more prevalent with military veterans, with a possible caveat being a comorbidity with mental illness. As such, substance use is not seen as a significant contributor to the differences in incarceration rates between veterans and non-veterans.

Homelessness

Homelessness and incarceration: As discussed in Chapter 1, incarceration is a strong contributor to homelessness. However, homelessness is also a risk factor for incarceration. Unsheltered homeless individuals are at an increased risk of having negative contact with the criminal justice system. In an evaluation of more than 64,000 homeless individuals, Roundtree and colleagues (Roundtree et al., 2019) found unsheltered individuals were 10 times more likely than sheltered homeless to have police contacts and at least seven times as likely to spend a night in jail over a six-month period. Two factors which cannot be easily separated from homelessness are the high association with substance use and mental illness, both associated with future incarceration.

The risks homelessness poses to incarceration are increased by the negative effect incarceration has on housing. Studies have found individuals discharged from incarceration are up to 10 times as likely (Couloute, 2018) to become homeless as those not previously incarcerated. This acceleration of homelessness creates an increasing risk of reincarceration.

Veterans and homelessness: Currently there is little published direct evidence that being homeless prior to enlistment predicts joining the military. However, Bareis and Mezuk (Bareis & Mezuk, 2016) compared military veterans to civilians, focusing, in part, on economic insecurity as a child. They found that 21% of those in the military during the all-volunteer era had experienced their family moving due to finances compared to civilians (15%).

There is a strong association between homelessness and incarceration in veterans (Moschion & Johnson, 2019). In a large meta-analysis of 79 studies which included over 1.2 million veterans who had a history of incarceration, 40% of previously incarcerated veterans had a history of homelessness (Edwards et al., 2025). In a survey of 1602 incarcerated veterans, 27% identified being homeless at sometime in the 12 months prior to incarceration (Elbogen et al., 2023). In an evaluation of 7260 veterans, those with a history of incarceration were five times as likely to be experiencing homelessness or housing instability, the largest predictor (Umucu et al., 2024).

There are differences between homeless veterans and non-veterans. In an evaluation of 6200 homeless veterans and 96,000 homeless non-veterans, Leite and Vieira da Silva (2025) found veterans tend to be older, male, and had 12 or more years of education. They had a primary trauma-related diagnosis, and were less likely to have never been married, generally consistent with the overall veteran population. Veterans were also more likely to be unemployed than non-veterans and have a serious mental illness but were less likely to report a substance use disorder, including alcohol, factors which have been shown to mediate rates of homelessness (Orak et al., 2023).

National rates of homelessness, that is, the percentage experiencing homelessness, are difficult to calculate due to different state-reporting methods, different housing alternatives, and the inability to combine databases. Additionally, rates are affected by the various services where increased service use could indicate a higher number of homeless individuals or the same number of homeless individuals but more seeking services. Data from the Department of Housing and Urban Development (HUD; Mast, 2023) combined VA and HUD data to provide the best estimate of homelessness rates between veterans and non-veterans. Consistently since 2008, veterans have demonstrated a higher homeless rate compared to non-veterans and though rates have declined for both veteran and non-veterans, data from 2020 found the homeless rate for veterans was 12.4% higher than that for non-veterans.

Finding: Homelessness has a complicated and reciprocal association with incarceration and is highly overlapped with substance use and mental illness. However, there is strong evidence that being homeless is associated with increased incarceration. Additionally, there is evidence that homelessness is more prevalent in US veterans than non-veterans. As such, homelessness is seen as a significant contributor to the differences in incarceration rates between veterans and non-veterans. However, the effects of mental illness should be considered in this factor.

Mental Illness

Mental illness and incarceration: NIH data finds that 6% of the US adult population, 4.8% of males, 7.1% of females, had a serious mental illness (National Institutes of Mental Illness, 2024); younger adults, age 18–25, were at higher risk, 11.6%. Mental illness has been shown to be a predictor of criminal justice involvement, though the strength of the association varies by population and methods of the study. For example, Luciano (Luciano et al., 2014) followed 198 individuals with mental illness for three years. Rates of incarceration over the follow-up time ranged from 15% of those with depressive diagnoses to 85% of those with psychotic disorders. Nakic and colleagues (2022) found that in a nationally representative sample of 36,000 US adults, almost 7% of those with mental illness had been incarcerated compared to less than 5% of those without a psychiatric disorder. However, this study found variables such as gender, socioeconomic status, and antisocial personality were more highly associated, and once these variables were statistically controlled, only psychotic disorders and borderline personality disorder demonstrated an increased risk for incarceration.

Estimating the prevalence rates of non-substance use mental illness in the US prison population is difficult due to factors such as lack of focused attention and different assessment techniques. The most comprehensive review was conducted by the US Department of Justice (Maruschak et al., 2021a). This evaluation sampled prisoners from 364 State and Federal prisons, conducting face-to-face interviews with 24,848 prisoners. Prisoners were evaluated for recent psychological distress and a history of being told they had mental illness by a health care professional. The findings demonstrated the significant rate of mental illness. Thirteen percent reported they were experiencing current serious psychological distress while 40% reported having a history of mental illness, rates higher than seen in the general population. In combination, over half of all those incarcerated in prison experienced either current or past indications of mental illness. The most prominent diagnosis was major depressive disorder (43%) followed by bipolar disorder and non-PTSD-related anxiety disorders, 27% and 23%, respectively.

Veterans and incarceration: In a retrospective evaluation of 100,000 veterans, veterans with schizophrenia had between a 300% and 500% increase in risk of incarceration, depending on age cohort (Lin et al., 2022). Using Department of Justice numbers from the early 2010s (Bronson et al., 2015), the most recent available, 41,000 incarcerated individuals in state and federal prisons were surveyed about their mental health. Veterans reported being treated for mental health problems and were taking prescription medications for mental health problems at a higher rate than non-veterans. Overall, almost half, 48% had been told they had a mental disorder by a mental health professional compared to only 36% of non-veterans. After statistically controlling for nonmental illness variables, two diagnoses were higher in the veteran population, PTSD, 23% vs 14% and personality disorders (antisocial or borderline), 26% vs 22%. LePage et al. (2016) also found in a matched group of veterans and non-veterans that only bipolar disorder had a higher rate in veterans leaving prison compared to veterans not incarcerated; however, this sample was limited to those who had seen VA for health care.

Veterans and mental illness: Data about mental illness rates in veterans is inconsistent. Na and colleagues (Na et al., 2023) evaluated 1257 combat veterans surveyed for the National Health and Resilience in Veterans study. This study found 12% of all veterans and 20% of OEF/OIF veterans had a high rate of screening positive for major depressive disorder, 9%, and generalized anxiety disorder, 16% (Na et al., 2023). Betancourt and colleagues (Betancourt et al., 2023) evaluating Center for Disease data from 2003 to 2021 found that after controlling for age, veterans had higher rates of a number of medical conditions than non-veterans, but had significantly lower overall rates of poor mental health; however, the criteria for mental health concerns was self-report of "one or more days out of 30 with poor mental health." These discrepancies are noteworthy and may suggest significant differences in the way data is collected and the specific veteran experiences of those assessed.

Findings: Mental illness is associated with higher rates of incarceration. However, though mixed, there is limited data to show mental illness, excluding PTSD, is more significantly prevalent in veterans. As such, currently, it appears mental illness is an unlikely contributor to the differences in incarceration rates between veterans and non-veterans.

Unemployment

Unemployment and incarceration: Unemployment is associated with an increased rate of incarceration. Almost 40% of prisoners in state and federal prison (Maruschak & Snell, 2023) were unemployed in the 30 days prior to arrest, and 25% were not looking for employment. In the veteran population, unemployment was a significant predictor of incarceration, increasing the odds of incarceration by 32% (Kelton et al., 2023).

Unemployment and veterans: Since moving to an all-volunteer military, recruitment into the armed services has been impacted by economic forces, specifically, during times of economic hardship, wage stagnation, and unemployment. Data from the early 2000s found that a 10% decrease in national employment rates increased military recruitment by 2–4% (Warner, 2012).

Though unemployment may be associated with joining the military, Department of Labor statistics find veteran unemployment rates are comparable if not somewhat lower than non-veterans. Comparing monthly unemployment from 2015 to 2025, veterans experienced an average of 0.7% lower monthly adjusted unemployment compared to non-veterans (US Department of Labor, 2025). Though the Department of Labor statistics do not account for type of employment, income, etc., there is no compelling data to suggest poorer employment for veterans.

Findings: Though unemployment is a significant factor associated with incarceration, the data does not support that veteran unemployment is related to differences in incarceration rates between veterans and non-veterans.

Several Additional Factors Associated with Incarceration

Veteran treatment courts (VTC) are specialized courts focused on assuring veterans receive treatment when appropriate, rather than incarceration. With over 700 courts nationally, these courts focus on veterans with substance or mental health contributors to their crimes, connecting veterans to services and volunteer mentors. Though not all courts will accept those with felonies, the functions of the courts will diminish the number of veterans going to prison. Overall, the results of these courts have been positive (e.g., Hartley & Baldwin, 2019), though it has been noted that most reports of effectiveness have lacked scientific rigor (Byrne et al., 2024) and the VTC systems are not standardized (Hummer et al., 2024).

Types of crimes resulting in prison are another factor and data suggests veterans and non-veterans are currently in prison for different crimes at different rates. For example, a higher percentage of non-veterans are in prison due to drug and property crimes than veterans. Though incarceration for broad violent crimes is approximately equal, a significantly higher percentage of veterans are incarcerated in state prison for violent sexual crime than non-veterans, 26% vs 12% respectively, and 7% and 1% respectively in federal prison (Maruschak et al., 2021b). Even after controlling for important clinical and childhood variables, veterans were still 35% more likely to be convicted of a sexual crime (Finlay et al., 2019), resulting in longer sentences.

Sentence length can also be a contributor. Longer sentences will not affect the overall number of individuals convicted but may artificially affect the interpretation of a current prisoner make up. Data from the Bureau of Justice Statistics finds that veterans, as a group, have similar sentence lengths (Maruschak et al., 2021b), but this report did not compare sentences across different crimes.

One interesting finding is that veterans had lower rates of having 1–10-year sentences, but higher rates of more than 10-year and life sentences.

The type of military discharge may also be a contributor. Almost 18% of veterans in prison received an other-than-honorable, bad conduct, or dishonorable discharge from the military, compared to approximately 7% receiving those types of discharges from the armed services in the OEF/OIF era. These types of discharges can affect access to VA services and benefits. Though most dishonorable discharges are for military crimes rising to the level of felonies, many other-than-honorable and bad conduct discharges are related to mental health or substance use issues.

Summary

Though there are a number of factors that are associated with higher incarceration rates within the veteran population, not all are likely explanations of the difference in veteran and non-veteran incarceration. Several factors, including race and childhood negative events which are associated with incarceration, are also predictors of joining the military. PTSD and TBI, both associated with military service and present at higher rates than the general population, are associated with increased incarceration rates. Finally, homelessness, a factor affecting more veterans than non-veterans, is a likely contributor to the differences in incarceration rates.

Obviously, we cannot say that all the factors are causative as some may have a direct effect on incarceration (e.g., homelessness increasing contact due to vagrancy laws), indirect effects (e.g., TBI potentially resulting in increased anger and aggression), or cooccurring associations (e.g., race or homelessness both being associated with broad socioeconomic factors).

One fact that the information highlights is the relatively limited knowledge we have about the incarceration experience and the need to explore new areas that may be part of the veterans' criminal justice experience. These are most likely to be uncovered through a deeper understanding of the lived experience of veterans involved in the legal system and an increased focus on areas that emerge from this better understanding. The need and methods for these evaluations will be discussed in the next chapters.

References

Akhanemhe, R., Stevelink, S. A. M., Corbett, A., Ballard, C., Brooker, H., Creese, B., Aarsland, D., Hampshire, A., & Greenberg, N. (2024). Is lifetime traumatic brain injury a risk factor for mild cognitive impairment in veterans compared to non-veterans? *European Journal of Psychotraumatology, 15*(1), 1–10. https://doi.org/10.1080/20008066.2023.2291965

Ashekun, O., Zern, A., Langlois, S., & Compton, M. T. (2023). Adverse childhood experiences and arrest rates among individuals with serious mental illnesses. *The Journal of the American Academy of Psychiatry and the Law, 51*(3), 329–336. https://jaapl.org/content/early/2023/06/05/JAAPL.220096-22

Baranyi, G., Cassidy, M., Fazel, S., Priebe, S., & Mundt, A. P. (2018). Prevalence of posttraumatic stress disorder in prisoners. *Epidemiologic Reviews, 40*(1), 134–145. https://doi.org/10.1093/epirev/mxx015

Bareis, N., & Mezuk, B. (2016). The relationship between childhood poverty, military service, and later life depression among men: Evidence from the Health and Retirement Study. *Journal of Affective Disorders, 206*, 1–7. https://doi.org/10.1016/j.jad.2016.07.018

Beatty, L. G., & Snell, T. L. (2021). *Profle of prison inmates, 2016* (NCJ 255037). U.S. Department of Justice, Office of Justice Programs, Bureau of Justice Statistics https://bjs.ojp.gov/content/pub/pdf/ppi16.pdf

Bennett, M. D., Jr., McDaniel, J. T., & Albright, D. L. (2023). Chronic disease multimorbidity and substance use among African American men: Veteran-non-veteran differences. *Ethnicity & Health, 28*(8), 1145–1160. https://doi.org/10.1080/13557858.2023.2224949

Betancourt, J. A., Dolezel, D. M., Shanmugam, R., Pacheco, G. J., Stigler Granados, P., & Fulton, L. V. (2023). The health status of the US Veterans: A longitudinal analysis of surveillance data prior to and during the COVID-19 pandemic. *Healthcare, 11*(14). https://doi.org/10.3390/healthcare11142049

Blosnich, J. R., Dichter, M. E., Cerulli, C., Batten, S. V., & Bossarte, R. M. (2014). Disparities in adverse childhood experiences among individuals with a history of military service. *JAMA Psychiatry, 71*(9), 1041–1048. https://doi.org/10.1001/jamapsychiatry.2014.724

Boden, M. T., & Hoggatt, K. J. (2018). Substance use disorders among veterans in a nationally representative sample: Prevalence and associated functioning and treatment utilization. *Journal of Studies on Alcohol and Drugs, 79*(6), 853–861. https://doi.org/10.15288/jsad.2018.79.853

Bray, R. M., Pemberton, M. R., Lane, M. E., Hourani, L. L., Mattiko, M. J., & Babeu, L. A. (2010). Substance use and mental health trends among U.S. military active duty personnel: Key findings from the 2008 DoD Health Behavior Survey. *Military Medicine, 175*(6), 390–399. https://doi.org/10.7205/MILMED-D-09-00132

Bronson, J., Carson, E. A., Noonan, M., & Berzofsky, M. (2015). *Veterans in prison and jail, 2011–12* (NCJ 249144). U.S. Department of Justice, Office of Justice Programs, Bureau of Justice Statistics. https://bjs.ojp.gov/content/pub/pdf/vpj1112.pdf

Buehler, E. D., & Kluckow, R. (2024). *Correctional populations in the United States, 2022 – Statistical tables* (NCJ 308699). https://bjs.ojp.gov/document/cpus22st.pdf

Byrne, J. M., Kras, K. R., Rapisarda, S. S., & Socia, K. M. (2024). New research on veterans treatment courts: An overview of the community participatory research on veterans in specialized programming project. *Victims and Offenders, 19*(1), 5–31. https://doi.org/10.1080/15564886.2023.2295882

Carson, E. A. (2022). *Prisoners in 2021* (NCJ 305125). U.S. Department of Justice, Office of Justice Programs, Bureau of Justice Statistics. https://bjs.ojp.gov/sites/g/files/xyckuh236/files/media/document/p21st.pdf

Cesur, R., Sabia, J. J., & Tekin, E. (2022). Post–September 11 War deployments and crime among veterans. *Journal of Law and Economics, 65*(2), Article 3. https://chicagounbound.uchicago.edu/jle/vol65/iss2/3

Chassay, L., & Kremer, K. P. (2025). Latent classes of incarcerated people's behavioral health: Differences by childhood adversity and criminal history. *Victims & Offenders, 20*(2), 346–370. https://doi.org/10.1080/15564886.2022.2146824

Couloute, L. (2018). *Nowhere to go: Homelessness among formerly incarcerated people*. Prison Policy Initiative. www.prisonpolicy.org/reports/housing.html

Durand, E., Chevignard, M., Ruet, A., Dereix, A., Jourdan, C., & Pradat-Diehl, P. (2017). History of traumatic brain injury in prison populations: A systematic review. *Annals of Physical and Rehabilitation Medicine, 60*(2), 95–101. https://doi.org/10.1016/j.rehab.2017.02.003

Edwards, E. R., Fortuna, A., Holliday, R., Addison, H., & Tsai, J. (2025). Prevalence of mental health conditions, substance use disorders, suicidal ideation and attempts, and experiences of homelessness among veterans with criminal-legal involvement: A meta-analysis. *Clinical Psychology Review, 115,* 102533.https://doi.org/10.1016/j.cpr.2024.102533

Elbogen, E. B., DuBois, C. M., Finlay, A. K., Clark, S., Kois, L. E., Wagner, H. R., & Tsai, J. (2023). How often does homelessness precede criminal arrest in veterans? Results from the US survey of prison inmates. *American Journal of Orthopsychiatry, 93*(6), 486–493. https://doi.org/10.1037/ort0000693

Escolas, S. M., Luton, M., Ferdosi, H., Chavez, B. D., & Engel, S. D. (2020). Traumatic brain injuries: Unreported and untreated in an army population. *Military Medicine, 185*(Suppl 1), 154–160. https://doi.org/10.1093/milmed/usz259

Farrington, D., Bergstrøm, H., & Jolliffe, D. (2025). Childhood predictors of successful self-reported delinquents. *Psychology, Crime & Law, 31*(3), 249–269. https://doi.org/10.1080/1068316X.2023.2228972

Farrington, D. P. (2011). Families in crime. In J. Q. Wilson & J. Peersilia (Eds.), *Crime and public policy* (pp. 130–157). Oxford University Press.

Federal Bureau of Investigations. (2019). *Crime in the US, 2019.* https://ucr.fbi.gov/crime-in-the-u.s

Finlay, A. K., McGuire, J., Bronson, J., & Sreenivasan, S. (2019). Veterans in prison for sexual offenses: Characteristics and reentry service needs. *Sexual Abuse: A Journal of Research and Treatment, 31*(5), 560–579. https://doi.org/10.1177/1079063218793633

Geller, A., Cooper, C., Garfinkel, I., Schwartz-Soicher, O., & Mincy, R. (2012). Beyond absenteeism: Father incarceration and child development. *Demography, 49*(1), 49–76. https://doi.org/10.1007/s13524-011-0081-9

Greenberg, G. A., & Rosenheck, R. A. (2009). Mental health and other risk factors for jail incarceration among male veterans. *Psychiatric Quarterly, 80*(1), 41–53. https://doi.org/10.1007/s11126-009-9092-8

Greer, N., Sayer, N. A., Spoont, M., Taylor, B. C., Ackland, P. E., MacDonald, R., McKenzie, L., Rosebush, C., & Wilt, T. J. (2020). Prevalence and severity of psychiatric disorders and suicidal behavior in service members and veterans with and without traumatic brain injury: Systematic review. *Journal of Head Trauma Rehabilitation, 35*(1), 1–13. https://doi.org/10.1097/HTR.0000000000000478

Hartley, R. D., & Baldwin, J. M. (2019). Waging war on recidivism among justice-involved veterans: An impact evaluation of a large urban veterans treatment court.

Criminal Justice Policy Review, 30(1), 52–78. https://doi.org/10.1177/0887403416650490

Herrenkohl, T. I., Jung, H., Jungeun, O. L., & Moo-Hyun, K. (2017). Effects of child maltreatment, cumulative victimization experiences, and proximal life stress on adult crime and antisocial behavior (250506). U.S. Department of Justice, Office of Justice Programs. www.ojp.gov/pdffiles1/nij/grants/250506.pdf

Horton, K. B. (2021). Assessing the correlation between parental incarceration and relational aggression: Factor structure of the Diverse Adolescent Relational Aggression Scale (DARAS). *Journal of Aggression, Maltreatment & Trauma, 30*(4), 491–508. https://doi.org/10.1080/10926771.2020.1747129

Hummer, D., Byrne, J. M., Rapisarda, S. S., Socia, K. M., & Kras, K. R. (2024). No veteran left behind? Perspectives on vtc eligibility criteria for justice-involved veterans in multiple jurisdictions across the United States. *Victims and Offenders, 19*(1), 59–79. https://doi.org/10.1080/15564886.2023.2288963

Hunter, S., Kois, L. E., Peck, A. T., Elbogen, E. B., & LaDuke, C. (2023). The prevalence of traumatic brain injury (TBI) among people impacted by the criminal legal system: An updated meta-analysis and subgroup analyses. *Law and Human Behavior, 47*(5), 539–565. https://doi.org/10.1037/lhb0000543

Irwin, V., Wang, K., Jung, J., Kessler, E., Tezil, T., Alhassani, S., Filbey, A., Dillig, R., & Bullock Mann, F. (2024). Report on the condition of education 2024 (NCES 2024-144). U.S. Department of Education. https://nces.ed.gov/pubs2024/2024144.pdf

Jensen, E., Jones, N., Rabe, M., Pratt, B., Medina, L., Orozco, K., & Spell, L. (2021). 2020 U.S. population more racially and ethnically diverse than measured in 2010. U.S. Census Bureau. www.census.gov/library/stories/2021/08/2020-united-states-population-more-racially-ethnically-diverse-than-2010.html

Jung, H., Herrenkohl, T. I., Klika, J. B., Lee, J. O., & Brown, E. C. (2015). Does child maltreatment predict adult crime? Reexamining the question in a prospective study of gender differences, education, and marital status. *Journal of Interpersonal Violence, 30*(13), 2238–2257. https://doi.org/10.1177/0886260514552446

Karr, J. E., Rippey, C. S., Hubert, T. J., Stein, M. B., Adams, T. G., & Pietrzak, R. H. (2025). Traumatic brain injury in US veterans: Prevalence and associations with physical, mental, and cognitive health. *Archives of Physical Medicine and Rehabilitation, 106*(4), 537–547. https://doi.org/10.1016/j.apmr.2024.11.010

Kelton, K., Van Voorhees, E. E., Elbogen, E. B., Workgroup, V. A. M.-A. M., & Dillon, K. H. (2023). Correlates of incarceration history among military veterans. *Military Psychology, 35*(6), 577–589. https://doi.org/10.1080/08995605.2022.2141049

Khan, M. R., Scheidell, J. D., Rosen, D. L., Geller, A., & Brotman, L. M. (2018). Early age at childhood parental incarceration and STI/HIV-related drug use and sex risk across the young adult lifecourse in the US: Heightened vulnerability of black and hispanic youth. *Drug and Alcohol Dependence, 183*, 231–239. https://doi.org/10.1016/j.drugalcdep.2017.11.006

Kornblith, E. S., Yaffe, K., Langa, K. M., & Gardner, R. C. (2020). Prevalence of lifetime history of traumatic brain injury among older male veterans compared with civilians: A nationally representative study. *Journal of Neurotrauma, 37*(24), 2680–2685. https://doi.org/10.1089/neu.2020.7062

Kyckelhahn, T., & Kerbel, A. (2023). Education levels of federally sentenced prisoners. United States Sentencing Commission. www.ussc.gov/sites/default/files/pdf/research-and-publications/research-publications/2023/20231218_Education.pdf

Lee, J. O., Herrenkohl, T. I., Jung, H., Skinner, M. L., & Klika, J. B. (2015). Longitudinal examination of peer and partner influences on gender-specific pathways from child abuse to adult crime. *Child Abuse and Neglect, 47*, 93–93.

Lee, R., & Luo, F. (2024). Parental incarceration in childhood and violent delinquent behaviors in adulthood: Race/ethnicity and sex differences. *Journal of Family Trauma, Child Custody & Child Development, 21*(1), 41–56. https://doi.org/10.1080/26904586.2023.2200773

Leite, Â., & Vieira da Silva, C. (2025). Trends in homelessness and social sustainability: Veterans vs. non-veterans in the US. *Healthcare, 13*(9), 967. https://doi.org/10.3390/healthcare13090967

LePage, J. P., Bradshaw, L. D., Cipher, D. J., Crawford, A. M., & Parish-Johnson, J. A. (2016). The association between recent incarceration and inpatient resource use and death rates: Evaluation of a US veteran sample. *Public Health, 134*, 109–113. https://doi.org/10.1016/j.puhe.2016.01.009

Lin, D., Kim, H., Wada, K., Aboumrad, M., Powell, E., Zwain, G., Benson, C., & Near, A. M. (2022). Unemployment, homelessness, and other societal outcomes in patients with schizophrenia: A real-world retrospective cohort study of the United States Veterans Health Administration database: Societal burden of schizophrenia among US Veterans. *BMC Psychiatry, 22*. https://doi.org/10.1186/s12888-022-04022-x

Logan, M. W., McNeeley, S., & Morgan, M. A. (2021). Not-so-special forces? Revisiting the "veteran effect" in the context of prison research. *Journal of Criminal Justice, 72*. https://doi.org/10.1016/j.jcrimjus.2020.101762

Luciano, A., Belstock, J., Malmberg, P., McHugo, G. J., Drake, R. E., Xie, H., Essock, S. M., & Covell, N. H. (2014). Predictors of incarceration among urban adults with co-occurring severe mental illness and a substance use disorder. *Psychiatric Services, 65*(11), 1325–1331. https://doi.org/10.1176/appi.ps.201300408

Maruschak, L. M., & Bronson, J. (2021). Alcohol and drug use and treatment reported by prisoners (NCJ 252641). U.S. Department of Justice, Office of Justice Programs, Bureau of Justice Statistics. https://bjs.ojp.gov/sites/g/files/xyckuh236/files/media/document/adutrpspi16st.pdf

Maruschak, L. M., Bronson, J., & Alper, M. (2021a). Indicators of mental health problems reported by prisoners (NCJ 252643). U.S. Department of Justice, Office of Justice Programs, Bureau of Justice Statistics. https://bjs.ojp.gov/media/document/44841

Maruschak, L. M., Bronson, J., & Alper, M. (2021b). Parents in prison and their minor children (NCJ 252645). U.S. Department of Justice, Office of Justice Programs, Bureau of Justice Statistics. https://bjs.ojp.gov/content/pub/pdf/pptmcspi16st.pdf

Maruschak, L. M., & Snell, T. L. (2023). Employment of state and federal prisoners prior to incarceration, 2016 (NCJ 305983). U.S. Department of Justice, Office of Justice Programs, Bureau of Justice Statistics. https://bjs.ojp.gov/sites/g/files/xyckuh236/files/media/document/esfppi16.pdf

Mast, B. D. (2023). Veteran and nonveteran homelessness rates: New estimates. *Cityscape*, *25*(2), 379–386. www.jstor.org/stable/48736633

Miller, A. R., Martindale, S. L., Rowland, J. A., Walton, S., Talmy, T., & Walker, W. C. (2024). Blast-related mild TBI: LIMBIC-CENC focused review with implications commentary. *NeuroRehabilitation, 55*(3), 329–345. https://doi.org/10.3233/NRE-230268

Moore, D. F., Jaffee, M. S., & Ivins, B. J. (2010). Hospitalization associated with traumatic brain injury in the active duty US Army: 2000–2006. *NeuroRehabilitation, 26*(3), 199–212. https://doi.org/10.3233/NRE-2010-0556

Moschion, J., & Johnson, G. (2019). Homelessness and incarceration: A reciprocal relationship? *Journal of Quantitative Criminology, 35*(4), 855–887. https://doi.org/10.1007/s10940-019-09407-y

Muentner, L., McLaughlin, K. K., & Shlafer, R. (2024). Substance use among rural adolescents with incarcerated parents: Evidence from a state-wide sample. *The Journal of Rural Health, 40*(2), 338–347. https://doi.org/10.1111/jrh.12806

Na, P. J., Schnurr, P. P., & Pietrzak, R. H. (2023). Mental health of US combat veterans by war era: Results from the national health and resilience in veterans study. *Journal of Psychiatric Research, 158*, 36–40. https://doi.org/10.1016/j.jpsychires.2022.12.019

Nakase-Richardson, R., Stevens, L. F., Tang, X., Lamberty, G. J., Sherer, M., Walker, W. C., Pugh, M. J., Eapen, B. C., Finn, J. A., Saylors, M., Dillahunt-Aspillaga, C., Adams, R. S., & Garofano, J. S. (2017). Comparison of the VA and NIDILRR TBI model system cohorts. *The Journal of Head Trauma Rehabilitation, 32*(4), 221–233. https://doi.org/10.1097/HTR.0000000000000334

Nakic, M., Stefanovics, E. A., Rhee, T. G., & Rosenheck, R. A. (2022). Lifetime risk and correlates of incarceration in a nationally representative sample of US adults with non-substance-related mental illness. *Social Psychiatry and Psychiatric Epidemiology, 57*(9), 1839–1847. https://doi.org/10.1007/s00127-021-02158-x

National Center for PTSD. (2025a). How common is PTSD in adults. www.ptsd.va.gov/understand/common/common_adults.asp

National Center for PTSD. (2025b). How common is PTSD in veterans. www.ptsd.va.gov/understand/common/common_veterans.asp

National Institutes of Mental Illness. (2024). Mental illness. www.nimh.nih.gov/health/statistics/mental-illness#part_2541

National Institutes of Neurological Disorders and Stroke. (Retrieved 2025). Traumatic brain injury (TBI). www.ninds.nih.gov/health-information/disorders/traumatic-brain-injury-tbi

Orak, U., Kelton, K., Vaughn, M. G., Tsai, J., & Pietrzak, R. H. (2023). Homelessness and contact with the criminal legal system among U.S. combat veterans: An exploration of potential mediating factors. *Criminal Justice & Behavior, 50*(3), 392–409. https://doi.org/10.1177/00938548221140352

Pew Research Center. (2019). The American veteran experience and the post-9/11 generation. https://pewrsr.ch/32uqNJs

Pew Research Center. (June 2024). Most black Americans believe U.S. institutions were designed to hold black people back. www.pewresearch.org/?p=171871

Roos, L. E., Afifi, T. O., Martin, C. G., Pietrzak, R. H., Tsai, J., & Sareen, J. (2016). Linking typologies of childhood adversity to adult incarceration: Findings from a nationally representative sample. *American Journal of Orthopsychiatry, 86*(5), 584–593. https://doi.org/10.1037/ort0000144

Roundtree, J., Hess, N., & Lyke, A. (2019). Health conditions among unsheltered adults in the U.S. California Policy Lab. www.capolicylab.org/wp-content/uploads/2023/02/Health-Conditions-Among-Unsheltered-Adults-in-the-U.S..pdf

Schwab, K., Terrio, H. P., Brenner, L. A., Pazdan, R. M., McMillan, H. P., MacDonald, M., Hinds, S. R., & Scher, A. I. (2017). Epidemiology and prognosis of mild traumatic brain injury in returning soldiers: A cohort study. *Neurology, 88*(16), 1571–1579. https://doi.org/10.1212/WNL.0000000000003839

Snowden, D., Oh, S., Salas-Wright, C., Vaughn, M., King, E., Snowden, D. L., Salas-Wright, C. P., & Vaughn, M. G. (2017). Military service and crime: New evidence. *Social Psychiatry & Psychiatric Epidemiology, 52*(5), 605–615. https://doi.org/10.1007/s00127-017-1342-8

Substance Abuse and Mental Health Services Administration. (2022). Key substance use and mental health indicators in the United States: Results from the 2021 National Survey on Drug Use and Health (HHS Publication No. PEP22-07-01-005, NSDUH Series H-57).

Talaugon, A. R., & Turanovic, J. J. (2025). Childhood exposure to family violence, residential instability, and parental incarceration: Compounding household adversities and adolescent delinquency. *Journal of Research in Crime & Delinquency, 62*(3), 387–428. https://doi.org/10.1177/00224278241280903

Taylor, E. N., Timko, C., Nash, A., Owens, M. D., Harris, A. H. S., & Finlay, A. K. (2020). Posttraumatic stress disorder and justice involvement among military veterans: A systematic review and meta-analysis. *Journal of Traumatic Stress, 33*(5), 804–812. https://doi.org/10.1002/jts.22526

Torregrossa, W., Raciti, L., Rifici, C., Rizzo, G., Raciti, G., Casella, C., Naro, A., & Calabrò, R. S. (2023). Behavioral and psychiatric symptoms in patients with severe traumatic brain injury: A comprehensive overview. *Biomedicines, 11*(5). https://doi.org/10.3390/biomedicines11051449

Trevillion, K., Williamson, E., Thandi, G., Borschmann, R., Oram, S., & Howard, L. M. (2015). A systematic review of mental disorders and perpetration of domestic violence among military populations. *Social Psychiatry and Psychiatric Epidemiology, 50*(9), 1329–1346. https://doi.org/10.1007/s00127-015-1084-4

Trivedi, R. B., Post, E. P., Sun, H., Pomerantz, A., Saxon, A. J., Piette, J. D., Maynard, C., Arnow, B., Curtis, I., Fihn, S. D., & Nelson, K. (2015). Prevalence, comorbidity, and prognosis of mental health among US veterans. *American Journal of Public Health, 105*(12), 2564–2569. https://doi.org/10.2105/AJPH.2015.302836

Umucu, E., Lee, B., Chang, C., Szymkowiak, D., & Tsai, J. (2024). Geographic and psychosocial correlates of homelessness or unstable housing among US veterans in the midwest. *American Journal of Community Psychology, 74*, 142–151. https://doi.org/10.1002/ajcp.12751

U.S. Census Bureau. (2023). Educational attainment in the United States: 2022. www.census.gov/data/tables/2022/demo/educational-attainment/cps-detailed-tables.html

U.S. Department of Defense. (2023). 2023 demographics: Profile of the military community. https://download.militaryonesource.mil/12038/MOS/Reports/2023-demographics-report.pdf

U.S. Department of Labor. (2025). Labor force statistics from the current population survey. https://data.bls.gov/timeseries/LNS14049526&series_id=LNS14049601

U.S. Department of Veterans Affairs. (2011). Educational attainment of veterans: 2000 to 2009. National Center for Veterans Analysis and Statistics. www.va.gov/vetdata/docs/SpecialReports/education_FINAL.pdf

U.S. Department of Veterans Affairs. (2020). Demographic characteristics of veterans who separated in 2011 and 2017. www.data.va.gov/dataset/Demographic-Characteristics-of-Veterans-Who-Separa/c6pc-frdg/about_data

Ward, J., Wenger, J. B., & Kroeger, T. (2024). The evolution of veteran educational attainment gaps over the life cycle. *Journal of Demographic Economics*, 1–24. https://doi.org/https://doi.org/10.1017/dem.2024.5

Warner, J. T. (2012). The effect of the civilian economy on recruiting and retention. In Department of Defense (Ed.), *Report of the 11th quadrennial review of military compensation*. Department of Defense.

Wittine, L. M., Ketchum, J. M., Silva, M. A., Hammond, F. M., Chung, J. S., Loyo, K., Lezama, J., & Nakase-Richardson, R. (2025). Mortality among veterans following traumatic brain injury: A veterans administration traumatic brain injury model system study. *Journal of Neurotrauma, 42*(7–8), 745–757. https://doi.org/10.1089/neu.2024.0043

Woodard, T., & Copp, J. E. (2016). Maternal incarceration and children's delinquent involvement: The role of sibling relationships. *Children & Youth Services Review, 70*, 340–348. https://doi.org/10.1016/j.childyouth.2016.10.003

Zhao, Q. (2025). Prevalence and risk factors of mental health and substance use problems among asian american offenders: A nationally representative study. *Journal of Ethnicity in Substance Abuse*, *16*, 1–17. https://doi.org/10.1080/15332640.2025.2532716

3

THE NEED TO INCORPORATE LIVED EXPERIENCES

Introduction

In Chapters 1 and 2 we broadly reviewed the factors that predict incarceration and the negative life events that are consequences or associated with leaving prison. The domains that were reviewed are very robust and easily measured. These include housing, employment, health diagnoses, criminal history, and demographic information. They are frequently included in large data collections including those conducted by agencies and organizations such as the Veterans Health Administration, the Department of Justice, and the Center for Disease Control.

The advantage of these variables is that they are objectively defined, easily measured, and logically associated with incarceration. They lend themselves to categorical or binary classifications which tend to be relatively black and white. These types of data are critical to our ability to quickly describe and understand populations of individuals. These types of data are often used in policy decisions, resource allocations, and outcome measures.

An example of a data collection and analysis government office is the Department of Justice's Bureau of Justice Statistics (BJS), the source of the Department of Justice information reviewed in Chapters 1 and 2. The BJS is one of the US government's 13 federally funded statistical agencies (Department of Justice; Bureau of Justice Statistics, 2025). BJS has as its mission

> to collect, analyze, publish, and disseminate information on crime, criminal offenders, victims of crime, and the operation of justice systems at all levels

DOI: 10.4324/9781003522300-3

of government. BJS also provides financial and technical support to state, local, and tribal governments to improve both their statistical capabilities and the quality and utility of their criminal history records.

The execution of this mission is critical to the understanding of the nation's criminal justice system. Because BJS collects data in a standardized way, comparisons can be made between different correctional levels, different years, and different states allowing for the tracking of changes and trends within the nation's criminal justice systems.

Another important collector of large national data is the Department of Labor's Bureau of Labor Statistics (BLS). Similar to the BJS, the BLS has a mission to measure "labor market activity, working conditions, price changes, and productivity in the U.S. economy to support public and private decision making" (Department of Labor; Bureau of Labor Statistics, 2025). The BLS plays an important role in guiding government policy on employment, labor productivity, national healthcare coverage, and employment wages.

The standardization of collected data has significant benefits. This ability to compare years is critical to evaluating national and local trends, ascertaining if large-scale policies are having an effect, and determining where resources may be best used. As an example, the Department of Justice's BJS has performed three large-scale evaluations looking at incarcerated veterans since 2000, first in 2004 (Noonan & Mumola, 2007), then again in 2011 (Bronson et al., 2015), and then again 2016 (Maruschak et al., 2021). These were part of larger data collections at those times. As mentioned, these large-scale standardized evaluations allow policymakers to look back and compare current and past figures; for example, 2011 report presented veteran data as far back as the 1970s which was able to trace the decline in percentage of veterans in prison mirroring the decline in the national number of veterans over that time reference. All of the reports collected data on the number, the age and gender, racial/ethnic makeup, and the branch of service of veterans incarcerated. Each reported information on the type of crime and time sentenced. The earlier two reported data on marital status and all reported on combat experience. The earlier two also reported on mental illness, a statistic missing from the most recent report. Interestingly only the earlier report collected data on histories of drug and alcohol use. Overall, these reports, some of the most comprehensive evaluations, tend to stay close to the same data collected.

There are several drawbacks on the reliance of these large data sets. One limitation is that researchers, statisticians, and policymakers are frequently trapped by the data that is collected, and that has always been collected. When data for large national databases is being collected, there may be a tendency to collect the same variables over time to ensure the data from one year can be compared to another year.

Another drawback is that the longer data is collected the less likely it is to stop being collected, even once its utility is no longer relevant. This makes it less likely that new data types will be collected, as new items may not be proven and there are limits to the data that can be collected due to time and effort of face-to-face interviews. More importantly, a natural consequence of data collection over time is that the repeated collection of the same or similar data limits the evaluation of new possible connections and associations. Researchers and policymakers may be required to further mine and refine their analyses of the same or similar concepts either confirming existing relationships or attempting to identify new associations, which as the data becomes more subtle, may have limited utility toward understanding or resolving the broad issues addressed.

What is increasingly clear is that reliance on traditional database-driven evaluations to clarify important aspects of interest has a limit to its broad utility unless the databases can be adjusted and refined. Because of these limits, it is important then that new domains are explored and defined.

One of the most important sources of new areas of exploration is the inclusion of those with knowledge gained from lived experiences (Dembele et al., 2024; Mah et al., 2025), referred to here as issue holders. Though meta-analyses, scoping reviews, and other systematic evaluations of existing published data can provide strong scientific evidence, they are limited to reviewing what is already known. To expand into new areas, issue holder knowledge must be incorporated through interviews and qualitative analyses. In a review of qualitative research, Beames and colleagues (Beames et al., 2021) identify several significant benefits. Qualitative research incorporating issue holders can target and identify gaps in existing research. It allows researchers to assess their theories and findings, comparing them to the relevance of issue holders. It can help researchers and policymakers determine what areas of future research should occur and whether these areas will be worth the effort. The inclusion of issue holders may also increase the trust and acceptance of the findings.

Relevant to expanding existing knowledge, issue holders have strong personal experiences that can assist to develop hypotheses on how variables are connected. These experiences can lead to a more comprehensive understanding and lead to quantitative studies. As seen in Chapters 1 and 2, there is ample information about core factors associated with the incarceration experience. However, it is important that those involved in the criminal justice system be given a voice to provide their insights into our understanding of the difficulties encountered and the important needs.

Examples of Lived Experience Research

The inclusion of those with lived experiences related to experiences in the criminal justice system has yielded many important findings, not all in the US.

Though not meant to be exhaustive, the following are several examples of how issue holder input is being incorporated into areas important to those involved in the criminal justice system.

Veteran Adaptation to Prison

Stacer and Solinas-Saunders (2024) evaluated how veterans adapt to prison. The two goals were to look for patterns of adaptation and describe how past military experiences influenced the prison experience. The research team interviewed 43 male veterans who were currently incarcerated in a state prison. Three central themes were identified. The first was discipline and respect. Veterans reported the discipline they learned in the military, how to not lash out or complain, and how to keep boundaries, kept them out of trouble and gave them a sense of pride and confidence. The second theme was being able to understand and follow daily routines and tight structure. Veterans found the structure and schedules of the prison was not too different from the structure in the military, allowing them to adapt. The third theme was the similarity of the environment. Veterans found communal life, being alert to one's surroundings, the need to give respect, the lack of privacy, and having limited possessions compared closely to the military life and that prison even felt like downtime in the military.

As can be seen here, the adjustment of veterans to incarceration may be smoother than non-veterans due to similarities with the military experience. This insight could not be obtained through standardized assessments to determine who may have the most difficulty adjusting to prison life.

Social Connections

In an evaluation of eight individuals held in prison in Norway (Solbakken & Wynn, 2022), participants were interviewed about social support and incarceration. This study identified the impacts of incarceration on social connections. These included the loss of friendships and fall in social status, and the inability to contact family due to security and bureaucracy. Participants identified the need to create new relationships with others in prison to help with mental health but those in prison must be careful with whom they trust. They also identified that self-isolation can lead to mental health problems and that prisoners needed to help other prisoners.

As can be seen, the information provided by the issue holders highlight the need for social connections as a way of addressing mental health challenges, which as seen in Chapters 1 and 2 are heavily tied to the incarceration experience.

Transition from Prison with an Opioid Addiction

Hoffman and colleagues (Hoffman et al., 2023) focused their efforts on understanding the factors that act as barriers and facilitators for those with opioid use disorders to reintegrate into the community after prison. The investigators interviewed 42 patients receiving treatment for opioid addictions who had been previously incarcerated, focusing on their experiences navigating and planning for reentry after prison. The interviews specifically targeted problems after release, the first 24 hours after release, and experiences with housing and employment. A number of key themes were identified. For example, in the first 24 hours after release, individuals with opioid addictions had to decide whether to begin use again or seek treatment, and that social support played a strong role in this decision. These decisions were complicated by difficulties navigating the possible social programs, accessing transportation, and the ability to access obtaining basic needs.

As can be seen from this study, critical knowledge could be and was gained about the difficulties those leaving prison face within the first 24 hours after leaving prison, knowledge which can be instrumental in developing programs and processes to improving successful transition.

Perceptions of Veterans Courts

As noted in Chapter 2, veterans treatment courts (VTC) are becoming more prevalent. Typically targeting crimes associated with substance use or mental illness, these courts work to divert veterans from prison by facilitating engagement in treatment. Herzog and colleagues (Herzog et al., 2019) interviewed 13 veterans who were actively involved in a VTC. The interviews focused on the veterans' opinions about what was helpful and unhelpful in the VTC process.

Several key findings were uncovered. Veterans found the courts beneficial, feeling the courts provided them with a second chance. Veterans identified their assigned mentors, who had experienced a similar history of legal difficulties, as instrumental to success. They felt their positive regard for the courts was influenced by the personalized experience of the court. Though a specific factor of the specific court being evaluated, the judge was an effective element as he was a veteran himself with an experience of military trauma.

The findings here would not be able to be collected using traditional techniques; however, the findings are important toward identifying ways of improving the VTCs and increasing veteran engagement.

Reintegration after Prison

Brine and colleagues (Brine et al., 2021) conducted a small study that evaluated the experiences of issue holders being released from federal prison in Canada, focusing on what was needed for successful reentry. Interviewing four volunteers with mental illness who were doing well in the community, the researchers asked the issue holders about the most important factors, the role of social relationships, and the role of employment.

Symptoms of mental illness were seen as a significant barrier, including stress and hallucinations, and having access to treatment was a benefit. Not surprisingly, ceasing substance use was an important factor as it led to increased criminal behavior. Other factors found important were employment or volunteering, social support from family, and religious beliefs factors that could be capitalized upon by reentry programs.

Peer Specialists

Peer specialists, those with similar lived experience, have been used in assisting veterans transition from prison (Brine et al., 2021). However, the fact that these programs are successful does not assist us in understanding what components of a program make them effective. Issue holders' perception of what these peer relationships offer may be able to provide important information about what makes these relationships successful.

Richardson and colleagues (Richardson et al., 2025) interviewed 25 veterans about their experiences with a peer specialist. A number of important themes were identified. One of the most important was that veterans reported they had challenges with initial trust working with a new person they didn't know. The veterans identified three primary themes that built the relationship with the peer; these were (1) the peer being available at all times, (2) realizing the peer had similar experiences, and (3) the peer being able to connect the veteran to resources.

These themes can be used to improve the effectiveness of peer support in a previously incarcerated population by incorporating them into the peers' work and efforts.

Summary

The examples presented here are not meant to be a comprehensive review of what we have learned through interviews with issue holders who have lived experiences with the criminal justice system. It does, however, demonstrate that important information can be and should be collected directly from issue holders.

Issue holders with prison experience are a key component to understanding the mechanisms that drive incarceration and success after prison. These interviews allow researchers to go beyond the 10,000-foot view of an issue, letting us understand what is going on in the daily lives of issue holders. For example, broad data sets on homelessness are very well equipped to provide large amounts of data about the numbers of those experiencing homelessness, the time spent being homeless, and their specific types of living arrangement, for example, street, shelter, etc. However, these large collections of data are limited to counting and categorizing information about what leads to homelessness, what is keeping people homeless, and what resources are used to help people exit homelessness and remain housed. These upper-level collections tend to reduce and flatten the nuances and the experiences of issue holders into simple categories. An increased focus on the lived experiences of issue holders is needed to take us beyond "score-keeping" data and move us to improving the programs and policies that improve the lives of veterans and others. This is not to say that data should remain at the qualitative level. For the data collected from issue holders to be beneficial, it must ultimately be converted into action and, when possible, quantified so that comparisons can be made and progress tracked.

In this chapter, we have demonstrated examples of incorporating issue holder's lived experiences into our understanding of those involved in the criminal justice system. As can be seen, issue holders have unique personal experiences which, when uncovered, can provide insight to the difficulties they encounter, the ways they cope with difficulties, and the processes which help them succeed. In the next chapters, we will turn our attention to veterans recently released from incarceration focusing on understanding veteran identity and how this identity affects seeking treatment, coping, and interactions with healthcare providers.

References

Beames, J. R., Kikas, K., O'Gradey-Lee, M., Gale, N., Werner-Seidler, A., Boydell, K. M., & Hudson, J. L. (2021). A new normal: Integrating lived experience into scientific data syntheses. *Frontiers in Psychiatry, 12*. https://doi.org/10.3389/fpsyt.2021.763005

Brine, K., Power, J., Smith, H. P., & Nolan, A. (2021). A qualitative study of success in postrelease federal inmates with mental health issues. *Journal of Correctional Health Care, 27*(1), 40–50. https://doi.org/10.1089/jchc.19.02.0009

Bronson, J., Carson, E. A., Noonan, M., & Berzofsky, M. (2015). Veterans in prison and jail, 2011–12 (NCJ 249144). U.S. Department of Justice, Office of Justice Programs, Bureau of Justice Statistics. https://bjs.ojp.gov/content/pub/pdf/vpj1112.pdf

Dembele, L., Nathan, S., Carter, A., Costello, J., Hodgins, M., Singh, R., Martin, B., & Cullen, P. (2024). Researching with lived experience: A shared critical reflection between co-researchers. *International Journal of Qualitative Methods*, 1–14. https://doi.org/10.1177/16094069241257945

Herzog, J. R., Ferdik, F., Scott, D., Denney, A., & Conklin, S. (2019). Participant perceptions of veterans treatment courts: A qualitative assessment and systems model. *Journal of Veteran Studies, 4*(2), 78–93. https://doi.org/DOI: 10.21061/jvs.v4i2.108

Hoffman, K. A., Thompson, E., Gaeta Gazzola, M., Oberleitner, L. M. S., Eller, A., Madden, L. M., Marcus, R., Oberleitner, D. E., Beitel, M., & Barry, D. T. (2023). "Just fighting for my life to stay alive": A qualitative investigation of barriers and facilitators to community re-entry among people with opioid use disorder and incarceration histories. *Addiction Science and Clinical Practice, 18*(1), 16. https://doi.org/10.1186/s13722-023-00377-y

Mah, H., Dobson, R., & Thomson, A. (2025). The importance of lived experience: A scoping review on the value of patient and public involvement in health research. *Health Expectations, 28*(2), 1–11. https://doi.org/10.1111/hex.70205

Maruschak, L. M., Bronson, J., & Alper, M. (2021). Veterans in Prison (NCJ 252646). US Department of Justice. Retrieved from https://bjs.ojp.gov/content/pub/pdf/vpspi16st.pdf

Noonan, M. E., & Mumola, C. J. (2007). *Veterans in state and federal prison, 2004* (NCJ 217199). U.S. Department of Justice, Office of Justice Programs, Bureau of Justice Statistics. https://bjs.ojp.gov/content/pub/pdf/vsfp04.pdf

Richardson, E., Flike, K., Hyde, J., Petrakis, B. A., McInnes, D. K., & Kim, B. (2025). "It's more than a ride" veteran perceptions of peer specialist qualities and activities that were most valuable for post-incarceration reentry: A qualitative analysis. *Health and Justice, 13*(1), 2. https://doi.org/10.1186/s40352-024-00303-7

Solbakken, L. E., & Wynn, R. (2022). Barriers and opportunities to accessing social support in the transition from community to prison: A qualitative interview study with incarcerated individuals in Northern Norway. *BMC Psychology, 10*. https://doi.org/10.1186/s40359-022-00895-5

Stacer, M. J., & Solinas-Saunders, M. (2024). Incarcerated veterans and their adaptation to prison. *American Journal of Criminal Justice, 49*(4), 552–575. https://doi.org/10.1007/s12103-024-09754-y

U.S. Department of Justice; Bureau of Justice Statistics. (2025). Bureau of Justice Statistics. https://bjs.ojp.gov/

U.S. Department of Labor; Bureau of Labor Statistics. (2025). Bureau of Labor Statistics. www.bls.gov/

4

VETERAN IDENTITY, TREATMENT SEEKING, AND SERVICE PROVISION

Introduction

A veteran's identity is multifaceted, formed by the distinct values, norms, experiences, and cultural expectations of military life. This identity strongly influences how veterans view themselves, affecting their actions and interactions, especially with healthcare and social services. Resilience, discipline, self-reliance, camaraderie, and a strong sense of duty are often central to veteran identity. The way veterans interact with and perceive treatment and support systems after service is significantly shaped by these internalized values.

We will examine in this chapter how the distinct characteristics of veteran identity shape veterans' treatment-seeking behaviors and their relationships with healthcare and social service providers. This study will pinpoint how veteran identity helps or hinders their use of healthcare and social services, showing how veterans' beliefs affect their experiences. To improve service provision and address transition barriers for veterans, this chapter thoroughly examines this relationship, offering insights and actionable strategies.

Individual life courses and perspectives from lived experience inform our analysis. These frameworks provide a structured approach to understanding the complex relationships between veteran identity, healthcare engagement, and social service use throughout veterans' lives. Understanding how veterans perceive and negotiate their identities within various contexts, this chapter stresses the vital role of aligning service delivery with their cultural values and personal histories. The sections of this chapter will analyze how veteran identity affects treatment, healthcare, and social service engagement. Later chapters

DOI: 10.4324/9781003522300-4

introduce substantive veterans' stories that point to key turning points that structure veterans' reintegration experiences and their incarceration pathways.

It is important to foreground that treatment-seeking behaviors and service provision are not isolated aspects of veteran reintegration. The choices veterans make around whether and how to engage with services often intersect with pivotal turning points that, as later chapters will show, can influence patterns of behavior linked to criminal justice involvement. These choices, whether to seek help, delay it, or avoid it entirely, intersect with other stressors that can escalate into situations carrying legal risk. Understanding these early decision points is essential to seeing how identity-based healthcare engagement, or the lack thereof, may serve as precursors to justice involvement. In clarifying these identity-based and systemic barriers in the treatment domain, this chapter lays essential groundwork for understanding how they shape incarceration pathways discussed in Chapter 5.

Understanding Veteran Identity: Theoretical and Empirical Insights

Veteran identity encompasses deeply internalized values, beliefs, and behaviors formed through rigorous military training and shared military experiences. Beyond mere group identification, this identity reflects a comprehensive set of formal and informal norms, shaped profoundly by collective challenges, structured expectations, and cultural values inherent in military service (Heward et al., 2024). Veterans' internalization of military norms significantly impacts their attitudes and behaviors related to healthcare utilization, mental health support, community interactions, and civilian reintegration processes. Recognizing the complex interplay between veterans' identities and their postmilitary psychosocial experiences is crucial for developing effective and culturally responsive interventions to facilitate successful civilian reintegration and overall well-being. Resilience, self-reliance, camaraderie, discipline, and loyalty are central to veterans' value system (Lancaster & Hart, 2015). These values are systematically reinforced during military service, where individual behavior is guided by strict adherence to hierarchical structures, organizational norms, and group cohesion. Veterans integrate these expectations and carry them into postservice life as a way to make sense of decision-making and interactions within healthcare and social service settings.

One of the primary theoretical frameworks used to understand veteran identity and behavior is social identity theory, which proposes that individuals derive significant aspects of their self-concept from their membership in social groups (Tajfel & Turner, 1979). Within this framework, the military serves as a powerful social group that shapes individual behavior, perceptions, and emotional experiences. Social identity theory explains how veterans often maintain strong attachments to military identities, which can result in positive group affiliation but also contribute to difficulties adapting to civilian life and institutions (Lancaster & Hart, 2015).

Scholars have documented how military identity influences psychosocial functioning, self-perception, and interpersonal relationships postservice (Lancaster & Hart, 2015). Veterans who strongly identify with military culture and values often experience substantial challenges when navigating civilian contexts that differ markedly in their norms, expectations, and structures (Mobbs & Bonanno, 2018). This identity shift can create internal tensions, leading to feelings of alienation, loss of purpose, and reduced self-efficacy, significantly impacting veterans' willingness and ability to engage with healthcare and social services.

The period of veterans' transition from military to civilian environments constitutes a complex phase of identity renegotiation, demanding significant psychological and social adjustments. Recent studies highlight that veterans often grapple with identity conflicts due to fundamental differences between military and civilian life structures, including shifts from predictable hierarchies and clearly delineated roles to more fluid and ambiguous civilian frameworks (Joseph et al., 2023). Contrasts can significantly undermine veterans' sense of self-efficacy, purpose, and belonging, leading to heightened psychological stress and challenges in adapting effectively to civilian social roles and expectations (Bond et al., 2022).

The interplay between veteran identity and attitudes toward mental health and substance use treatment is also critically influential during this transitional phase. Empirical research underscores how internalized military norms around emotional toughness, autonomy, and resilience contribute to veterans' hesitation in seeking professional psychological support (Hitch et al., 2023). Concerns regarding perceived stigma, fears about judgment from peers, and skepticism about healthcare providers' capacity to understand their unique military experiences significantly discourage veterans from accessing or maintaining mental health interventions (Meyer et al., 2023). Thus, culturally informed and veteran-specific mental health approaches are vital in bridging this gap and improving engagement among transitioning veterans.

Qualitative research provides a uniquely valuable approach to understanding veterans' experiences and perspectives regarding healthcare interactions, particularly due to its ability to deeply explore the intricate dimensions of veteran identity. The long-format interview methods inherent in qualitative studies allow veterans to articulate detailed narratives of their personal experiences, clearly revealing explicit dissatisfaction with treatments perceived as ineffective or misaligned with their identity expectations. Veterans frequently describe interactions where healthcare providers misunderstand or dismiss their military background, prompting disengagement from formal care and encouraging reliance on alternative, often maladaptive coping strategies (True et al., 2015). Qualitative methods are particularly suited to capturing the complexities and nuances of veteran identity, including how deeply held values and cultural norms shaped through military service inform attitudes and behaviors toward healthcare. In-depth qualitative insights can substantially improve culturally competent healthcare practices, ensuring they are genuinely responsive to veterans' identity-informed needs (Finley et al., 2015).

Exploring veteran identity through qualitative research also provides crucial insights into veterans' interactions with social service providers. Veteran identity directly shapes their expectations, perceptions, and engagement with available social services. Qualitative methods effectively capture the nuances of veterans' feelings of misunderstanding or marginalization, often experienced when service providers lack appropriate cultural competence regarding military life and its lasting impacts (Meyer et al., 2016). These qualitative narratives clearly highlight how negative experiences can reinforce feelings of institutional mistrust, exacerbating veterans' sense of social isolation and prompting avoidance behaviors that complicate their successful reintegration into civilian life.

Institutional interactions play a pivotal role in influencing veterans' trust and their subsequent willingness to seek and engage with essential support services. Research consistently demonstrates that interactions marked by cultural competence, empathetic communication, and responsiveness substantially increase veterans' trust in providers and enhance their proactive engagement with available resources (Koenig et al., 2014). Conversely, experiences characterized by bureaucratic hurdles, perceived dismissiveness, or inadequate cultural understanding intensify mistrust and discourage veterans from seeking necessary care. Programs utilizing other veterans as support providers haven proven effective, thereby improving engagement and mental health outcomes through shared experiences, mutual understanding, and cultural validation (Chinman et al., 2010). Recognizing military cultural norms, values, and expectations, tailored interventions resonate deeply with veterans' identities, increasing both their acceptance and efficacy (Resnick & Rosenheck, 2008). Strategies should address veterans' psychosocial needs from their perspective and experiences. Healthcare providers, social service institutions, and policymakers should enhance understanding of military culture, values, language, and experiences, enabling more effective communication, empathy, and trust-building with veteran clients (Meyer & Wynn, 2018). In this way, peer-support initiatives into healthcare and social service systems are ones that center a veteran standpoint to mitigate barriers related to institutional mistrust and treatment engagement (Chinman et al., 2010).

These identity-driven dynamics do not merely affect how veterans relate to healthcare and social services; they also influence broader life trajectories, including risk factors associated with justice involvement. When identity conflicts result in disengagement from supportive services, unmet needs can escalate into crises that intersect with other stressors, increasing vulnerability to adverse legal outcomes. For some veterans, unresolved identity conflicts during adjustment periods can trigger coping behaviors, such as substance misuse or withdrawal from supportive networks. Over time, these coping strategies may increase vulnerability to arrest or incarceration. We highlight these tensions here and set the stage for Chapter 5's deeper exploration of these behaviors as inflection points on justice-involved pathways.

Veteran Identity and Treatment-Seeking Behaviors: Navigating Healthcare Systems

The intersection of military identity and healthcare engagement often creates internal conflicts and external barriers, complicating veterans' willingness and ability to access essential healthcare services. Exploring this relationship is crucial for developing targeted strategies to improve treatment engagement, responsiveness, and overall health outcomes among veterans navigating healthcare systems (Blais & Renshaw, 2013). When the values and expectations veterans carry from military service are not acknowledged or supported in the care they receive, it can create a sense that the system does not recognize who they are or what they need. This disconnect can open a space where veterans seek ways of coping outside formal services, sometimes relying on strategies that provide short-term relief but increase long-term risks. As later chapters will show, persistent unmet needs can intersect with justice involvement and lay a pathway to incarceration.

Veteran Identity and Treatment Engagement

Military culture, with its distinct values of resilience, self-reliance, and strength, shapes veterans' attitudes toward mental health and substance use interventions. Research indicates that these cultural expectations create internal pressures to manage psychological distress independently, often resulting in delayed or foregone care (Currier et al., 2017). Veterans frequently internalize military norms, leading to negative self-assessments when considering professional help for mental health or substance use challenges. Veteran identity encompasses various strengths cultivated during military service, including resilience, discipline, self-reliance, and a profound sense of camaraderie. These strengths represent significant potential resources for veterans transitioning from military service to civilian life. Recognizing and leveraging these inherent attributes can substantially improve healthcare and social service provision, creating more effective, culturally sensitive, and engaging support systems tailored explicitly to veterans' unique needs and experiences. Over time, unresolved health or psychosocial issues linked to such avoidance may contribute to patterns of instability or risk-taking behaviors that emerge in the incarceration narratives of veterans in our study.

One of the most significant advantages derived from veteran identity is resilience. Developed through rigorous military training and service, resilience equips veterans with the capacity to adapt effectively in the face of adversity and stress (Pietrzak et al., 2009). Healthcare providers and social services can actively leverage veterans' resilience by incorporating strength-based treatment approaches, which emphasize veterans' capacity to overcome challenges and develop adaptive coping strategies. This would align closely with veterans' own expectations developed during their military service and possibly enhance their motivation and engagement with treatment and services.

Veterans also frequently internalize strong values of discipline and structure from their military service. Structured, goal-oriented interventions resonate strongly with these values, enhancing treatment adherence and effectiveness. Research demonstrates that healthcare interventions incorporating clear structure, consistent routines, and goal-oriented strategies align closely with veterans' identity-informed expectations, significantly improving outcomes (Sayer et al., 2010). Veterans have articulated the importance of structure and discipline in their healthcare experiences, noting that treatments with clear objectives and well-defined steps are most effective in sustaining their engagement and motivation.

Veteran self-reliance, another critical aspect of military identity, offers valuable insights into designing effective healthcare and social service interventions. Many veterans prefer treatments that enable and reinforce their sense of independence, autonomy, and personal accountability. Service provision models that actively involve veterans in treatment planning, decision-making, and self-management align closely with these identity expectations, improving engagement and satisfaction. One of our veterans put forward their positive experience in a self-management-focused healthcare program: "They respected my input and let me decide how I wanted to approach my recovery. That made a huge difference." The qualitative insights throughout the book's chapters underscore how prioritizing veterans' views on self-reliance can help us understand their views about treatment effectiveness and feelings about institutional trust.

Veterans' hesitance to pursue health treatment often stems from deeply ingrained military expectations emphasizing strength, independence, and emotional resilience. Acknowledging emotional vulnerability or psychological struggles can appear to contradict these internalized cultural values, creating significant internal tension. One veteran vividly expressed this conflict, stating, "I didn't want people thinking less of me; in the military, admitting you have a problem means you can't handle it. I tried dealing with it on my own." This perspective underscores the complex interplay between military identity, internalized stigma, and treatment avoidance, illustrating how adherence to cultural expectations can inadvertently discourage veterans from accessing formal mental health support. These identity-based expectations can lead veterans to rely heavily on personal coping strategies, which may inadvertently exacerbate underlying mental health conditions and limit meaningful engagement with available healthcare resources.

Confidentiality concerns further compound veterans' reluctance to access formal treatment services. Veterans may fear that seeking assistance for mental health or substance use issues could negatively affect their professional standing, personal relationships, or perceived reliability, which are values closely tied to their military identity. These concerns reflect the military culture's emphasis on accountability, trustworthiness, and strength, making the potential breach of confidentiality especially impactful. One veteran explicitly articulated these apprehensions, stating, "You never really trust that it won't get back to your unit or your employer. So you keep it to yourself." This reflects the veteran's internalized understanding that maintaining a perception of resilience and self-sufficiency is crucial, even in civilian contexts. Fears around confidentiality and stigma may significantly inhibit veterans from seeking necessary treatments, prompting them instead to manage conditions independently. This self-reliant behavior aligns with their military cultural values but may lead to untreated mental health conditions, prolonged emotional distress, and increased reliance on less-effective coping mechanisms, thereby compounding their psychosocial vulnerabilities. Reluctance to engage with care due to confidentiality concerns is not simply a healthcare utilization issue. For some veterans, untreated conditions and reliance on maladaptive coping mechanisms during these critical periods were cited as key moments on our veterans' path toward incarceration.

This critical intersection between veteran identity, key life turning points, and healthcare engagement significantly informs the pathways leading toward incarceration, a relationship that will be examined in detail throughout subsequent chapters. Specifically, upcoming chapters will explore how veterans' internalized cultural values and significant transitional moments intersect, driving behaviors and coping strategies that directly influence their trajectories into the criminal justice system.

Veterans' qualitative accounts consistently reflect this tension between military expectations and the need for treatment. One veteran clearly described the internal conflict: "In the military, you handle your problems on your own. Asking for help feels like admitting defeat." Another veteran similarly noted, "You're trained to push through pain, both physically and mentally. It makes reaching out feel impossible." These statements highlight how deeply military cultural expectations shape veterans' treatment-seeking behaviors, reinforcing barriers to effective healthcare engagement.

Gaps in Current Treatment Paradigms

Current healthcare paradigms frequently fail to adequately address the specific cultural and experiential needs of veterans, resulting in decreased treatment effectiveness and engagement. Traditional mental health and substance use treatment models often do not incorporate military cultural competence, creating systemic barriers to care (Meyer et al., 2016). Veterans consistently report feeling misunderstood or marginalized by healthcare providers who lack insight into military values, experiences, and expectations, thus perpetuating cycles of mistrust and disengagement. This disconnect highlights an urgent need for healthcare systems to adopt approaches that explicitly recognize and integrate the veteran standpoint, utilizing theory and methodology that directly reflect veterans' lived realities. Addressing these gaps is not only a matter of improving health outcomes; it is also a preventive strategy for reducing justice system contact. Several veterans in our study linked unresolved service needs, stemming from culturally incongruent care, to escalating crises that preceded their incarceration with the criminal justice system.

The lack of culturally tailored interventions specifically designed for veterans is a notable gap within existing treatment paradigms. While some programs incorporate veteran-specific content, many healthcare systems still operate under generic frameworks that inadequately address veterans' unique identity-driven needs. Recent research underscores the value of employing a veteran standpoint theory, emphasizing the importance of understanding healthcare experiences from veterans' perspectives to better tailor interventions and improve outcomes (Meyer & Wynn, 2018; Brys et al., 2018). Treatment models lacking this depth of military cultural competence significantly diminish veterans' engagement, treatment adherence, and overall outcomes, often reinforcing veterans' perception of healthcare systems as unresponsive or irrelevant to their needs.

To effectively address these gaps, healthcare providers and institutions must prioritize the integration of military cultural competence into their treatment models. This involves not only recognizing and understanding veterans' specific experiences, expectations, and coping strategies but also actively incorporating veterans' perspectives into the development, implementation, and evaluation of treatment protocols (Tanielian & Jaycox, 2008). Healthcare models grounded in veteran standpoint theory, characterized by qualitative data collection methods that center veteran voices, can significantly improve the relevance, responsiveness, and effectiveness of care delivery.

Provider training programs should emphasize comprehensive education in military culture, norms, and experiences, equipping providers with the skills necessary for effective communication, empathy, and treatment planning tailored explicitly to veterans' needs (Koenig et al., 2014). Training initiatives must go beyond traditional didactic methods, incorporating experiential learning, veteran narratives, and practical applications of veteran-specific care approaches. Incorporating veteran-specific peer support into healthcare delivery can significantly enhance trust, engagement, and treatment outcomes by utilizing shared experiences and mutual understanding (Chinman et al., 2010). Shared experiences may also foster broader systemic change by embedding authentic veteran perspectives throughout veteran treatment plans

Veteran Identity and Experiences with Social Service Providers

Veteran interactions with social services reflect veteran expectations derived from their military experiences, particularly notions of efficiency, clarity, accountability, and responsiveness. Military training instills structured, clear, and predictable procedures; thus, veterans frequently expect civilian social services to replicate these organizational features. When civilian institutions fail to meet these expectations, veterans commonly experience frustration, disillusionment, and mistrust, reducing their willingness to engage proactively and sustainably with available services. Scholars document several systemic deficiencies and gaps within current social service provisions, particularly regarding cultural competence and institutional responsiveness to veterans' unique needs and viewpoints (Tsai & Rosenheck, 2015). Interactions perceived as inefficient, insensitive, inadequate, or indifferent impedes veterans' motivation to engage and diminishes their trust in social services.

Veterans' stories suggest these deficiencies and their impacts. For instance, one veteran expressed frustration with institutional responsiveness, stating, "Nobody even at HUD [U.S. Department of Housing and Urban Development] was answering phones." Another veteran explicitly highlighted bureaucratic hurdles: "If I had money to get an apartment I wouldn't be sitting in your office [VA Housing]." These and other veteran narratives show perceived and real institutional unresponsiveness and bureaucratic inefficiency can significantly discourage veterans from accessing and utilizing critical social support services.

Veteran identity influences interactions with social services through internalized cultural expectations. Veterans often interpret perceived inefficiencies or misunderstandings within social services as dismissive or disrespectful to their military-informed values and experiences. A veteran described this sentiment clearly, stating: "In the military, we handle things quickly and efficiently. Civilian offices feel slow and disorganized, and it makes it hard to trust they can help me." These experiences of perceived institutional incompetence or indifference exacerbate feelings of alienation, isolation, and frustration among veterans, directly reducing their motivation for continued engagement. Veterans' narratives offer crucial insights into their subjective interpretations of institutional interactions, highlighting the direct implications of identity-driven expectations on their trust, engagement, and psychosocial outcomes. Veterans' explicit descriptions of negative social service encounters clearly demonstrate how identity-informed perceptions significantly shape their willingness and ability to engage with available services.

From a life course point of view, critical life transitions significantly influence long-term behavior patterns and psychosocial outcomes. Negative social service interactions represent critical turning points that substantially shape veterans' reintegration trajectories. These encounters cumulatively influence veterans' overall engagement, trust, and reliance on institutional support, significantly impacting their vulnerabilities to adverse outcomes, including incarceration. Exploring veteran identity helps to clarify these dynamics by highlighting internal conflicts veterans experience between their military-informed expectations and civilian institutional realities (Demers, 2011). Veterans consistently articulate frustration with civilian institutions that appear inefficient, impersonal, or indifferent, contrasting sharply with military structures' clarity and responsiveness. This internal conflict exacerbates veterans' alienation, mistrust, and disengagement from critical social support services. This is where the overlap with incarceration risk becomes more apparent. When veterans describe withdrawal from social services after negative experiences, many also connected this withdrawal to a cascade of instability, such as loss of housing, loss of income, and worsening substance use. Highlighted in later chapters, these negative experiences played an important role in turning points toward justice system involvement.

Filling these critical gaps in social service provisions requires targeted interventions explicitly focused on enhancing cultural competence and institutional responsiveness. Social service providers must receive specialized training in military cultural competence, explicitly addressing veterans' expectations, experiences, and cultural norms (Meyer et al., 2016). This training significantly improves providers' understanding, empathy, and responsiveness, reducing perceived indifference and bureaucratic inefficiencies. Enhancing institutional transparency, accountability, and responsiveness is equally critical. Veterans consistently express frustration with unclear or inefficient bureaucratic processes, significantly hindering their effective engagement with social services. Institutions should prioritize clear, straightforward communication regarding procedures, expectations, and available resources, reducing bureaucratic hurdles and enhancing veterans' trust and engagement (Keene et al., 2018).

Peer-led and community-based initiatives also offer significant potential for addressing veterans' identity-driven barriers to social service engagement. Peer support programming leverages shared military experiences and cultural understandings to validate veterans' experiences, reducing stigma and fostering trust within social service interactions (Russell, 2009; Solomon, 2004). These programs provide critical emotional and practical support, significantly enhancing veterans' willingness and ability to engage proactively with available social services. These programs utilize veterans' shared military experiences, mutual understanding, and common identity to provide culturally competent and empathetic support. Peer-led initiatives significantly improve veterans' trust, engagement, and mental health outcomes by providing relatable role models and culturally resonant support strategies (Chinman et al., 2010).

Veterans consistently express a strong preference for peer-led programs, emphasizing the value of shared experiences and camaraderie as essential to their successful reintegration. One veteran succinctly articulated the importance of peer support, stating, "Having someone who's been where I've been makes all the difference. They understand without me having to explain." Peer-led programs, grounded in veterans' standpoint, can validate their experiences and enhance their engagement with healthcare and social services. Peer-led initiatives leverage veteran identity effectively, creating supportive contexts that directly address veterans' specific needs, preferences, and expectations. Our veterans spoke to how aligning services with veteran identity yields significant positive outcomes. One veteran described their experience with a structured peer-led mental health group as particularly beneficial, explaining, "It felt like being back with my unit again. We had structure, clear objectives, and peers who understood what I was going through." Another veteran highlighted the benefits of goal-oriented treatments aligned with their disciplinary expectations: "The program had clear goals, and I could see my progress. It motivated me to keep going."

Institutional transparency and accountability further can promote veteran engagement by clearly communicating treatment processes, expectations, and outcomes. Institutions providing clear, responsive communication and streamlined procedures significantly reduce veterans' frustrations and improve their willingness to engage proactively with healthcare and social services (Keene et al., 2018). One veteran specifically emphasized institutional responsiveness, stating, "When they clearly explained the steps and followed through promptly, I felt respected and willing to trust the process." Qualitative insights underscore the importance of transparent, accountable institutional practices in effectively addressing veterans' specific needs and improving their reintegration outcomes. Future chapters will return to these and other veteran accounts that demonstrate how identity-aligned healthcare and social service provision significantly enhance veterans' engagement, satisfaction, and outcomes.

Developing veteran-centered intervention models explicitly incorporating veterans' expectations and preferences can inform social services. For instance, structured, goal-oriented social service interventions align closely with military cultural norms, enhancing veterans' perceived effectiveness and engagement with services (Sayer et al., 2010). By explicitly acknowledging and addressing veterans' identity-driven expectations and needs, tailored interventions significantly reduce veterans' perceived institutional barriers, improving reintegration outcomes and reducing risks of incarceration.

Learning from Veteran Identity to Enhance Service Provision

Veterans' interactions with healthcare providers critically influence their treatment-seeking behaviors, particularly in the context of mental health and substance use treatment. Negative experiences, including perceived dismissiveness, lack of sensitivity, or inadequate acknowledgment of veterans' military backgrounds, significantly undermine veterans' trust in healthcare systems and discourage continued engagement. These negative experiences, discussed in greater detail in Chapter 9, lead to feeling misunderstood and marginalized. In turn, veterans become isolated as they cannot find people who understand them, their concerns, or their (lack of) motivation to pursue care services. Of course, this process of withdrawal exacerbates untreated mental health symptoms and substance use disorders, potentially contributing to increased rates of chronic illness and social difficulties.

Research increasingly emphasizes the need for culturally competent healthcare providers who recognize and integrate the distinct elements of military identity and experiences into care strategies (Heward et al., 2024; Meyer & Wynn, 2018). Despite growing awareness and some targeted training programs, many veterans continue to encounter providers who lack familiarity with the nuances of military culture, exacerbating feelings of frustration and alienation. This gap in cultural competence can manifest through misunderstandings related to the implications of combat exposure, military hierarchies, or the profound sense of identity derived from military service, further complicating the therapeutic relationship and impeding effective care delivery. Improving the cultural competence, transparency, and accountability of healthcare and social services is not merely about increasing satisfaction or engagement. It is also about disrupting pathways to incarceration that veterans themselves describe as rooted in identity-informed disengagement during critical transitions.

One veteran described a particularly discouraging encounter, stating, "I felt like my provider didn't understand anything about military life. It made me less willing to go back." Another veteran articulated a similar sentiment regarding mental health treatment discontinuation: "They didn't get it. They had no clue about what being in combat meant." These statements reflect a broader trend where the absence of military cultural competence among providers creates critical barriers, significantly diminishing veterans' willingness to seek or continue formal treatment. Scholars have documented veterans often view healthcare interactions through the lens of their service-related identity, where experiences of marginalization or misunderstanding can trigger feelings of isolation and mistrust, directly impacting treatment outcomes and adherence

(Cheney et al., 2018; Miller et al., 2020). For veterans, healthcare interactions extend beyond mere clinical encounters; they represent opportunities to have their identities recognized and validated within a broader societal context. When providers fail to acknowledge the profound impact of military experiences, veterans may interpret this as a rejection or invalidation of their identity, significantly weakening therapeutic alliances and diminishing treatment efficacy. This disconnect requires targeted interventions, provider education, and healthcare systems explicitly attuned to veterans' unique cultural perspectives, experiences, and expectations.

As will be shown in later chapters, our veterans frequently describe substance misuse explicitly as a strategy to manage conflicts arising from unmet expectations in civilian contexts. Our interviews with veterans show how identity-informed expectations influence their substance use behaviors, significantly shaping their coping strategies and increasing vulnerabilities to long-term negative outcomes, including incarceration. Similarly, externalized perceptions of control also interact significantly with veteran identity, shaping veterans' responses to civilian institutional interactions and treatment engagement. Veterans who perceive their ability to influence healthcare outcomes as limited often experience internal conflicts with their ingrained military values of control and self-reliance (Mobbs & Bonanno, 2018). These conflicts can lead veterans toward maladaptive coping behaviors (e.g., self-medication or healthcare avoidance) as strategies to regain perceived control over their situations. This qualitative insight highlights the critical relationship between veterans' external perceptions of control, their internalized identity expectations, and subsequent coping behaviors, emphasizing the necessity of recognizing these conflicts in treatment provision.

Negative service experiences, particularly in healthcare and social service contexts, was another critical identity-related conflict, reinforcing veterans' mistrust of institutions and reliance on unhealthy coping behaviors. Veterans often report that negative interactions, characterized by provider indifference, bureaucratic hurdles, or perceived insensitivity, directly contradict their ingrained expectations of competence, efficiency, and respect fostered during military service (True et al., 2015). These experiences contribute significantly to veterans' withdrawal from formal services and increase their vulnerabilities to maladaptive coping strategies.

Veteran identity intersects with broader psychosocial risk factors (i.e., isolation, trauma exposure, and emotional distress). Veterans who perceive their expectations as unmet or invalidated within civilian institutions often experience increased emotional distress, isolation, and reliance on maladaptive coping mechanisms. One veteran described isolation clearly resulting from identity-related conflicts, stating: "I felt completely disconnected from providers who didn't understand military life. Eventually, I withdrew completely, relying on substances to manage isolation and stress." Veteran accounts illustrate the complex interactions between veteran identity, institutional interactions, and broader psychosocial vulnerabilities, emphasizing the critical importance of addressing these interconnected factors in treatment and support provision.

Veteran standpoints can inform interventions seeking to minimize harmful coping behaviors. Interventions that recognize veterans' identity-informed expectations and incorporate these perspectives into treatment approaches can work to address identity conflicts, improving engagement, satisfaction, and outcomes (Meyer & Wynn, 2018). These interventions should validate veterans' background, specifically their internalized values and expectations.

If the aim was to enhance cultural competence, transparency, and accountability within healthcare and social services, our research shows the importance of addressing identity-related conflicts. Healthcare providers must receive specialized training in military cultural competence, ensuring effective communication, empathy, and responsiveness to veterans' specific needs and expectations (Meyer et al., 2016; Sayer et al., 2010). Improved institutional transparency, clear communication, and streamlined processes further address veterans' perceptions of institutional inefficiency or indifference, significantly reducing barriers to engagement.

The intersection of veteran identity with other critical turning-point behaviors significantly influences veterans' coping strategies, institutional interactions, and psychosocial vulnerabilities. A main argument in this book is that risk factors associated with incarceration for veterans are tied to veterans' sense of self *as veterans*. Throughout this book, we make practical and policy recommendations anchored in veterans' lived experiences, perspectives, and identity-informed expectations. The goal is to ensure healthcare and social service providers can significantly enhance veterans' reintegration outcomes, reduce reliance on harmful coping behaviors, and effectively mitigate risks of adverse outcomes, including incarceration.

Research and program development should prioritize veterans' voices, ensuring care strategies authentically reflect their lived experiences and identity-specific needs, thereby enhancing trust, engagement, and overall treatment efficacy. Engaging veterans directly in co-designing healthcare programs and training curricula for providers could offer meaningful pathways to integrating genuine military cultural competence. Additionally, longitudinal studies investigating the impact of culturally competent care on veteran health outcomes are necessary to provide robust evidence for systemic change. By foregrounding veterans' perspectives and fostering genuine collaboration between veterans and healthcare providers, the healthcare system can better meet veterans' complex and specific needs, ultimately improving their quality of life and treatment outcomes. Learning about veteran identity provides a powerful and effective framework for enhancing healthcare and social service provision. Aligning interventions from veterans' standpoint, service delivery can significantly improve treatment engagement, trust, and psychosocial outcomes. This strategy not only validates and supports veterans' unique identities and experiences but also reduces their vulnerabilities during reintegration into civilian life.

Summary

This chapter highlights how veterans' internalized military values and expectations significantly influence their interactions with healthcare systems, treatment-seeking behaviors, and coping strategies postservice. Veterans' self-perceptions, informed by experiences of discipline, resilience, and self-reliance, fundamentally shape their responses to healthcare providers and social service systems, often resulting in unmet needs, institutional mistrust, and reliance on maladaptive coping behaviors (e.g., substance misuse). The intersection between these internalized expectations and the realities veterans encounter within civilian institutions represents a critical challenge that shapes their reintegration experiences and can increase their vulnerabilities to adverse outcomes, including incarceration.

Building upon this foundation, Chapter 5 will further theorize and detail the critical transitions and trajectories experienced by veterans, specifically focusing on their pathways toward incarceration. By examining the significant moments, choices, and experiences that shape veterans' journeys, Chapter 5 will provide a nuanced exploration of how these transitions directly impact veterans' psychosocial outcomes and vulnerabilities. This forthcoming analysis will deepen the understanding of veterans' postservice experiences, illuminating critical intervention points and further supporting efforts to effectively address and disrupt pathways leading toward incarceration.

References

Blais, R. K., & Renshaw, K. D. (2013). Stigma and demographic correlates of help-seeking intentions in returning service members. *Journal of Traumatic Stress*, *26*(1), 77–85. https://doi.org/10.1002/jts.21772

Bond, G. R., Al-Abdulmunem, M., Drake, R. E., Davis, L. L., Meyer, T., Gade, D. M., Frueh, B. C., Dickman, R. B., & Ressler, D. R. (2022). Transition from military service: Mental health and well-being among service members and veterans with service-connected disabilities. *The Journal of Behavioral Health Services & Research*, *49*(3), 282–298. https://doi.org/10.1007/s11414-021-09778-w

Brys, N. A., Whittle, J., & Safdar, N. (2018). Development of a veteran engagement toolkit for researchers. *Journal of Comparative Effectiveness Research*, *7*(6), 595–602. doi.org/10.1186/s12913-018-3346-9

Cheney, A. M., Koenig, C. J., Miller, C. J., Zamora, K. A., Wright, P., Stanley, R., Fortney, J., Burgess, J. F., & Pyne, J. M. (2018). Veteran-centered barriers to VA mental healthcare services use. *BMC Health Services Research*, *18*, 591. https://doi.org/10.1186/s12913-018-3346-9

Chinman, M., Shoai, R., & Cohen, A. (2010). Using organizational change strategies to guide peer support technician implementation in the Veterans Administration. *Psychiatric Rehabilitation Journal, 33*(4), 269–277. https://doi.org/10.2975/33.4.2010.269.277

Currier, J. M., McDermott, R. C., & McCormick, W. H. (2017). Mental health treatment related stigma and professional help-seeking among student veterans. *Psychological Services, 14*(4), 531–542. https://doi.org/10.1037/ser0000129

Demers, A. (2011). When veterans return: The role of community in reintegration. *Journal of Loss and Trauma, 16*(2), 160–179. https://doi.org/10.1080/15325024.2010.519281

Finley, E. P., Garcia, H. A., Ketchum, N. S., McGeary, D. D., McGeary, C. A., Stirman, S. W., & Peterson, A. L. (2015). Utilization of evidence-based psychotherapies in Veterans Affairs posttraumatic stress disorder outpatient clinics. *Psychological Services, 12*(1), 73–82. https://doi.org/10.1037/ser0000014

Heward, C., Li, W., Chun Tie, Y., & Waterworth, P. (2024). A scoping review of military culture, military identity, and mental health outcomes in military personnel. *Military Medicine, 189*(11–12), e2382–e2393. https://doi.org/10.1093/milmed/usae276

Hitch, C. M., Toner, P., & Armour, C. (2023). A qualitative systematic review of enablers and barriers to help-seeking for veterans that have completely left the military within the context of mental health and alcohol. *Journal of Veterans Studies, 9*(1), 15–30. https://doi.org/10.21061/jvs.v9i1.376

Joseph, J. S., Smith-MacDonald, L., Filice, M. C., & Smith, M. S. (2023). Reculturation: A new perspective on military-civilian transition stress. *Military Psychology, 35*(3), 193–203. https://doi.org/10.1080/08995605.2022.2094175

Keene, D. E., Rosenberg, A., Schlesinger, P., Guo, M., & Blankenship, K. M. (2018). Navigating limited and uncertain access to subsidized housing after prison. *Housing Policy Debate, 28*(2), 199–214. https://doi.org/10.1080/10511482.2017.1336638

Koenig, C. J., Maguen, S., Monroy, J. D., Mayott, L., & Seal, K. H. (2014). Facilitating culture centered communication between healthcare providers and veterans transitioning from military deployment to civilian life. *Patient Education and Counseling, 95*(3), 414–420. https://doi.org/10.1016/j.pec.2014.03.016

Lancaster, S. L., & Hart, R. P. (2015). Military identity and psychological functioning: A pilot study. *Military Behavioral Health, 3*(1), 83–87. https://doi.org/10.1080/21635781.2014.995254

Meyer, E. G., Writer, B. W., & Brim, W. (2016). The importance of military cultural competence. *Current Psychiatry Reports, 18*(26). https://doi.org/10.1007/s11920-016-0662-9

Meyer, E. G., & Wynn, G. H. (2018). The importance of US military cultural competence. In L. Roberts & C. Warner (Eds.), *Military and veteran mental health* (pp. 15–33). Springer. https://doi.org/10.1007/978-1-4939-7438-2_2

Meyer, J. F., Wattenberg, M. S., Kosman, K. A., Budd, M. A., Duffy, M. J., Agrawal, A., Richmond, J. S., Hough, S., Meltzer, B., Schein, A. Z., Poster, M. F., & Bradley, J. C. (2023). Stigma and barriers to care for mental health treatment for military and veteran populations. In C. H. Warner & C. A. Castro (Eds.), *Veteran and military mental health: A clinical manual* (pp. 45–85). Springer Nature Switzerland AG. https://doi.org/10.1007/978-3-031-18009-5_4

Miller, C. J., Shin, M., Pugatch, M., & Kim, B. (2021). Veteran perspectives on care coordination between Veterans Affairs and community providers: A qualitative

analysis. *The Journal of Rural Health, 37*(2), 437–446. https://doi.org/10.1111/jrh.12526
Mobbs, M. C., & Bonanno, G. A. (2018). Beyond war and PTSD: The crucial role of transition stress in the lives of military veterans. *Clinical Psychology Review, 59*, 137–144. https://doi.org/10.1016/j.cpr.2017.11.007
Pietrzak, R. H., Johnson, D. C., Goldstein, M. B., Malley, J. C., & Southwick, S. M. (2009). Psychological resilience and postdeployment social support protect against traumatic stress and depressive symptoms in soldiers returning from Operations Enduring Freedom and Iraqi Freedom. *Depression and Anxiety, 26*(8), 745–751. https://doi.org/10.1002/da.20558
Resnick, S. G., & Rosenheck, R. A. (2008). Integrating peer-provided services: A quasi-experimental study of recovery orientation, confidence, and empowerment. *Psychiatric Services, 59*(11), 1307–1314. https://doi.org/10.1176/ps.2008.59.11.1307
Russell, R. T. (2009). Veterans treatment court: A proactive approach. *New England Journal of Criminal and Civil Confinement, 35*(2), 357–372.
Sayer, N. A., Noorbaloochi, S., Frazier, P., Carlson, K., Gravely, A., & Murdoch, M. (2010). Reintegration problems and treatment interests among Iraq and Afghanistan combat veterans receiving VA medical care. *Psychiatric Services, 61*(6), 589–597. https://doi.org/10.1176/ps.2010.61.6.589
Solomon, P. (2004). Peer support/peer provided services underlying processes, benefits, and critical ingredients. *Psychiatric Rehabilitation Journal, 27*(4), 392–401. https://doi.org/10.2975/27.2004.392.401
Tajfel, H., & Turner, J. C. (1979). An integrative theory of intergroup conflict. In W. G. Austin & S. Worchel (Eds.), *The social psychology of intergroup relations* (pp. 33–47). Monterey, CA: Brooks/Cole.
Tanielian, T., & Jaycox, L. H. (Eds.). (2008). Invisible wounds of war: Psychological and cognitive injuries, their consequences, and services to assist recovery. RAND Corporation. www.rand.org/pubs/monographs/MG720.html
True, G., Rigg, K. K., & Butler, A. (2015). Understanding barriers to mental health care for recent war veterans through photovoice. *Qualitative Health Research, 25*(10), 1443–1455. https://doi.org/10.1177/1049732314562894

5

TRAJECTORIES AND TRANSITIONS AND HOW THEY GUIDE OUR UNDERSTANDING OF VETERAN INCARCERATION EXPERIENCES

Introduction

Understanding the experiences of veterans involved with the criminal justice system necessitates a thorough exploration of the broader patterns of life stability and significant life changes they encounter. This chapter provides a detailed examination of these long-term patterns and critical life events, revealing how they collectively shape the paths veterans follow, particularly concerning their potential involvement in incarceration. Focusing on the nuanced relationship between military service, civilian reintegration, and encounters with criminal justice institutions allows for a deeper comprehension of veterans' unique experiences, presenting opportunities for meaningful intervention.

Long-term behavioral patterns, often shaped by consistent life circumstances and environments, reflect how individuals navigate various societal contexts, relationships, and institutional interactions (Benson & Elder, 2011; Weese, n.d.). Within the veteran population, these consistent patterns are informed significantly by military experiences, encompassing rigorous discipline, structured environments, hierarchical relationships, and communal interdependence. Military service can offer stability, particularly for individuals from challenging backgrounds, and provides a foundation upon which veterans build their subsequent life experiences and expectations. However, these established patterns of behavior may not always support veterans during significant life shifts (e.g., military discharge, family reunification, broader psychosocial reintegration) that introduce substantial disruption and adaptation demands to new social, economic, and relational contexts (Castro & Kintzle, 2014).

DOI: 10.4324/9781003522300-5

Critical life shifts, defined as significant events altering existing stable patterns, can dramatically reshape an individual's life direction, expectations, and behaviors (Grimell, 2024; Morris & Hanna, 2023). Military discharge represents a primary event for veterans, marking the transition from highly structured military environments to the relative ambiguity of civilian life. This change, often accompanied by economic instability, loss of institutional identity, and relational disruptions, significantly influences veterans' behavior patterns and coping strategies. Veterans frequently describe the destabilizing nature of discharge, emphasizing the abrupt loss of structure, clear responsibilities, and social support previously provided by military service. For example, one veteran explicitly described their discharge as disorienting, noting, "Leaving the military felt like stepping into uncertainty; I didn't have clear guidance anymore, and civilian life felt overwhelming." Transitions have a profound impact on veterans' postservice trajectories.

Economic and employment-related changes represent another significant transitional area impacting veterans' reintegration experiences. Transitioning to civilian employment often introduces challenges related to mismatches between military training and civilian job requirements, job instability, and financial insecurity (Harrod et al., 2017). These challenges not only disrupt veterans' economic stability but also influence their psychological well-being and coping strategies. Veterans described economic struggles as critical factors contributing to their involvement with substances, mental health concerns, and potential criminal behavior. One veteran clearly described employment-related stress, stating, "After the service, finding steady employment was difficult; nothing matched my skills, and the stress led me to make poor choices." This insight underscores how economic instability acts as a critical transitional experience shaping veterans' behavioral patterns and increasing their vulnerabilities.

Relational transitions, particularly those involving family structures and social connections, similarly exert significant influence on veterans' postservice experiences. Military deployments, separations, and frequent relocations often strain family and personal relationships, leading to relationship breakdowns, isolation, and emotional distress during reintegration (Knobloch & Theiss, 2012). Relational disruptions directly affect veterans' mental health and coping behaviors, often pushing them toward maladaptive coping strategies like substance misuse or isolation. Upon returning home, this veteran shared, "Family life felt foreign; we had all changed so much. It was easier to isolate and cope alone than face the family tensions." These narratives illustrate the complex emotional and behavioral impacts relational transitions have on veterans' lives, significantly shaping their trajectories postservice.

Health-related shifts, including physical injuries, chronic pain, and mental health conditions developed during military service, represent additional significant transitional experiences for veterans. These health-related challenges substantially influence veterans' quality of life, interactions with healthcare institutions, and coping strategies (Currier et al., 2015). Veterans frequently report inadequate healthcare experiences that exacerbate their reliance on maladaptive coping strategies, significantly increasing their risks for adverse psychosocial outcomes, including potential incarceration. One veteran explicitly linked health challenges and inadequate care to substance use: "Managing my injuries and PTSD was overwhelming; when treatments failed, substance use became my only relief." This reflection underscores how health-related transitions and inadequate healthcare experiences significantly shape veterans' behavioral patterns and vulnerabilities.

Recognizing these complex patterns and critical transitional experiences is essential for developing effective intervention strategies tailored explicitly to veterans' unique needs and contexts. Interventions designed to support veterans must emphasize comprehensive approaches addressing economic stability, employment support, relational counseling, healthcare accessibility, and community-based resources. Targeted programs incorporating structured, culturally competent approaches, peer-led initiatives, and institutional reforms hold substantial potential for enhancing veterans' resilience during transitional periods (Resnick & Rosenheck, 2008; Tanielian & Jaycox, 2008).

This chapter provides a comprehensive analysis of critical patterns and transitions influencing veterans' pathways toward incarceration. By explicitly understanding and addressing the complex interplay of transitions, which include military discharge, economic challenges, relational disruptions, and healthcare inadequacies, stakeholders can develop informed, culturally competent interventions that effectively address veterans' needs. This comprehensive understanding provides a robust foundation for systemic improvements aimed at enhancing veterans' successful reintegration and reducing vulnerabilities to adverse outcomes, including incarceration.

Veteran Experiences within Broader Social and Historical Contexts

Understanding veterans' incarceration experiences requires a detailed examination of individual lives set against broader societal and historical contexts. This approach emphasizes how personal choices, social relationships, and institutional interactions combine over time to shape veterans' life pathways. It acknowledges that individual actions occur within a structured social context, recognizing the dynamic interaction between personal agency and societal factors.

The timing of life events holds significant implications for veterans, particularly given that military service often aligns with critical developmental phases. Early adulthood is a period characterized by identity development, formation of long-term relationships, and key decisions that shape personal and professional futures. Military service during this formative period provides a unique, structured environment that fosters discipline, clear responsibilities, and strong peer relationships, potentially redirecting individuals from adverse backgrounds toward more constructive pathways. MacLean and Elder (2007) note military involvement positively affects individuals' developmental trajectories, offering resources and support structures previously unavailable.

However, transitioning from the structured military setting to civilian life introduces substantial instability. The shift from a highly organized environment to civilian society, often characterized by ambiguity and isolation, can undermine veterans' previously stable patterns. This disruption frequently occurs during critical periods in adulthood when individuals are expected to establish stable careers, personal relationships, and community integration. Without comprehensive transition support or effective management of underlying mental health challenges (e.g., PTSD, anxiety, or depression) veterans may experience increased risks for unemployment, homelessness, and involvement with the criminal justice system (Brignone et al., 2017).

Social relationships significantly influence veterans' experiences following military service. The strength and stability of interpersonal relationships (whether familial, peer-based, or community-related) can greatly facilitate or hinder veterans' successful reintegration. Strong relationships provide emotional support, practical assistance, and a sense of belonging, mitigating the challenges veterans encounter in adjusting to civilian environments. In contrast, relationships weakened by military deployment, prolonged separations, or reintegration stressors often leave veterans feeling isolated and disconnected. Research has documented veterans' struggles in relating to civilian peers, noting profound feelings of misunderstanding and alienation that contribute to social withdrawal and maladaptive coping strategies, including substance use (Knobloch & Theiss, 2012).

The balance between individual agency and social constraints also plays a critical role in veterans' postservice experiences. While veterans actively strive to redefine their civilian identities and establish new life goals, structural barriers frequently hinder their efforts. Limited access to comprehensive healthcare services, institutional bureaucratic challenges, societal stigmatization of mental health, and difficulties translating military skills into civilian employment collectively impede veterans' autonomy and choices. These barriers exacerbate vulnerabilities, prompting some veterans to adopt maladaptive behaviors that can escalate to criminal activities and subsequent incarceration (Harrod et al., 2017).

Economic instability following military service further compounds veterans' challenges. Veterans often encounter employment difficulties arising from mismatched military-to-civilian skill translations, inadequate job opportunities, and financial insecurity. Economic instability not only influences mental and physical health but also heightens vulnerability to risky behaviors. Veterans consistently describe employment struggles as stressful and disorienting, emphasizing how limited career opportunities can foster feelings of inadequacy, frustration, and instability. Economic stressors have been linked to substance misuse, which further complicate reintegration processes and elevate incarceration risks (Harrod et al., 2017).

Health challenges also substantially shape veterans' postmilitary experiences. Chronic physical injuries, psychological trauma, and mental health conditions are prevalent among veterans, influencing their quality of life and interactions with healthcare systems. Veterans often express dissatisfaction with healthcare services, citing inadequate responsiveness, impersonal care approaches, and ineffective treatments as reasons for disengagement from formal care. These negative healthcare experiences drive veterans toward alternative coping mechanisms, further exacerbating existing mental and physical health challenges (Sayer et al., 2010).

Interconnected challenges require culturally competent interventions specifically tailored to veterans' unique needs and experiences. Effective interventions include integrated mental and physical health services, peer-led support programs, and structured employment and economic-assistance initiatives. Comprehensive support structures that address economic stability, relational networks, and healthcare accessibility can significantly improve veterans' reintegration outcomes. Institutions must prioritize clear, responsive, and accountable service delivery, ensuring veterans receive effective and culturally aligned support.

Leveraging shared experiences and cultural understanding among veterans, significantly enhance emotional and practical support during reintegration. As will be discussed in future chapters, these shared experiences can be essential in reducing isolation, stigma, and institutional mistrust, effectively addressing their reintegration challenges and vulnerabilities. Specifically, programs anchored on shared veteran experiences and understandings provide culturally resonant support, significantly improving veterans' engagement and outcomes.

Transparent procedures, clear communication, and institutional accountability measures can also reduce veterans' frustrations and mistrust postservice. Improving institutional effectiveness and responsiveness fosters proactive engagement among veterans, encouraging their reliance on formal support systems and reducing their vulnerability to maladaptive coping mechanisms and incarceration.

Analyzing veterans' postmilitary experiences through a holistic understanding of individual actions, relational influences, and structural contexts provides deeper insights into their reintegration challenges and vulnerabilities. Effective interventions must recognize the interconnectedness of economic, relational, healthcare, and institutional factors, providing comprehensive, culturally competent, and responsive support. Addressing these complex dynamics comprehensively enables veterans to successfully transition into civilian life, reducing their vulnerabilities to adverse outcomes, including involvement with the criminal justice system.

Trajectories Leading to Incarceration

The pathways leading veterans toward involvement with the criminal justice system result from intricate and multifaceted interactions spanning their entire lives. Factors including early-life adversities, military experiences, and postservice adjustments intersect, creating cumulative vulnerabilities that elevate their susceptibility to criminal justice interactions. To fully comprehend these interconnected pathways, it is essential to acknowledge how challenges encountered at different life stages interact sequentially, shaping individuals' long-term outcomes.

Early-Life Experiences and Their Long-Term Implications

Early-life experiences around familial instability, poverty, neglect, or exposure to violence, establish foundational vulnerabilities that significantly influence an individual's psychological development and coping mechanisms. Adverse childhood experiences (ACEs) are strongly correlated with increased risks of mental health disorders like depression, anxiety, posttraumatic stress disorder (PTSD), and substance use issues later in life (Anda et al., 2006; Felitti et al., 1998). These early experiences often create an enduring predisposition toward maladaptive coping behaviors and emotional regulation challenges. For many veterans, joining the military initially serves as an escape from these adverse environments, offering structured routines, economic security, and strong social connections previously unavailable. However, underlying vulnerabilities may resurface or intensify under military stressors, especially during deployments or combat exposure, exacerbating their susceptibility to subsequent criminal justice involvement (Blosnich et al., 2014).

For veterans, childhood experiences often create a predisposition toward challenges that resurface under the pressures and stresses of military and postmilitary life. While the structured military environment may temporarily mitigate these early vulnerabilities by providing stability, economic security, and supportive social networks, the underlying issues typically persist, resurfacing prominently during periods of stress, transition, or adversity (Blosnich et al., 2014). Therefore, understanding and addressing early-life adversities are vital for developing comprehensive interventions aimed at reducing vulnerabilities throughout veterans' subsequent life stages.

Military Experiences

Military service can act as both a protective and destabilizing force in veterans' lives. For many individuals, the military offers structure, discipline, camaraderie, and clear role definitions that provide a stabilizing influence, especially for those emerging from challenging early-life circumstances (Mobbs & Bonanno, 2018). Military training fosters personal agency, resilience, and a sense of identity, empowering many veterans to redirect negative life patterns toward more positive trajectories.

However, military experiences, especially exposure to combat or trauma, can introduce significant psychological burdens. Trauma exposure frequently results in long-term mental health conditions, including PTSD, anxiety, depression, and substance abuse issues (Ramchand et al., 2015). The structured environment that initially fosters resilience can paradoxically become a source of vulnerability when veterans face traumatic experiences without adequate mental health support. Stigma related to mental health treatment further deters veterans from seeking necessary care, exacerbating emotional and psychological challenges, and potentially escalating to maladaptive coping behaviors and interactions with criminal justice systems (Sharp et al., 2015).

The transition from military service to civilian life constitutes another pivotal phase in veterans' lives, significantly influencing their adjustment outcomes. This transition often entails substantial challenges, including loss of identity associated with military roles, economic instability, social disconnection, and feelings of isolation or alienation. Veterans commonly report difficulties translating military experiences and skills into civilian employment, which may result in financial hardship and instability. Economic strain, coupled with social isolation and inadequate access to healthcare, can lead veterans toward substance misuse or social withdrawal (Mobbs & Bonanno, 2018). The transition from structured military environments to civilian contexts represents a critical period characterized by uncertainty, identity challenges, and difficulties establishing stable economic and social roles (Mobbs & Bonanno, 2018). Veterans commonly report significant struggles during reintegration, including identity loss, social isolation, and difficulty translating military skills to civilian employment (Harrod et al., 2017). The escalation of these coping responses frequently heightens vulnerabilities to encounters with law enforcement, particularly through offenses related to homelessness, substance-related crimes, or survival behaviors, such as trespassing or petty theft (Tsai et al., 2016).

Discharge and its Consequences

The nature of military discharge (e.g., honorable, general, or dishonorable) also influences veterans' subsequent access to critical support services, including healthcare, mental health treatment, and economic assistance (Brignone et al., 2017). Veterans receiving less-than-honorable discharges often face substantial barriers to critical resources, heightening their vulnerability to homelessness, untreated mental health conditions, substance misuse, and criminal behavior. Therefore, policy changes to broaden eligibility and support for veterans regardless of discharge status are vital for reducing vulnerabilities during the critical transitional period postservice.

Addressing Homelessness and Substance Misuse

Homelessness and substance use represent interconnected issues significantly influencing veterans' pathways to incarceration. Homelessness often arises from economic instability, lack of affordable housing, untreated mental health conditions, or disrupted social support systems, all factors prevalent among veterans transitioning to civilian life (Tsai & Rosenheck, 2015). Homelessness frequently increases interactions with law enforcement, often related to survival behaviors, thereby heightening incarceration risks.

Similarly, substance misuse often emerges as a coping mechanism for untreated psychological trauma, chronic pain, or stress associated with civilian reintegration. Substance misuse exacerbates veterans' social isolation, economic instability, and legal troubles, significantly escalating incarceration vulnerability (Sayer et al., 2010). Integrating comprehensive mental health, housing, employment, and substance use support services is critical for addressing these interconnected challenges effectively.

Interconnected Lives: How Social Connections Shape Veterans' Experiences

Understanding veterans' pathways after military service, including their susceptibility to involvement with the criminal justice system, demands careful exploration of their social connections and relationships. Human lives unfold within social environments and interpersonal relationships, significantly influencing decision-making processes and life outcomes (Elder & Giele, 2009; Kahn & Antonucci, 1980). These relational dynamics play critical roles during major life events or periods of substantial change, profoundly affecting personal stability and adaptation.

Military service creates intense social bonds forged through shared hardship, mutual dependence, and collective identity. Participants interviewed for this research frequently highlighted the importance of these military relationships as essential sources of emotional strength, practical support, and psychological stability during challenging periods. They described how friendships formed in military contexts often provided vital coping resources, facilitating effective management of stress and adversity. For instance, veterans noted that their fellow service members offered crucial emotional support and practical guidance, enabling them to navigate complex situations more effectively.

Yet, the conclusion of active military service can abruptly disrupt these relationships, significantly altering veterans' social support networks and their coping mechanisms. Participants expressed substantial difficulty in effectively communicating their military experiences and emotional challenges to civilian acquaintances, even to close family members. Recent studies similarly demonstrate that veterans frequently perceive civilian interactions as lacking the depth of understanding provided by their military peers, intensifying their sense of alienation and emotional isolation (Kintzle et al., 2018). This disconnection often intensifies psychological distress and heightens vulnerability to maladaptive coping behaviors.

Family relationships, specifically, are central to veterans' adjustment following military service. The qualitative narratives from our research emphasize how successful civilian reintegration is often contingent upon robust and adaptable family support systems. Participants described family relationships as either protective, offering emotional reassurance and practical assistance, or as sources of added stress and isolation when family members struggled to comprehend the veteran's postservice challenges. For example, strained family interactions significantly exacerbated veterans' emotional vulnerability, leading to heightened stress and feelings of isolation, as also supported by recent empirical findings (Creech et al., 2014).

Community connections similarly play a pivotal role in veterans' reintegration experiences. Veterans frequently articulate the difficulty in forming new civilian relationships due to civilians' limited understanding of military culture and experiences. This lack of mutual understanding often fosters a profound sense of estrangement and detachment from civilian social contexts. Participants emphasized the critical need for new relationships and social networks that authentically comprehend and validate their unique experiences, thereby promoting successful community integration and emotional well-being.

The importance of social connections as foundational elements influencing veterans' experiences underscores the necessity for targeted interventions that explicitly support the maintenance and development of supportive relational networks. Qualitative data from this research highlight how enhancing familial understanding, improving community awareness, and cultivating genuine social integration can effectively address veterans' social isolation, reducing their risks of negative coping behaviors and involvement with the criminal justice system. Recent research supports this perspective, emphasizing community-based programs tailored to veterans' specific relational needs as essential for successful reintegration (Chinchilla et al., 2019).

It is also vital to note that these qualitative insights serve as groundwork for deeper exploration into how veterans' identities and their personal developmental experiences interact within their broader life circumstances, themes explored in subsequent chapters. These interconnected social dynamics provide a crucial context for examining how veterans' sense of self and their life experiences shape critical turning points, including pathways toward potential incarceration. Understanding these relational patterns from veterans' perspectives facilitates more effective, culturally sensitive intervention strategies that honor their unique experiences and social needs.

In conclusion, examining veterans' experiences through their relational connections provides essential insight into their adjustment pathways after military service. Identifying and strengthening these social networks through targeted interventions significantly supports veterans' emotional stability, community integration, and overall psychological health, mitigating their vulnerabilities to negative outcomes. The qualitative narratives and contemporary research underscore that relational interconnectedness is pivotal in shaping veterans' postservice experiences, offering practical implications and direction for policy and community support programs.

Intervention Approaches Informed by Veterans' Lived Experiences

Effectively managing the complexities and cumulative challenges faced by veterans requires interventions explicitly tailored to their unique lived experiences. Qualitative insights from veterans' personal narratives offer valuable guidance for designing and implementing targeted strategies. Veterans' firsthand accounts highlight that addressing their specific vulnerabilities and utilizing their inherent strengths are essential to fostering successful reintegration and reducing the risk of involvement in the criminal justice system.

Qualitative interviews from our study underscore that effective intervention strategies must start by recognizing and addressing childhood adversities and the enduring vulnerabilities they create. Veterans often describe childhood trauma, economic hardships, and unstable family environments as foundational factors influencing their later life decisions and coping mechanisms. Recent research supports this viewpoint, emphasizing that trauma-informed care and early intervention strategies significantly improve long-term outcomes (McCauley et al., 2015; Bowen et al., 2016). Thus, integrating trauma-informed services into veterans' healthcare and social support systems is vital for mitigating early-life adversities' long-term consequences (Katz, 2012).

Additionally, comprehensive mental health support during and immediately after military service emerges as a crucial intervention component. Veterans repeatedly highlight insufficient mental health care as a primary contributor to their postservice struggles. Interviews reveal veterans' experiences of mental health stigma, inadequate support, and lack of access to culturally competent treatments, which exacerbate mental health conditions and encourage reliance on maladaptive coping strategies. Recent scholarship confirms these findings, suggesting that culturally responsive mental health care models significantly enhance veterans' engagement, reduce stigma, and improve overall mental health outcomes (Treichler et al., 2023).

Economic stability and employment assistance represent further critical elements of comprehensive intervention. Veterans consistently report substantial difficulties transitioning their military skills into civilian job markets, often resulting in unemployment, economic stress, and associated mental health challenges. Qualitative narratives from our research illustrate that employment stability is vital for psychological well-being and successful civilian integration. Recent studies reinforce these insights, demonstrating that employment programs specifically tailored to veterans' skillsets and experiences significantly improve economic stability, reduce mental health distress, and decrease risks for incarceration (Bond et al., 2022).

Housing security and homelessness prevention programs also emerge as essential intervention strategies. Veterans frequently describe homelessness as a pivotal factor exacerbating their vulnerabilities and interactions with the criminal justice system. Qualitative accounts indicate that comprehensive housing assistance programs tailored explicitly to veterans' unique circumstances significantly mitigate homelessness-related risks. Contemporary research supports these qualitative findings, demonstrating that integrated housing, employment, and healthcare services substantially reduce veterans' vulnerabilities to homelessness and incarceration (Weese, n.d.).

Summary

As was mentioned in Chapter 4, peer-led support initiatives consistently receive high praise in veterans' qualitative narratives. Veterans emphasize the significant benefits derived from peer support networks, which provide emotional validation, practical assistance, and shared understanding of military experiences. Our qualitative findings emphasize peer support as uniquely effective in reducing isolation, stigma, and mistrust toward formal support services. Recent empirical research corroborates these qualitative insights, showing peer-led initiatives' effectiveness in enhancing veterans' mental health, social integration, and overall resilience (Mercier et al., 2023).

Veterans describe institutional interactions marked by bureaucracy, perceived indifference, and inadequate cultural understanding as significant barriers to successful reintegration. Integrating veterans' perspectives directly into healthcare and social service provision significantly enhances institutional responsiveness and effectiveness. Recent literature emphasizes the importance of embedding culturally competent practices and transparent communication within institutional frameworks, demonstrating improved veteran trust and proactive engagement (Sellers et al., 2023).

Finally, building on veterans' strengths of resilience, discipline, and structured routines learned during military service, can be a powerful strategy for improving outcomes. Veterans highlight the importance of structured, goal-oriented approaches aligning closely with their military-acquired skills and values. Recent evidence supports this, indicating that structured interventions explicitly utilizing veterans' strengths significantly improve engagement, motivation, and overall psychosocial outcomes (Mael et al., 2022).

Learning from veterans' qualitative experiences, contemporary research, and a clear understanding of their lived realities, comprehensive intervention strategies can be tailored to effectively address their unique needs. Utilizing a veteran-informed perspective to inform these interventions ensures their relevance, responsiveness, and overall effectiveness. An integrated approach offers the best opportunity to facilitate successful reintegration, improve psychological well-being, reduce maladaptive coping behaviors, and significantly decrease vulnerability to involvement in the criminal justice system.

References

Anda, R. F., Felitti, V. J., Bremner, J. D., Walker, J. D., Whitfield, C., Perry, B. D., Dube, S. R., & Giles, W. H. (2006). The enduring effects of abuse and related adverse experiences in childhood. A convergence of evidence from neurobiology and epidemiology. *European Archives of Psychiatry and Clinical Neuroscience, 256*(3), 174–186. https://doi.org/10.1007/s00406-005-0624-4

Benson, J. E., & Elder, G. H. Jr. (2011). Young adult identities and their pathways: A developmental and life course model. *Developmental Psychology, 47*(6), 1646–1657. https://doi.org/10.1037/a0023833

Blosnich, J. R., Dichter, M. E., Cerulli, C., Batten, S. V., & Bossarte, R. M. (2014). Disparities in adverse childhood experiences among individuals with a history of military service. *JAMA Psychiatry, 71*(9), 1041–1048. https://doi.org/10.1001/jamapsychiatry.2014.724

Bond, G. R., Al-Abdulmunem, M., Ressler, D. R., Drake, R. E., Davis, L. L., Meyer, T., Gade, D. M., Frueh, B. C., & Dickman, R. B. (2022). Evaluation of an employment intervention for veterans transitioning from the military: A randomized controlled trial. *The Journal of Nervous and Mental Disease, 210*(5), 321–329. https://doi.org/10.1097/NMD.0000000000001472

Bowen, G. L., Jensen, T. M., Martin, J. A., & Mancini, J. A. (2016). The willingness of military members to seek help: The role of social involvement and social responsibility. *American Journal of Community Psychology, 57*(1–2), 203–215. https://doi.org/10.1002/ajcp.12030

Brignone, E., Fargo, J. D., Blais, R. K., Carter, M. E., Samore, M. H., & Gundlapalli, A. V. (2017). Non-routine discharge from military service: Mental illness, substance use disorders, and unemployment. *American Journal of Preventive Medicine, 52*(5), 557–565. https://doi.org/10.1016/j.amepre.2016.11.015

Castro, C. A., & Kintzle, S. (2014). Suicides in the military: The post-modern combat veteran and the Hemingway effect. *Current Psychiatry Reports, 16*(8), Article 460. https://doi.org/10.1007/s11920-014-0460-1

Chinchilla, M., Gabrielian, S., Hellemann, G., Glasmeier, A., & Green, M. (2019). Determinants of community integration among formerly homeless veterans who received supportive housing. *Frontiers in Psychiatry, 10*, 472. https://doi.org/10.3389/fpsyt.2019.00472

Creech, S. K., Hadley, W., & Borsari, B. (2014). The impact of military deployment and reintegration on children and parenting: A systematic review. *Professional Psychology: Research and Practice, 45*(6), 452–464. https://doi.org/10.1037/a0035055

Currier, J. M., Holland, J. M., Drescher, K., & Foy, D. (2015). Initial psychometric evaluation of the Moral Injury Questionnaire-Military version. *Clinical Psychology & Psychotherapy, 22*(1), 54–63. https://doi.org/10.1002/cpp.1866

Elder, G. H., & Giele, J. Z. (Eds.). (2009). *The craft of life course research.* Guilford Press.

Felitti, V. J., Anda, R. F., Nordenberg, D., Williamson, D. F., Spitz, A. M., Edwards, V., Koss, M. P., & Marks, J. S. (1998). Relationship of childhood abuse and household dysfunction to many leading causes of death in adults. The Adverse Childhood Experiences (ACE) Study. *American Journal of Preventive Medicine*, *14*(4), 245–258. https://doi.org/10.1016/s0749-3797(98)00017-8

Grimell, J. (2024). You can take a person out of the military, but you can't take the military out of the person: Findings from a ten-year identity study on transition from military to civilian life. *Frontiers in Sociology*. https://doi.org/10.3389/fsoc.2024.1406710

Harrod, M., Miller, E. M., Henry, J., & Zivin, K. (2017). "I've never been able to stay in a job": A qualitative study of veterans' experiences of maintaining employment. *Work: A Journal of Prevention, Assessment and Rehabilitation*, *57*(2), 259–268. https://doi.org/10.3233/WOR-172551

Kahn, R. L., & Antonucci, T. C. (1980). Convoys over the life course: Attachment, roles, and social support. In P. B. Baltes & O. G. Grim (Eds.), *Life span development and behavior* (Vol. 3, pp. 253–286). Academic Press.

Katz, L. S., Cojucar, G., Beheshti, S., Nakamura, E., & Murray, M. (2012). Military sexual trauma during deployment to Iraq and Afghanistan: Prevalence, readjustment, and gender differences. *Violence and Victims, 27*(4), 487–499. https://doi.org/10.1891/0886-6708.27.4.487

Kintzle, S., Barr, N., Corletto, G., & Castro, C. A. (2018). PTSD in U.S. veterans: The role of social connectedness, combat experience and discharge. *Healthcare, 6*(3), 102. https://doi.org/10.3390/healthcare6030102

Knobloch, L. K., & Theiss, J. A. (2012). Experiences of U.S. military couples during the post-deployment transition: Applying the relational turbulence model. *Journal of Social and Personal Relationships*, 29(4), 423–450. https://doi.org/10.1177/0265407511431186

MacLean, A., & Elder, G. H., Jr. (2007). Military service in the life course. *Annual Review of Sociology*, *33*, 175–196. https://doi.org/10.1146/annurev.soc.33.040406.131710

McCauley, H. L., Blosnich, J. R., & Dichter, M. E. (2015). Adverse childhood experiences and adult health outcomes among veteran and non-veteran women. *Journal of Women's Health, 24*(9), 723–729. https://doi.org/10.1089/jwh.2014.4997

Mael, F., Wyatt, W., & Iyer, U. J. (2022). Veterans to workplace: Keys to successful transition. *Military Psychology, 34*(5), 516–529. https://doi.org/10.1080/08995605.2021.2016307

Mercier, J. M., Hosseiny, F., Rodrigues, S., Friio, A., Brémault-Phillips, S., Shields, D. M., & Dupuis, G. (2023). Peer support activities for veterans, serving members, and their families: Results of a scoping review. *International Journal of Environmental Research and Public Health, 20*(4), Article 3628. https://doi.org/10.3390/ijerph20043628

Mobbs, M. C., & Bonanno, G. A. (2018). Beyond war and PTSD: The crucial role of transition stress in the lives of military veterans. *Clinical Psychology Review*, *59*, 137–144. https://doi.org/10.1016/j.cpr.2017.11.007

Morris, J., & Hanna, P. (2023). The military to civilian transition: Exploring experiences of transitions to "civvy street" and implications for the self. *Journal of Veterans Studies*, *9*(3), 74–88. https://doi.org/10.21061/jvs.v9i3.458

Ramchand, R., Rudavsky, R., Grant, S., Tanielian, T., & Jaycox, L. (2015). Prevalence of, risk factors for, and consequences of posttraumatic stress disorder and other mental health problems in military populations deployed to Iraq and Afghanistan. *Current Psychiatry Reports, 17*(5), Article 37. https://doi.org/10.1007/s11920-015-0575-z

Resnick, S. G., & Rosenheck, R. A. (2008). Integrating peer-provided services: A quasi-experimental study of recovery orientation, confidence, and empowerment. *Psychiatric Services*, *59*(11), 1307–1314. https://doi.org/10.1176/ps.2008.59.11.1307

Sayer, N. A., Noorbaloochi, S., Frazier, P., Carlson, K., Gravely, A., & Murdoch, M. (2010). Reintegration problems and treatment interests among Iraq and Afghanistan combat veterans receiving VA medical care. *Psychiatric Services*, *61*(6), 589–597. https://doi.org/10.1176/ps.2010.61.6.589

Sellers, J. A., & Kitchen, N. M. (2023). National comparison of veterans and non-veterans medical center patient satisfaction ratings: An HCAHPS survey data analysis. *Journal of Veterans Studies, 9*(3), 89–97. https://doi.org/10.21061/jvs.v9i3.451

Sharp, M. L., Fear, N. T., Rona, R. J., Wessely, S., Greenberg, N., Jones, N., & Goodwin, L. (2015). Stigma as a barrier to seeking healthcare among military personnel with mental health problems. *Epidemiologic Reviews*, *37*(1), 144–162. https://doi.org/10.1093/epirev/mxu012

Tanielian, T., & Jaycox, L. H. (Eds.). (2008). *Invisible wounds of war: Psychological and cognitive injuries, their consequences, and services to assist recovery*. RAND Corporation. www.rand.org/pubs/monographs/MG720.html

Treichler, E. B. H., Reznik, S. J., Oakes, D., Girard, V., & Zisman-Ilani, Y. (2023). Military culture and collaborative decision-making in mental healthcare: Cultural, communication and policy considerations. *BJPsych Open, 9*(5). https://doi.org/10.1192/bjo.2023.516

Tsai, J., Link, B., Rosenheck, R. A., & Pietrzak, R. H. (2016). Homelessness among a nationally representative sample of US veterans: Prevalence, service utilization, and correlates. *Social Psychiatry and Psychiatric Epidemiology, 51*(6), 907–916. https://doi.org/10.1007/s00127-016-1210-y

Tsai, J., & Rosenheck, R. A. (2015). Risk factors for homelessness among US veterans. *Epidemiologic Reviews, 37*(1), 177–195. https://doi.org/10.1093/epirev/mxu004

Weese, K. (n.d.). Integrating employment and housing services for homeless veterans: Implementation lessons from the field [PowerPoint slides]. US Department of Veterans Affairs. https://static1.squarespace.com/static/5e0f94086070a506a2cef5ec/t/62a8f1b67022e8396091738a/1655239095810/Integrating+Emp+and+Housing.pdf

6

BUILDING DIALOGUE AND TRUST AROUND VETERAN LIVED EXPERIENCES

Introduction

This chapter presents an overview of the veteran participants who took part in the study, beginning with statistical information that situates them demographically and socially. This includes data on where participants were from, as well as their socioeconomic status, employment and housing situations, legal histories, and mental health characteristics. Establishing these baseline characteristics provides essential context for understanding the varied life circumstances from which participants entered the study. Such information not only grounds the qualitative narratives in concrete background data but also enables readers to better interpret how personal history and social position may shape veterans' experiences with incarceration and reintegration.

Following this descriptive foundation, the analysis turns to a qualitative exploration of why participants' lived experiences with incarceration were central to the study's objectives. While quantitative indicators can describe the scope of justice involvement among veterans, they cannot by themselves explain how individuals understand, interpret, and give meaning to their own experiences. Capturing these perspectives was vital for examining incarceration not simply as a legal or institutional outcome, but as a process intertwined with identity, relationships, and broader life trajectories. This deeper qualitative component reflects the study's commitment to situating incarceration within the context of veterans' own narratives and interpretations.

A significant focus is placed on veteran standpoint and identity, particularly the widely documented tendency toward skepticism or distrust of government research and researchers. This dimension of identity has important implications

DOI: 10.4324/9781003522300-6

for both data collection and interpretation, as it shapes the conditions under which veterans are willing to participate and disclose personal experiences. Many veterans also describe feeling greater rapport with clinicians or service providers who share a military background and can relate directly to their service experiences. In this study, one author's veteran status served as an important bridge to trust-building, helping participants feel understood and respected, and thereby facilitating more open and detailed accounts. This section also reflects on how similar approaches may assist future research in overcoming barriers related to trust and access within this population.

Later we describe the development and application of a novel interview script designed specifically for the study. Informed by the life course perspective, the instrument aimed to capture a detailed understanding of both the impact and the interconnections among key psychosocial factors, such as mental health, substance use, homelessness, unemployment, military experiences, and legal histories, in shaping incarceration outcomes. By integrating these domains within a single interview structure, the study sought to examine not only the presence of individual factors but also the ways they intersect in veterans' lived experiences. Grounded Theory was employed to elicit rich, in-depth accounts, and grounded analytic principles guided the process of identifying and exploring relationships among the various psychosocial domains.

Finally, the methodological approach to identifying and analyzing central experiential concepts and themes from the interviews is outlined, with attention to how the analytic process supported the study's aims. This includes an acknowledgment of the study's methodological limitations, such as constraints on generalizability and potential selection biases, as well as recommendations for how future research might address these issues. By situating the findings within both their strengths and their limitations, this study contributes to a more transparent and cumulative knowledge base on veteran incarceration and reintegration.

Recruitment Strategies

The first stage of the research involved recruiting veteran participants from targeted settings. This section offers a detailed account of the recruitment sites, including the institutional and community contexts in which veterans were approached. Providing this information serves two purposes: it clarifies the pathways through which participants entered the study, and it offers a snapshot of their circumstances at the time of data collection. Many were experiencing housing instability, active substance use, and mental health challenges. These conditions shape both veterans' immediate needs and their perspectives on incarceration and reentry. Presenting these recruitment details allows readers to better understand how the composition of the sample was shaped by the environments in which veterans were engaged and how these contexts may have influenced the narratives collected.

Veterans were recruited from several locations within VA North Texas Health Care System (VANTHCS). These locations included the in-patient and outpatient substance use programs, homeless programs, and transitional programs. VANTHCS provides substance use services in the form of both in-patient and outpatient programs. The in-patient program is a traditional 30-day residential program where veterans receive intensive biopsychosocial services, which often begins with detoxification and includes a balanced individualized treatment plan that features psychological and psychiatric care and social services. Outpatient substance use programs provide veterans with the same individualized biopsychosocial services and often provide veterans leaving the in-patient program with a bridge to receive continued services.

VANTHCS also provides veterans experiencing homelessness with a variety of biopsychosocial services. Within VANTHCS there is a homeless domiciliary, which provides veterans with temporary housing while simultaneously providing them with mental health, substance use, and social services. Much like the in-patient substance use program, veterans are provided individualized treatment plans which feature psychological and psychiatric care and social services aimed at impacting the barriers to housing. Many of these barriers are interrelated. For example, not being able to maintain sobriety can negatively impact a veteran's ability to successfully hold a job, which can negatively impact their ability to maintain housing. The care and services are ultimately aimed at improving their chances of obtaining housing, which often includes addressing the related issues of sobriety and employment.

Within these locations we implemented several recruitment methods. First, we engaged in direct recruitment by having members of the study team directly recruiting veterans at orientation and community meetings. Second, providers and professional staff, consisting of psychologists, psychiatrists, and social service providers, were made aware of the study and directly recruited veterans at patient meetings and groups. Finally, flyers were disseminated at orientation meetings and posted within common areas of the hospital, such as outpatient waiting rooms, in-patient common areas, and emergency rooms' waiting areas.

COVID-19 Impact on Recruitment

The Novel Coronavirus (COVID-19) pandemic had, and continues to have, serious and often deadly health consequences to the population. Aside from the harmful health implications of COVID, it also presented unique challenges to research communities. Our research was not immune from these challenges.

In response to COVID-19, VA instituted two policies that directly impacted our research. First, VA suspended many in-person residential treatment programs, shifting to virtual programs to fill the need. Second, all in-person, non-critical, research activities were suspended.

To address these potentially limiting factors, we adapted our recruiting methods. First, we received IRB authorization to conduct telephone interviews with veterans. Second, we expanded our recruitment location to include the Sam Rayburn Memorial Veterans Center, Bonham VA Medical Center. The Bonham VA is within the VANTHCS system and was one of a limited number of residential substance use treatment programs that remained open during COVID-19. We also pivoted our recruiting strategy by using Bonham VA providers to disseminate study flyers.

Once eligible veterans were identified, they were enrolled and participated in our study using telephone or VA Video Connect (VVC) system. Adapting our recruiting locations and methods allowed us to maintain momentum in interviewing veterans, whereas many studies had to completely halt all research-related activities.

Consent and Audio-Recording Processes

Our study was approved by the Dallas VA Institutional Review Board (IRB), under study #19-093. All the interviews were audio-recorded using an encrypted recording device and all files were placed on a dedicated and encrypted hard drive. All the participants provided written consent for in-person interviews. For telephone interviews, participants provided verbal consent, and a copy of the consent paperwork was mailed when possible. Verbal consent was documented through voice recording software. Prospective participants were informed that although some of their statements or comments may later be published, the research staff would protect their anonymity and confidentiality.

Inclusion and Exclusion Criteria

Admittedly, our inclusion and exclusion criteria were modest. The inclusion criteria had three components. First, veterans must be interested in participating in the study. Second, they must have a history of incarceration. Finally, they must consent to the interview. As will be discussed later in the chapter, we were primarily interested in the behaviors, or turning points, in veterans' most recent incarceration. Most of our veterans had multiple incarcerations across their lifetimes. Therefore, we wanted to focus on the most recent arrest to maintain fidelity to their memories of the events and circumstances leading up to and during their arrest.

Our exclusion criteria had one requirement. If veterans had a cognitive impairment or psychosis that precluded their ability to accurately follow study instructions, they were excluded from the study. We conducted a chart review of prospective participants to identify any disqualifying mental health conditions.

Transcription

In addition to collecting detailed notes (see Analytic Approach section later for more detail), we also transcribed all interviews for qualitative analysis. This allowed us to go back and review all interviews in greater detail, identifying and exploring turning point behaviors, their relationship to incarceration and, equally important, their relationship to other behaviors.

The Centralized Transcription Services Program (CTSP) at the VA Salt Lake City Health Care System (VASLCHCS) provided transcription services. All interviews were transcribed using the naturalized process, which captures all utterances of the conversation (Oliver et al., 2005). Naturalized transcriptions capture all the nuances of the interview which provided us with a more comprehensive understanding of veterans' incarceration experiences, behaviors, and views.

Novel Interview Script

Created by the author(s), the novel interview script identified specific behaviors the veteran engaged in immediately leading up to, and during, their most recent arrest leading to incarceration. Most veterans had multiple incarcerations across their lifetime. However, by focusing on their most recent arrest leading to incarceration, veterans were more likely to accurately recall nuanced details and behaviors that led to the incident.

The script was also guided by known psychosocial risk factors with incarceration, such as homelessness and unemployment. The script prompted participants to recall the role and impact, if any, of homelessness or unemployment on their most recent arrest leading to incarceration. The interview script also allowed us to probe and explore the role and impact of clinical indicators in veterans' incarceration. These clinical indicators included substance use and/or mental health disorders.

We acknowledge that contemporary literature and research identify the link between substance use, mental health, and social dysfunction (e.g., homelessness and unemployment) on incarceration. However, we contend there needs to be a more nuanced and granular understanding of how these factors impact incarceration. Furthermore, there is a need to understand how these factors interact with one another. Factors such homelessness and unemployment often do not exist separately, or within a silo, within veterans' lives. Instead, they often interact with one another to influence incarceration across veterans' life course. Our interview script allowed us to address these two noted deficiencies. We explored the incarceration turning point more in-depth and examined how these factors interacted upon incarceration collectively.

Overcoming Distrust and Building Dialogue

Veterans feature many positive attributes, such as selflessness in service to our country that often includes time away from family and loved ones. Time away is often a result of training, deployments, and assignments. For example, a "remote" assignment is one that lasts for one year but requires the servicemember to serve the posting unaccompanied, often without their family. So, while the servicemember is deployed for a year away from home, their family members and loved ones do not follow them to their assignment, remaining at home. Remote assignments, in addition to temporary duty assignments, training, and deployments, can place an extraordinary amount of strain on servicemembers and their families as they try to navigate childcare, finances, household chores, and personal relationships while on the assignment.

However, servicemembers, in general, and minority servicemembers specifically, share a tenuous relationship with research and the research community. This strained relationship can be traced to medical research and questions regarding consensual participation (McManus et al., 2005). Examples include George Washington's forced inoculation against smallpox among members of his army and the infamous Tuskegee Syphilis Study in which African American men, infected with syphilis, did not provide consent and were denied effective treatment to track the disease's progression (McManus et al., 2005).

Distrust with Research and Researchers

Given the history of unethical research practices, distrust was a key construct within our research project. Not only was it critical to acknowledge the existence of and extent of distrust, but we also took steps to explicitly limit its impact. Recent studies have found that veterans are broadly distrustful of government institutions, which includes the VA healthcare system (Cheney et al., 2018; Jones et al., 2021). The study by Cheney et al. (2018) found that veteran distrust of VA healthcare system was grounded in an overall lack of confidence stemming from multiple factors, including an absence of follow-ups by providers, scheduling problems, and staffing issues. Following recent highly publicized problems with veteran access to care at certain VA hospitals, Jones et al. (2021) note higher levels of distrust among minority veterans (e.g., women, Black, and Hispanic) compared to non-minority veterans.

In the context of veteran identity, distrust toward research and researchers cannot be separated from the broader patterns of mistrust toward government institutions, which many participants associated with prior disappointments, perceived bureaucratic indifference, or experiences of being marginalized within systems meant to serve them. From a standpoint theory perspective (Harding, 2004; Smith, 1987), this distrust represents not just a barrier to recruitment but a reflection of veterans' situated knowledge. Veterans distrust is shaped by an awareness of their social position as both former servicemembers and as individuals navigating civilian institutions. Qualitative research is uniquely suited to capture how this standpoint shapes decisions about participation, disclosure, and engagement with services. Without these in-depth accounts, policy and programmatic responses risk misinterpreting disengagement as apathy or resistance, rather than understanding it as a reasoned stance grounded in lived experience. By integrating these insights, the present study begins to bridge the gap between veterans' identity-based perspectives and the design of research and interventions intended to support them.

Distrust can extend beyond healthcare organizations. Specifically, distrust has been found to permeate into research departments and individual researchers (Chrystal et al., 2022; Grewe et al., 2021; Littman et al., 2018). In the study by Chrystal et al. (2022), women veterans' hesitancy to engage and participate in VA research was tied to their distrust of research as a whole and researchers in general. Grewe et al. (2021) document distrust and dissatisfaction among Gulf War veterans toward VA and Department of Defense (DoD) that extended to research activities. Similarly, veterans of the recent campaigns in Afghanistan and Iraq valued transparency in VA research, indicating their willingness to participate in research is directly tied to the trustworthiness of researchers and the value of the research to the veteran community (Littman et al., 2018).

Non-Veteran Providers

Another source of distrust stems from an absence of shared experiences between medical and mental health providers and veterans. This distrust stems from an absence of understanding derived from similar experiences. The absence of shared experiences between veterans and medical, mental health, and social service providers can negatively impact relationships and lead to feelings of distrust. According to studies, veterans seeking healthcare services have cited the lack of providers who have served in the armed forces and can directly relate to their experiences as a source of distrust (Cheney et al., 2018; Flynn et al., 2019). In the study conducted by Cheney et al. (2018), veterans cited a lack of understanding of common experiences by those who have not served in the military as a barrier to receiving mental health care services. Flynn et al. (2019) identified several barriers to participatory research and found that veterans are more willing to extend trust to fellow veterans who are active members on research teams.

Acknowledging and limiting distrust among veterans in general, and minority veterans specifically, was crucial to the success of our study given the population we intended to study. In addition, increasing trust in our study can have a ripple effect by affecting future studies ability to recruit and enroll veterans.

Methods to Develop Trust

Veteran-to-Veteran Connection

Another method for developing trust stems from the Veteran Engagement Group (VEG) concept. With VEGs, veterans outside of the existing research community are brought in to help develop trust. Another way to help instill and cultivate trust is having a veteran on VA side of the research group. In this case, one of the authors is a veteran of the US armed forces. Having a researcher who is a veteran himself was leveraged by our research project.

Researchers who have served in the military can perhaps be seen as the first step in establishing trust and rapport among veterans. Veterans seeking healthcare services have cited the lack of providers who have served in the armed forces and can directly relate to their experiences as a source of distrust (Cheney et al., 2018; Chinman et al., 2006).

This source of trust (i.e., having a fellow veteran who has similar experiences) is likely grounded in a distinct veteran identity. Veteran identity is a self-concept grounded in one's military experiences (Harada et al., 2002). A distinct veteran identity is grounded in a host of factors, such as service era, combat exposure, gender, trauma, race, and ethnicity (Hack et al., 2017).

Because one of the authors is a veteran of the US armed forces, our research explicitly leveraged their status as a veteran to 'tap' into the core tenet of shared experiences within veteran identity. The goal was to instill and develop trust among prospective research candidates. During direct recruitment of prospective candidates, the author was open about his military service to lay the foundation of trust. While only anecdotal evidence exists, initial communication between the author and prospective participants was positively influenced by the knowledge of shared experiences.

Altruism

Finally, our research project counted on another trait inherent within the veteran community to foster trust. This trait is what we referred to as "altruism." Research has found that a central motivating factor for participation in research and peer-based programming among veterans is the innate desire to help other veterans (Chrystal et al., 2022; Grewe et al., 2021; Hundt et al., 2015; Littman et al., 2018).

For example, Chrystal et al. (2022) found that, among women veterans, a primary motivation for participating in VA research is altruistic in helping other women veterans. In their research on Gulf War veterans, Grewe et al. (2021) found that an important motivating factor in participating in research is their desire to help other veterans and servicemembers. In their research on veterans' motivations for engaging in peer support for PTSD, Hundt et al. (2015) found the desire to help other veterans as a central motivating factor, even raising to the level of feeling obligated to help other veterans. Finally, Littman et al. (2018) found that, among Afghanistan and Iraq veterans, the decision to engage in health-related research was heavily influenced by the sense that their participation would help other veterans.

This facet of veteran identity quickly became evident in the recruitment processes for our research. While conducting in-person recruitment by the author, who is a veteran, numerous veterans openly admitted their motivation to participate in our research. While only anecdotal, many veterans openly expressed their motivation to participate in our study was due to their desire to help other veterans avoid the mistakes or pitfalls they encountered. Many veterans expressed an altruistic and selfless viewpoint in helping other veterans avoid the pitfalls and negative experiences associated with incarceration by sharing their personal experiences and lessons learned.

While not a direct factor in developing trust, if used properly, it could be viewed as a facilitator of trust. Our finding was that veterans' intrinsic desire to help other veterans, coupled with the author's service in the armed forces, combined to establish trust in our research and increase recruitment.

Interview Process

The principles within Grounded Theory guided the interview process. Following a Grounded Theory approach, our sample size for the pilot research was determined by theoretical "saturation." This occurs when no new conceptual information is discovered in the data (Morse, 1991). The development and identification of transitions and turning points emerged through the simultaneous and iterative process of collecting and analyzing data captured through the interview process (Creswell & Poth, 2018). Through theoretical sampling, we conducted simultaneous and continuous coding and comparisons of new and completed interview data to identify emerging behaviors associated with incarceration. The findings were used to guide future interviews and can be characterized as a cyclical process (Creswell & Poth, 2018). Within initial pass coding, preliminary analyses were conducted following the conclusion of each interview to identify categories and subcategories within the incarceration event. Interview data obtained from each participant was constantly compared before returning to conduct new interviews. We reached theoretical saturation at the conclusion of 16 interviews. A full discussion on the findings will be discussed in Chapter 7.

Analytic Approach

Data from veteran interviews were formally evaluated for central concepts and themes. The focus of the analyses was on the rich and contextual meanings associated with divergent incarceration experiences. Guided by the life course perspective, the analyses focused on exploring and identifying mitigating behaviors linked with incarceration.

At the conclusion of each interview, the research staff conducted an initial pass of open coding. This process resulted in the identification of categories and subcategories of behaviors within the incarceration event. These behaviors were compared with previous interviews and the findings were used to direct future interviews. This coding scheme identified instances of incarceration behaviors based on known characteristics of the population. Some of these characteristics include, but are not limited to, behavioral and substance addictions, mental health disorders, housing instability, unemployment, and poor prosocial networks. This process allowed the research team to theoretically develop transitions and turning points within the life course paradigm.

Preliminary thematic findings from the pilot research provided optimism in identifying more nuanced behaviors in the substance use, such as mental health—incarceration relationship. For example, beyond merely identifying substance use as a turning point behavior in the incarceration equation, we identified the phrase "self-medicating" which was nearly unanimous across all interviews. This phrase was used by veterans to describe the use of licit or illicit drugs in lieu of the perceived ineffectiveness of prescribed psychiatric medications. Not only does this provide a more detailed understanding of substance use across veterans' life course but also provides a glimpse into the relationship between mental health, substance use, and incarceration. These are key issues we sought out to identify with our research.

Axial coding was used to view the links of various data points or categories to their subcategories within an interview (Strauss & Corbin, 2008). While this does not establish causal linkages, axial coding helped to establish links between veterans' behavior and other psychosocial factors. Foremost among these were the interactions between incarceration and the environment or incarceration and significant life events or traumatic experiences. Research findings support the linkages between criminal behavior and the environment (Damm & Dustmann, 2014; Katz et al., 2001; Ludwig et al., 2001) and significant life events or traumatic events (Elbogen et al., 2012).

Selective coding was also adopted to narrow broad categories of topics into more refined and nuanced categories. Qualitative software (ATLAS.ti) assisted in the process. By identifying repeated and common themes and topics, the software aided the process of organizing broad categories of veteran's experiences into more focused groupings. Investigators coded simultaneously and independently to ensure coding reliability.

Participants

Socioeconomic Characteristics

To capture a diversity of incarceration experiences we explicitly recruited a diverse group of veterans based on their race, ethnicity, and gender. By recruiting from the Bonham VA Medical Center, which serves rural veterans, we increased the diversity of lived experiences based on veterans' geographic location.

The average age of our participants was 50 years of age. Our participants were more likely to be Caucasian, non-Hispanic, males. They were more likely to have a GED/High School education and be divorced. Table 6.1 provides more details on our participants' characteristics.

Employment and Housing Status

Because of the relationship between employment, housing, and incarceration, we were explicit in recruiting veterans with lived experiences with unemployment and homelessness. In general, recruiting veterans from the in-patient residential substance use programs and outpatient substance use programs allowed us to recruit veterans with lived unemployment and homelessness experiences. More specifically, recruiting veterans from the homeless programs and homeless transition programs allowed us to identify veterans currently experiencing homelessness.

TABLE 6.1 Socioeconomic Characteristics

Race		n (%)
	Caucasian	10 (63%)
	African American	5 (31%)
	Asian	1 (6%)
Hispanic/Latino Ethnicity		2 (13%)
Gender (Female)		2 (13%)
Education		
	Some HS	2 (13%)
	GED/High School Graduate	11 (69%)
	Associates or Bachelors Degree	3 (19%)
Age		
	Mean±SD	50±13
Marital status		
	Married	3 (19%)
	Divorced	6 (38%)
	Single	4 (25%)
	Separated/Widowed	3 (19%)

Homelessness and unemployment share a reciprocal relationship with incarceration. Studies have found incarceration predicts homelessness and homelessness predicts incarceration (Elbogen et al., 2013; Tsai et al., 2014; Tsai & Rosenheck, 2015). Individuals with felonies often experience greater difficulties obtaining employment (Decker et al., 2015; Pew Charitable Trusts, 2010; Schmitt & Warner, 2011) and experience overall rates of unemployment ranging between 10 and 33 percentage points higher than the general population (Carson et al., 2021; Couloute & Kopf, 2018; Schmitt & Warner, 2011).

While veteran-specific data is limited, one study found that unemployment rates among veterans, in the month prior to arrest, was 28% in federal prisons and local jails and 23% in state jails (Mumola, 2000) while those released from prison earn between 33% and 50% less lifetime earnings and between 6 and 10 fewer years of employment (Gordon et al., 2023). Furthermore, nonincarcerated veterans have nearly five times higher odds of gaining employment compared to those who have been incarcerated (LePage et al., 2005).

Three quarters of our population (n = 12) were unemployed and nearly three quarters of our population (n = 11) were experiencing housing instability. Both unemployment and homelessness are common turning point themes identified from our interviews. A more detailed discussion on both these turning points, within the context of our population, occurs in the following chapter (Chapter 7). Table 6.2 provides a visual representation of the housing and employment characteristics of our population.

Substance Use Disorders (SUD) and/or Mental Health Disorders

Within offending populations, substance use disorders (SUD), and mental health disorders are very prevalent. SUD and mental health disorders often play a contributing role in incarceration and is well documented within the literature. Compared to non-veterans, veterans in prison are more likely to have substance use or mental health problems, with 43% meeting the criteria for alcohol dependence, 43% for drug dependence, and 54% reporting a recent mental health problem (Bronson et al., 2015; Noonan & Mumola, 2007; Williams et al., 2010). The rates of co-occurring mental health and substance use disorders have been estimated to range from 23% to 51% among Veteran populations in jail and community settings (Erickson et al., 2008; McGuire et al., 2003).

TABLE 6.2 Employment and Housing Status

	n (%)
Employment status (unemployed)	12 (75%)
Housing status (homeless)	11 (69%)

While research on veteran incarceration has grown, much of the contemporary literature still relies on quantitative or administrative datasets that, while valuable, cannot capture the interpretive processes through which veterans understand and respond to life events. This limits our ability to address key questions about *how* and *why* specific factors, such as mental health disorders and substance use disorders (SUD), influence pathways to incarceration. Addressing this gap requires qualitative research capable of revealing the lived, identity-informed perspectives of those most affected. To this end, we intentionally recruited veterans with documented SUD and/or mental health diagnoses, ensuring that the study would capture experiences at the intersection of these high-impact conditions. Prior to enrollment, we conducted retrospective chart reviews in the VA Computerized Patient Record System (CPRS) for each participant, allowing us to contextualize their narratives with accurate clinical histories. By combining these records with in-depth interviews, we were able to generate a granular, nuanced account of how SUD and mental health conditions interact over time, how they shape decision-making, and how they contribute to incarceration risk. To the extent these insights remain underrepresented in the current scholarly literature, this book helps bridge the gap between veterans' voices and identity-based experiences and the policy, evaluation, and programmatic discussions needed to address incarceration and reintegration more effectively.

Regarding mental health diagnoses, nearly 70% of our participants suffered from depression (n = 11). Regarding substance use disorders, three-quarters (n = 12) of our participants suffered from alcohol use disorder, with stimulant use disorder and nicotine use also being highly prevalent (63% respectively for each category). It is important to note that most of our participants had more than one mental health and/or substance use disorder. However, two of our participants did not have any mental health diagnoses at the time of our study. Table 6.3 provides a more detailed description of the mental health and substance use characteristics of our population.

TABLE 6.3 Mental Health and Substance Use Diagnoses

Mental Health Diagnoses		*n (%)*
	Depression	11 (69%)
	PTSD	6 (38%)
	Other	2 (13%)
Substance use diagnoses		
	Stimulants (Cocaine/Methamphetamine)	10 (63%)
	Opioids	4 (25%)
	Marijuana	6 (38%)
	Alcohol	12 (75%)
	Nicotine	10 (63%)

Incarceration Experiences

We also recruited veterans with a wide range of criminal charges/offenses that led to their incarceration. We did not discriminate against the level or type of criminal offense. That is, we recruited veterans with low level offenses, often referred to as a misdemeanor, and veterans with higher level offenses, often referred to as felonies. Many veterans we recruited had been incarcerated multiple times throughout their lifetime for a wide range of both misdemeanor and felony-level offenses.

One of our primary concerns centered on veterans' ability to accurately recall the details of their incarceration experiences. To address this concern, we only recruited veterans who had recently been incarcerated. This typically meant that we identified veterans who had been incarcerated or released from incarceration within the last year. This allowed veterans to accurately recall events which maintained fidelity to the interview and their experiences, beliefs, and views.

A more detailed conversation on the drug-crime relationship occurs in the following chapter (Chapter 7). However, it is worth noting here that the relationship is often grounded in economic motivation. In many instances, an individuals' primary motivation to commit crime is to gain financial means to support their substance use habits. Economic theory has been used to explain the relationship between an individual's drug use and their decision to engage in crime to support their addiction (Bennett & Holloway, 2005). In addition, the connection between committing property-related crimes to support a drug addiction is also well established in the literature (Bennett & Holloway, 2005; Klee & Morris, 2009; Sutherland et al., 2015).

It is worth noting that incarceration experiences are comprised of all veterans' unique crimes. If a veteran committed driving while intoxicated (DWI) and assault, Table 6.4 reflects these incidents in the respective categories. However, if a veteran had multiple driving while intoxicated (DWI) offenses over their lifetime, only once instance of DWI was documented. For example, seven veterans (44%) indicated at least one instance of alcohol-related (DWI or public intoxication) legal involvement. This format allows for a more generalized understanding of our populations' broader legal characteristics.

Our participants were more likely to have been incarcerated for property related crimes, such as burglary, theft, or shoplifting. Furthermore, nearly half of our participants ($n = 7$) had been incarcerated for intoxication-related crimes, such driving while intoxicated (DWI) or public intoxication (PI). More than a third of our population ($n = 6$) had been incarcerated for drug possession. This finding supports the substance use-incarceration nexus. More details on the incarceration experiences of our population can be viewed in Table 6.4.

TABLE 6.4 Incarceration Experiences

	n (%)
Drug possession	6 (38%)
Property crimes (burglary/theft/shoplifting)	10 (63%)
Assault	6 (38%)
DWI/public intoxication	7 (44%)
Trespassing	2 (13%)

Military Experience

While a detailed description of our participants' military experiences is unavailable, some of the general known experiences are worth noting, especially within the life course perspective. Although already discussed in greater detail in previous chapters, turning points, also referred to as changes in individuals' life course, can be triggered by various events (Elder, 1985; Sampson & Laub, 1990, 2010). More importantly, how an individual responds to these turning points often dictates pathways and trajectories (Elder, 1985; Sampson & Laub, 1990). Turning points can be both negative and positive, with positive turning points examples including marriage and employment and negative turning points examples including substance use or incarceration (Sampson & Laub, 1993).

Over a third of our participants (38% or n = 6) experienced combat in Afghanistan or Iraq and nearly 20% (n = 3) suffered from posttraumatic stress disorder (PTSD) or traumatic brain injury (TBI) following combat. Prior research shows veterans are at a higher risk for mental health issues such as PTSD, depression, and anxiety as compared to the general population (Hoge et al., 2004). These conditions can significantly impede veterans' ability to reintegrate into civilian life, while also affecting their personal relationships and employment outcomes. For example, veterans with PTSD or traumatic brain injury are almost two and three times, respectively, more likely to have criminal justice involvement (Holliday et al., 2023; Logan et al., 2021; Taylor et al., 2020).

Interestingly, just over one-third (n = 5) of our population reported having received formalized discipline, such as Court Martial or Article 15, while in the military. From a life course perspective, combat exposure, PTSD, TBI, and military discipline could be viewed as negative turning points. Given the connection between these factors and justice involvement, our populations' experiences with formalized discipline provides unique insight into the turning point-justice involvement relationship and how turning points may have contributed to the risk of incarceration across veterans' lives. Table 6.5 provides a more detailed overview of our populations' military experiences.

TABLE 6.5 Military Experience/History

	n (%)
Combat (Afghanistan/Iraq)	6 (38%)
PTSD/TBI following combat	3 (19%)
Discipline (Art. 15/court martial)	5 (31%)

Limitations

While the findings are promising, our study is not without limitations. First, our population is comprised of veterans recruited solely from the VANTHCS catchment area. While potentially a limitation, our decision to recruit from this area was born out of intent and necessity. We were explicit in our intent to recruit a population of veterans with histories of criminal justice involvement, mental health, and substance use which directed our recruitment efforts to in-patient and outpatient mental health and substance use clinics and homeless transitional programs at VANTHCS.

From a necessity perspective, VA response to COVID-19, which suspended several in-patient programs, did not impact in-patient operations at the Bonham VA. The Bonham VA continued to admit veterans to their inpatient substance use/mental health programs during the pandemic, which allowed us to redirect our recruiting efforts at that facility and continue our recruitment efforts with little to no impact on our studies' recruitment timeline.

The second limitation derives from the first. Our sample was comprised solely of treatment seeking veterans. Put differently, all veterans in our study were actively receiving medical and psychiatric care at VA. Therefore, we did not capture veterans outside of VA healthcare system. It is likely that non-treatment seeking veterans are likely to have different lived experiences with incarceration, mental health, substance use, and social service provision.

Another potential limitation with our study is linked to veterans' discharge status. Not all veterans are qualified to receive care at VA hospitals. Veteran care eligibility is directly tied to their discharge status. Referred to as a veterans' character of discharge, certain discharge levels from the military disqualify a veteran from receiving care. Generally, an honorable or general discharge qualifies a veteran for care, while a dishonorable discharge is a disqualifying discharge status. Therefore, all veterans in our study had either honorable or general discharge types. The lack of inclusion of veterans with dishonorable discharges within VA healthcare has been cited as having far reaching implications (Bedford, 2021; Edwards et al., 2024; McClean, 2021; Reid & Sims, 2024).

Finally, the relatively low number of women veterans in our study can be viewed as a limitation. Women veterans in our study accounted for 13% ($n = 2$)

of our participants. In many ways, the low number of women veterans in our study is reflective of both the overall number of women veterans and the number of women veterans in the justice system. The number of women veterans in the United States is relatively low. According to VA, in 2000 women veterans accounted for 4% of the total veteran population in the United States (US Department of Veterans Affairs (VA), 2025). Regarding the number of women veterans in the justice system, the overall numbers are also relatively low. According to a Bureau of Justice Statistics Report in 2004, veterans comprised approximately 10% of the population in state and federal prisons (Noonan & Mumola, 2007). Of this population, approximately 1% were women veterans (Noonan & Mumola, 2007).

Summary

Future research on women veterans in general, and justice-involved veterans specifically, is critically important. The women veteran population is projected to increase significantly in the coming years. According to VA, women veterans are projected to account for 17% of the entire veteran population in the United States by the year 2043 (US Department of Veterans Affairs, 2024). This expansive growth would make women veterans the fastest growing group of veterans (US Department of Veterans Affairs, 2025). Given the estimated increase in the overall number of women veterans, it could be argued that justice involved women are likely to increase. Future research on women veterans is incredibly important. Their experiences, views, and beliefs are unique. In addition, it is important to understand what, if any, differences exist between the factors associated with justice involvement between males and females.

References

Bedford, J. R. (2021). Other than honorable discharges: Unfair and unjust life sentences of decreased earning capacity. *University of Pennsylvania Journal of Law & Public Affairs, 6*(4). https://scholarship.law.upenn.edu/cgi/viewcontent.cgi?article=1085&context=jlpa

Bennett, T., & Holloway, K. (2005). The association between multiple drug misuse and crime. *International Journal of Offender Therapy and Comparative Criminology, 49*(1), 63–81. https://doi.org/10.1177/0306624X04269003

Bronson, J., Carson, E. A., Noonan, M., & Berzofsky, M. (2015). Veterans in prison and jail, 2011–12 (NCJ 249144). US Department of Justice, Office of Justice Programs, Bureau of Justice Statistics. https://bjs.ojp.gov/content/pub/pdf/vpj1112.pdf

Carson, E. A., Sandler, D. H., Bhaskar, R., Fernandez, L. E., & Porter, S. R. (2021). Employment of persons released from federal prison in 2010. US Department of Justice, Office of Justice Programs, Bureau of Justice Statistics (NCJ 303147). https://bjs.ojp.gov/content/pub/pdf/eprfp10.pdf

Cheney, A. M., Koenig, C. J., Miller, C. J., Zamora, K., Wright, P., Stanley, R., Fortney, J., Burgess, J. F., & Pyne, J. M. (2018). Veteran-centered barriers to VA mental healthcare service use. *BMC Health Services Research, 18*(1), 591–604. https://doi.org/10.1186/s12913-018-3346-9

Chinman, M., Young, A. S., Hassell, J., & Davidson, L. (2006). Toward the implementation of mental consumer provider services. *Journal of Behavioral Health Services & Research, 33*(2), 176–195.

Chrystal, J. G., Dyer, K. E., Gammage, C. E., Klap, R. S., Carney, D. V., Frayne, S. M., Yano, E. M. & Hamilton, A. B. (2022). Increasing engagement of women veterans in health research. *Journal of General Internal Medicine, 37*, 42–49. https://doi.org/10.1007/s11606-021-07126-4

Couloute, L., & Kopf, D. (2018). Out of prison & out of work: Unemployment among formerly incarcerated people. Prison Policy Initiative. www.prisonpolicy.org/reports/outofwork.html

Creswell, J. W., & Poth, C. N. (2018). *Qualitative inquiry & research design: Choosing among five approaches* (4th ed.). SAGE.

Damm, A. P., & Dustmann, C. (2014). Does growing up in a high crime neighborhood affect youth criminal behavior? *The American Economic Review, 104*(6), 1806–1832. https://doi.org/10.1257/aer.104.6.1806

Decker, S. H., Ortiz, N., Spohn, C., & Hedberg, E. (2015). Criminal stigma, race, and ethnicity: The consequences of imprisonment for employment. *Journal of Criminal Justice, 43*(2), 108–121. https://doi.org/10.1016/j.jcrimjus.2015.02.002

Edwards, E. R., Fortuna, A., Stimmel, M., Gorman, D., & Epshteyn, G. (2024). Impact of expanded eligibility for veterans with other than honorable discharges on treatment courts and VA mental health care. *Federal Practitioner, 41*(9), 278–286. https://doi.org/10.12788/fp.0511

Elbogen, E., Johnson, S., Newton, V., Straits-Troster, K., Vasterling, J., Wagner, H., & Beckham, J. (2012). Criminal justice involvement, trauma, and negative affect in Iraq and Afghanistan war era veterans. *Journal of Consulting and Clinical Psychology, 80*(6), 1097–1102. https://doi.org/10.1037/a0029967

Elbogen, E. B., Sullivan, C. P., Wolfe, J., Wagner, H. R., & Beckham, J. C. (2013). Homelessness and money mismanagement in Iraq and Afghanistan veterans. *American Journal of Public Health, 103*(Suppl 2), S248–S254. https://doi.org/10.2105/AJPH.2013.301335

Elder, G. H. (1985). Perspectives on the life course. In G. H. Elder, Jr. (Ed.), *Life course dynamics,* (pp. 23–49). Cornell University Press.

Erickson, S. K., Rosenheck, R. A., Trestman, R. L., Ford, J. D., & Desai, R. A. (2008). Risk of incarceration between cohorts of veterans with and without mental illness discharged from inpatient units. *Psychiatric Services, 59*(2), 178–183. https://doi.org/10.1176/ps.2008.59.2.178

Flynn, L., Krause-Parello, C., Chase, S., Connelly, C., Decker, J., Duffy, S., Lapiz-Bluym, M. D., Walsh, P., & Weglicki, L. (2019). Toward veteran-centered research: A veteran focused community engagement project. *Journal of Veterans Studies, 4*(2), 265–277. https://doi.org/10.21061/jvs.v4i2.119

Gordon, G., Jones, J. B., Neelakantan, U., & Athreya, K. (2023). Incarceration, employment, and earnings: Dynamics and differences. *Review of Economic Dynamics, 51*, 677–697. https://doi.org/10.1016/j.red.2023.06.007

Grewe, M. A., Khalil, L., Felder, K., Goldstein, K. M., McNeil, R. B., Sims, K. J., Provenzale, D., & Voils, C. I. (2021). Gulf war era veterans' perspectives on research: A qualitative study. *Life Sciences, 287*. https://doi.org/10.1016/j.lfs.2021.120113

Hack, S. M., DeForge, B. R., & Lucksted, A. (2017). Variation in veteran identity as a factor in veteran-targeted interventions. *Psychiatric Services, 68*(7). https://doi.org/10.1176/appi.ps.201600237

Harada, N. D., Damron-Rodriguez, J., Villa, V. M., Washington, D. L., Dhanani, S., Shon, H., Chattopadhyay, M., Fishbein, H., Lee, M., Makinodan, T., & Andersen, R. (2002). Veteran identity and race/ethnicity: Influences on VA outpatient care utilization. *Medical Care, 40*(1), I-117–I-128.

Harding, S. (2004). *The feminist standpoint theory reader: Intellectual and political controversies*. Routledge.

Hoge, C. W., Castro, C. A., Messer, S. C., McGurk, D., Cotting, D. I., & Koffman, R. L. (2004). Combat duty in Iraq and Afghanistan, mental health problems, and barriers to care. *The New England Journal of Medicine, 351*(1), 13–22. https://doi.org/10.1056/NEJMoa040603

Holliday, R., Smith, A., Kinney, A., Forster, J., Bahraini, N., Monteith, L., & Brenner, L. (2023). Research letter: Traumatic brain injury among veterans accessing VA justice related services. *Journal of Head Trauma Rehabilitation, 38*(2), 184–190. https://doi.org/10.1097/HTR.0000000000000822

Hundt, N. E., Robinson, A., Arney, J., Stanley, M. A., & Cully, J. A. (2015). Veterans' perspectives on benefits and drawbacks of peer support for posttraumatic stress disorder. *Military Medicine, 180*(8), 851–856. https://doi.org/10.7205/MILMED-D-14-00536

Jones, A. L., Fine, M. J., Taber, P. A., Hausmann, L. R. M., Burkitt, K. H., Stone, R. A., & Zickmund, S. L. (2021). National media coverage of the Veterans Affairs waitlist scandal. *Medical Care, 6*(3), S322–S326. https://doi.org/10.1097/MLR.0000000000001551

Katz, L. F., Kling, J. R., & Liebman, J. B. (2001). Moving to opportunity in Boston: Early results of a randomized mobility experiment. *The Quarterly Journal of Economics, 116*(2), 607–654. https://doi.org/10.1162/00335530151144113

Klee, H., & Morris, J. (2009). Crime and drug misuse: Economic and psychological aspects of the criminal activities of heroin and amphetamine injectors. *Addiction Research, 1*(4), 377–386. https://doi.org/10.3109/16066359409005204

LePage, J., Bluitt, M., House-Hatfield, T., McAdams, H., Burdick, M., Dudley, D., Michaels, S., Merrell, C., Otto, S., Lenger-Gvist, J., Eisworth, J., Newton, J. A., & Gaston, C. (2005). Improving success in a veterans homeless domiciliary vocational program: Model development and evaluation. *Rehabilitation Psychology, 50*(3), 297–304. https://doi.org/10.1037/0090-5550.50.3.297

Littman, A. J., True, G., Ashmore, E., Wellens, T., & Smith, N. L. (2018). How can we get Iraq and Afghanistan-deployed US Veterans to participate in health-related research? Findings from a national focus group study. *BMC Medical Research Methodology, 18*(88). https://doi.org/10.1186/s12874-018-0546-2

Logan, M. W., McNeeley, S., & Morgan, M. A. (2021). The effects of traumatic brain injury and post-traumatic stress disorder on prison adjustment and recidivism among military veterans: Evidence from Minnesota. *Psychiatric Quarterly, 92*(3), 1147–1158. https://doi.org/10.1007/s11126-021-09883-1

Ludwig, J., Duncan, G. J., & Hirschfield, P. (2001). Urban poverty and juvenile crime: Evidence from a randomized housing-mobility experiment. *The Quarterly Journal of Economics, 116*(2), 655–679. https://doi.org/10.1162/00335530151144122

McClean, H. (2021). Discharged and discarded: The collateral consequences of a less-than honorable military discharge. *Columbia Law Review, 121*. https://heinonline.org/HOL/P?h=hein.journals/clr121&i=2278

McGuire, J., Rosenheck, R. A., & Kasprow, W. J. (2003). Health status, service use, and costs among veterans receiving outreach services in jail or community settings. *Psychiatric Services*, *54*(2), 201–207. https://doi.org/10.1176/appi.ps.54.2.201

McManus, J., Mehta, S. G., McClinton, A. R., De Lorenzo, R. A., & Baskin, T. W. (2005). Informed consent and ethical issues in military medical research. *Academic Emergency Medicine, 12*, 1120–1126. https://doi.org/10.1197/j.aem.2005.05.037

Morse, J. M. (1991). Strategies for sampling. In J. M. Morse (Ed.), *Qualitative nursing research: A contemporary dialogue* (pp. 127–145). SAGE. https://doi.org/10.4135/9781483349015

Mumola, C. J. (2000). Veterans in prison or jail. (NCJ 178888). US Department of Justice, Office of Justice Programs. https://bjs.ojp.gov/content/pub/pdf/vpj.pdf

Noonan, M. E., & Mumola, C. J. (2007). Veterans in state and federal prison, 2004. US Department of Justice, Office of Justice Programs, Bureau of Justice Statistics. NCJ 217199. https://bjs.ojp.gov/content/pub/pdf/vsfp04.pdf

Oliver, D. G., Serovich, J. M., & Mason, T. L. (2005). Constraints and opportunities with interview transcription: Towards reflection in qualitative research. *Social Forces, 84*(2), 1273–1289. https://doi.org/10.1353/sof.2006.0023

Pew Charitable Trusts (2010). Collateral costs: Incarceration's effect on economic mobility. The Pew Charitable Trusts. www.pew.org/-/media/3975EB366428437FADA60843AA02C2FC.ashx

Reid, T., & Sims, K. M. (2024). (Dis)honorably discharged: Identifying policy gaps in military civilian reintegration. *Health Affairs Scholar, 2*(2). https://doi.org/10.1093/haschl/qxae021

Sampson, R., & Laub, J. (1990). Crime and deviance over the life course: The salience of adult social bonds. *American Sociological Review*, *55*, 609–627. https://doi.org/10.2307/2095859

Sampson, R., & Laub, J. (1993). *Crime in the making: Pathways and turning points through life*. Harvard University Press.

Sampson, R. J., & Laub, J. H. (2010). Age-graded theory of informal social control. In F.T Cullen & P. Wilcox (Eds.), *Encyclopedia of criminological theory* (pp. 806–813). SAGE.

Schmitt, J., & Warner, K. (2011). Ex-offenders and the labor market. *Working USA, 14*, 87–109. https://doi.org/10.1111/j.1743-4580.2011.00322.x

Smith, D. E. (1987). *The everyday world as problematic: A feminist sociology*. University of Toronto Press.

Strauss, A. L., & Corbin, J. M. (2008). *Basics of qualitative research: Techniques and procedures for developing grounded theory* (3rd ed.). SAGE.

Sutherland, R., Sindicich, N., Barrett, E., Whittaker, E., Peacock, A., Hicky, S., & Burns, L. (2015). Motivations, substance use and other correlates amongst property and violent offenders who regularly inject drugs. *Addictive Behaviors*, *45,* 207–213. http://dx.doi.org/10.1016/j.addbeh.2015.01.034

Taylor, E. N., Timko, C., Nash, A., Owens, M. D., Harris, A. H. S., & Finlay, A. K. (2020). Posttraumatic stress disorder and justice involvement among military veterans: A systematic review and meta-analysis. *Journal of Traumatic Stress, 33*(5), 804–812. https://doi.org/10.1002/jts.22526

Tsai, J., & Rosenheck, R. A. (2015). Risk factors for homelessness among US veterans. *Epidemiologic Reviews, 37*(1), 177–195. https://doi.org/10.1093/epirev/mxu004

Tsai, J., Rosenheck, R. A., Kasprow, W. J., & McGuire, J. F. (2014). Homelessness in a national sample of incarcerated veterans in state and federal prisons. *Administration and Policy in Mental Health and Mental Health Services Research, 41*(3), 360–367. https://doi.org/10.1007/s10488-013-0483-7

U.S. Department of Veterans Affairs. (2024). Serving her country: Exploring the characteristics of women veterans. Department of Veterans Affairs Office of Enterprise Integration, Office of Data Governance and Analytics, National Center for Veterans Analysis and Statistics. www.data.va.gov/stories/s/Women-Veterans-in-2023/wci3-yrsv/

U.S. Department of Veterans Affairs. (2025). Women veterans health care. www.womenshealth.va.gov/materials-and-resources/facts-and-statistics.asp

Williams, B. A., McGuire, J., Lindsay, R. G., Baillargeon, J., Cenzer, I. S., Lee, S. J., & Kushel, M. (2010). Coming home: Health status and homelessness risk of older pre-release prisoners. *Journal of General Internal Medicine, 25*(10), 1038–1044. https://doi.org/10.1007/s11606-010-1416-8

7

TURNING POINTS IN VETERANS' PATHWAYS TO INCARCERATION

Introduction

Identifying and understanding critical turning points, which are key life events or circumstances that significantly alter an individual's trajectory, provide essential insights into pathways toward incarceration among veterans. Our research sought to explore turning points from two distinct perspectives: those previously identified and well-documented within broader criminological and psychological literature, and those uniquely revealed through our qualitative investigation of veterans' lived experiences. This dual-focused analysis enhances our capacity to pinpoint, comprehend, and proactively intervene with at-risk veterans, with the goal of effectively disrupting the cycle of incarceration through targeted biopsychosocial interventions and rehabilitative support.

In this chapter, we specifically examine six turning points widely recognized in scholarly discourse yet critically relevant to the unique experiences of veterans. These include homelessness, poor prosocial networks, social isolation, unemployment, economic motivations, and impulsivity. While these turning points have been documented extensively, our research offers substantial qualitative enrichment, providing depth through firsthand accounts of veterans themselves. By leveraging veterans' own narratives, we vividly illustrate how these significant life events intertwine with their military identities, directly influencing their trajectories and increasing their vulnerabilities to incarceration.

This chapter serves as a foundation for subsequent discussions that introduce additional turning points uniquely illuminated through our qualitative analysis. Importantly, what distinguishes these additional turning points is our deeper theoretical and empirical exploration of veteran identity as a central mechanism

DOI: 10.4324/9781003522300-7

influencing their emergence and impact. By closely examining how veterans' identities and military experiences shape their interpretation and navigation of critical life events, we offer fresh, theoretically informed insights that significantly advance the existing scholarly understanding of incarceration risk among veterans. Thus, we underscore the critical importance of integrating veteran identity and standpoint into research and intervention strategies, ultimately enhancing the effectiveness and relevance of incarceration prevention efforts tailored specifically to veterans.

Theory Grounded in Veterans' Standpoint

This research is grounded in the life course perspective, a robust theoretical framework emphasizing the significance of timing, transitions, and trajectories in shaping individuals' lives (Elder, 1985; Sampson & Laub, 1990). Rather than extensively redefining previously established concepts, this chapter builds upon the foundational ideas detailed earlier by exploring the life course perspective through the novel lens of veteran identity. This innovative application provides a deeper understanding of how veterans assign subjective meanings to critical life events, particularly in relation to substance use, mental health, and other psychosocial challenges.

We want to make clear our research does not imply a direct causal relationship between veterans' experiences and their incarceration outcomes. Instead, we seek to draw attention to how veterans themselves interpret and construct meaning around pivotal life events, experiences, and decisions. Our approach centers veterans' subjective interpretations *as veterans* to enrich existing literature on the influences on and trajectories toward incarceration.

Within the life course framework, trajectories represent prolonged, relatively stable pathways or developmental patterns across various life domains, including employment, family relationships, and criminal behavior (Elder, 1985; Sampson & Laub, 1990, 2010). Conversely, transitions are more discrete, significant life events occurring over a shorter timeframe (e.g., gaining employment, marriage, becoming a parent, or entering incarceration) (Elder, 1985; Sampson & Laub, 1990). These transitions serve as turning points and critical junctures capable of significantly altering an individual's trajectory. Turning points can be either positive (e.g., employment, marriage, military service) or negative (e.g., substance use, employment instability, incarceration), each having considerable implications for subsequent life outcomes and behaviors (Sampson & Laub, 1993). Negative turning points, particularly incarceration, often disrupt housing stability, employment prospects, and interpersonal relationships, severely impacting overall quality of life and social integration (Sampson & Laub, 2010).

What distinguishes this research is its explicit focus on the intersection of veteran identity and societal contexts. The life course perspective acknowledges that societal factors, roles, and institutions continuously shape adults' lives, influencing how turning points arise and affect behavior (Sampson & Laub, 1990, 2010). Although previous research has identified broad risk factors associated with veteran incarceration, including substance use, housing instability, and limited prosocial engagement (Blonigen et al., 2014; Greenberg & Rosenheck, 2009; Tsai et al., 2014), there remains a significant gap in individual-level qualitative insights. Our study addresses this gap by employing qualitative interviews that enable veterans to narrate their personal experiences authentically.

These interviews capture detailed narratives of veterans' beliefs, perceptions, and lived experiences regarding critical turning points involving substance use, mental health challenges, and behaviors immediately preceding their most recent incarceration. By emphasizing veterans' most recent incarceration experiences, our qualitative approach enhances both the depth and accuracy of veterans' retrospective accounts. Ultimately, this innovative theoretical and empirical integration of veteran identity with the life course perspective provides a more nuanced understanding of the pathways leading toward incarceration, offering valuable implications for targeted, identity-informed interventions and policies designed specifically for veterans.

The subsequent sections of this chapter begin exploring veteran identity through detailed analyses of widely recognized turning points documented in existing literature. Again, these usually include homelessness, social isolation, unemployment, economic motivations, mental health, and limited prosocial networks. By integrating veterans' own narratives, we illustrate how their identities and subjective interpretations frame veterans' thoughts, feelings, and actions to these turning points. This methodological approach deepens scholarly comprehension, illuminating how individual-level experiences and subjective meanings intersect dynamically with broader structural contexts, ultimately influencing veterans' life trajectories and pathways toward incarceration.

Homelessness

According to the US Department of Veterans Affairs (VA), homelessness is defined as a condition where an individual lacks a fixed, regular, and adequate nighttime residence, including individuals who reside temporarily in shelters or spaces not intended for habitation, namely, cars, parks, or abandoned buildings (US Department of Veterans Affairs, 2021). For this study, homelessness specifically refers to periods of unstable housing immediately preceding incarceration, underscoring the critical timing that positions housing instability as a pivotal turning point within veterans' life trajectories. This definition emphasizes the significance of timing and transitions central to the life course framework and highlights the role veteran identity plays in interpreting these critical moments.

Homelessness rarely occurs as an isolated event; rather, it frequently interacts with other significant life challenges. Veterans in this study articulated clearly how these interconnected issues compounded their vulnerabilities, creating a multidimensional pathway toward incarceration. Crucially, these compounded experiences are shaped profoundly by veterans' identity, influencing their interpretation of events, responses to crises, and navigation of hardships. This intersectionality provides a deeper understanding of veteran experiences than is typically captured by quantitative research alone.

Extant research clearly establishes a strong correlation between homelessness and incarceration among veterans. Tsai and Rosenheck (2015) emphasize the variability of this association across veteran subpopulations. Between 25% and 70% of homeless veterans have a history of incarceration (Petrovich et al., 2014; Tejani et al., 2013; Tsai & Rosenheck, 2012). In 2019, national point-in-time data indicated approximately 37,085 veterans experienced homelessness, representing about 8% of the total homeless adult population (Henry et al., 2020). Additionally, veterans experiencing homelessness prior to incarceration typically report significantly higher rates of lifetime arrests (Tsai et al., 2014), particularly among those with severe mental health conditions, where incarceration rates reach as high as 67% (Roy et al., 2014). While these quantitative insights offer critical context, qualitative narratives provide deeper insights into veterans' subjective experiences and interpretations, highlighting the role of identity in shaping their trajectories.

Our qualitative data highlights how veteran identity directly informs thoughts, feelings, and actions related to homelessness. Veterans described how immediate survival needs, driven by homelessness, compelled critical decisions, sometimes involving criminal actions. One participant stated: "I'm homeless, you know, I'm thinking, well I need a place to sleep … They gave me the keys to a car and I took off in it … It was raining, I was homeless … to get out of the elements." Our participants also demonstrated significant self-awareness in recognizing homelessness as the critical turning point triggering their downward trajectory, particularly in light of their identities formed through military service. One participant explicitly connected housing instability with subsequent incarceration: "The first red flag was the fact that I didn't have a place of my own … It was the red flag … It was my downfall."

Of note here is how veterans explicitly reference their veteran identity as a critical mechanism through which they frame and interpret turning points. These narratives emphasize core values of self-reliance and personal stability and how homelessness disrupts in a profound way veterans' sense of identity and autonomy. Furthermore, homelessness amplified existing challenges of mental health issues and employment instability, exacerbating conflicts with their military-informed expectations for structure, routine, and clear objectives. Veterans articulated how their identities intertwined with housing instability, intensifying these struggles, and often highlighted how homelessness directly conflicted with their self-perceptions rooted in military values and standards.

As on veteran explained, "I was on the streets, and I just wasn't capable of holding a job down mentally. This isn't who I was before … how it was [referring to when they were in the military]" illustrating the loss of the stability and discipline intrinsic to their veteran identity. Another described the compounded barriers caused by both homelessness and a criminal record: "I'm homeless, nowhere, I ain't got nowhere to go … once I got these felonies, I couldn't even get an apartment." The psychological and existential dimensions of homelessness were profoundly evident and explicitly shaped by veteran identity. Veterans expressed feelings of desperation, diminished self-worth, and reduced agency directly connected to their military-influenced identity expectations of self-sufficiency and personal competence. One participant reflected on the internalized desperation shaped by their loss of status and control: "I was homeless and stuff, and you know, I was like, hell yeah, I'll take that. [referring to committing theft]" Another conveyed existential despair specifically linked to their identity-based perceptions of dignity and self-worth: "I'd rather go to jail than stay out here and die." These poignant narratives highlight how homelessness becomes an internalized, identity-shaping psychological turning point, transcending purely economic interpretations, and profoundly altering veterans' sense of self and life trajectory.

Homelessness imposed profound constraints on veterans' perceived choices and behavior, significantly limiting their sense of agency through disruptions to their identity-based expectations of stability, self-control, and structured environments developed during military service. One veteran recounted: "I let another drug addict move in with me … and we had drug dealers coming in and out of our home … Every penny started to go to my drugs … I decided to give it up and just leave." In this reflection, the veteran's identity, shaped by military experiences emphasizing discipline, order, and self-reliance, stands in stark contrast to the chaotic and uncontrolled environment described. The decision to "give it up and just leave" highlights a perceived loss of control and a forced surrender of core identity values, illustrating vividly how homelessness challenges veterans' deeply internalized beliefs about their autonomy and capability. Thus, homelessness as a turning point becomes especially impactful for veterans, deeply reshaping their self-perception and profoundly affecting their subsequent actions. This underscores the critical importance of integrating an identity-informed understanding of turning points within life course theory.

Synthesizing these qualitative insights from a life course perspective and a veteran identity standpoint reveals homelessness as a transformative turning point profoundly influenced by veteran identity and broader contexts. Understanding veterans' subjective interpretations enriches theoretical comprehension of turning points, highlighting the necessity for integrated, identity-informed intervention strategies. Effective approaches must go beyond mere housing solutions, incorporating comprehensive mental health services, employment assistance, and community-based interventions tailored explicitly to veterans' unique identities and experiences. A holistic approach to incarceration risk mitigation includes capturing the subjective dimension of veterans' lives that informs behavioral responses to key turning points.

Poor Prosocial Networks

Positive environmental reinforcers, such as sober family members, supportive friends, stable employment, and recreational activities, play an essential role in maintaining sobriety and encouraging prosocial behavior (Meyers et al., 2011; Miller et al., 1999). Conversely, poor prosocial networks, characterized by relationships with individuals actively involved in substance use, criminal behavior, or negatively influencing recovery, significantly increase the risk of substance misuse and criminal offending. Within the context of this study, poor prosocial networks encompass either a scarcity of positive, supportive relationships or the active presence of antisocial influences, both shaped and interpreted through veterans' specific identity perspectives.

Existing theoretical frameworks (i.e., Risk-Need-Responsivity (RNR) model) underscore the role prosocial and antisocial relationships play in criminal trajectories (Andrews & Bonta, 2024). Specifically, antisocial associates are identified as a primary risk factor strongly associated with criminal recidivism. Prosocial recreational activities, conversely, serve as protective factors, facilitating healthier social connections that can mitigate the risk of reoffending (Andrews & Bonta, 2024). Within veteran populations specifically, robust social support networks significantly reduce aggression and violent behaviors, highlighting the crucial influence of positive social relationships (Elbogen et al., 2012).

Veteran narratives in this study vividly illustrate how veteran identity critically informs their perceptions and behaviors related to social networks. Veterans described how seemingly superficial social interactions rapidly escalated into pivotal negative turning points. One participant illustrated, "I been in a car with some people … and we was [sic] drinking … smoking weed," demonstrating how casual interactions, when perceived through their veteran identity and associated vulnerabilities, significantly altered their life trajectories. Another veteran emphasized the profound negative consequences stemming from peer associations explicitly linked to their veteran identity: "We made a deal to go buy some crack … He dumped all of his drugs in there … like I knew he was trouble … I knew that there would be no good that came from picking him up and hanging out with him."

Veterans further demonstrated substantial self-awareness about how their veteran identities shaped their responses to relational deficiencies, marking critical downward trajectories. One participant succinctly highlighted, "the root cause was a lack of family relationships," underscoring how familial bonds are integral to their sense of stability shaped by their identity as veterans. Military culture emphasizes close-knit relationships, camaraderie, and mutual support, fostering an expectation that family or similarly supportive social connections provide a critical foundation for stability. The absence or breakdown of these relationships thus creates a particularly pronounced sense of instability and vulnerability, significantly affecting veterans' decision-making and emotional resilience. Another described the direct negative influence of peer associations explicitly connected to their veteran experiences: "I didn't hang around the good people … I had people using me … I thought they were my friends … Every one of them were drug addicts." For veterans, identity formed through military service often involves trust and reliance on a cohesive, supportive peer group. When postdischarge civilian peer relationships betray this foundational expectation of positive group cohesion, leading instead to exploitation and harm, the resultant feelings of betrayal and isolation profoundly shape veterans' subsequent choices and behaviors, accelerating their pathways toward negative outcomes.

The impact of poor social networks on substance use behaviors was explicitly articulated through veterans' identity-informed experiences. One veteran remarked, "No alcoholic drug addict wants to sit around straight or non-drinking people … it's just uncomfortable as hell … you want to be around people that are doing what you're doing," demonstrating how veteran identity shapes choices around peer associations. Another recounted social interaction supporting substance misuse: "Mostly on the weekends I ran around looking for drugs … you know, hanging out with a lot of people in the clubs." These accounts illustrate how veteran identity actively informs and perpetuates choices regarding substance use and associated behaviors.

Family and intimate relationships emerged clearly as pivotal determinants shaped by veteran identity. Narratives highlighted how familial influences compounded existing vulnerabilities, explicitly connected to their veteran experiences. One veteran recounted parental modeling shaping their substance use: "All my life since I was little, I've seen my mom drink, my dad drink … and I just thought that was the thing to do." Another described the compounded vulnerabilities shaped by marital relationships: "My wife drank, my friends used, and I didn't cut those ties." Similarly, a participant explained the explicit acceptance of substance use within intimate relationships shaped by veteran identity: "He was my husband … as long as I did things in moderation everything was okay." Veterans point out the need for family-inclusive interventions tailored explicitly to veteran experiences.

Narratives explicitly connected poor prosocial networks to criminal behaviors beyond substance use. Veterans described how negative peer influences directly facilitated criminal activities informed by their identity contexts. One veteran explained, "I bumped into some friends of mine … They gave me the keys, and I took off in it [stolen vehicle]." Another described participation in organized theft: "it was just me and a couple more guys that had formed this little group, but we was going out boosting [committing theft]." These examples clearly illustrate how veteran identity shapes responses to peer pressure, influencing decisions leading directly to criminal behaviors. Veterans also described scenarios where impromptu social meetings were poor social structures that undermined perceived good choices and agency. One veteran explicitly described feeling trapped, stating: "When I moved to where I was at … it wasn't a safe situation for me … When I did move in with this person … it was automatically a road to disaster … I never was going to clean up while in this environment."

These reflections show us the important role of veteran identity in life turning points. Veterans noted a contrast between civilian life and their prior military experiences that the y perceive as providing stability, structured relationships, and a secure environment. For instance, when one veteran stated, "it was automatically a road to disaster … I never was going to clean up while I was in this different environment," it illustrates precisely how civilian living situation starkly contrasts with the ordered and controlled environments veterans become accustomed to during military service. Similarly, the participant's observation, "My wife drank, my friends used, and I didn't cut those ties," and the narrative, "He was my husband … as long as I did things in moderation everything was okay," underscore how veterans' experiences of clear boundaries and disciplined routines during military service conflicted sharply with the ambiguous, permissive social norms of their postmilitary intimate relationships. Further, the scenario described by another veteran, "I bumped into some friends of mine … They gave me the keys, and I took off in it [stolen vehicle]", reveals the vulnerability veterans face in civilian life due to a lack of structured peer interactions, clear behavioral expectations, and consistent authority that military contexts typically provide. Collectively, these narratives explicitly illustrate how veteran identity, shaped by disciplined routines, clear structures, and predictable environments inherent in military experience, significantly influences veterans' perceptions and interpretations of their civilian social relationships and living situations, thereby profoundly impacting their decision-making processes and behavioral trajectories. Here again understanding veterans' subjective interpretations significantly enriches theoretical comprehension, emphasizing the necessity of targeted, identity-informed interventions.

Social Isolation

Social isolation, as defined by the American Psychological Association (APA, 2020a), refers to the voluntary and complete absence of contact with all social networks, including family, friends, and community activities. This is distinct from poor prosocial networks, as it denotes a total withdrawal from any type of social interaction, positive or negative. Within the Community Reinforcement Approach (CRA) framework, social isolation is negatively associated with substance use; as substance dependence intensifies, individuals increasingly withdraw from non-substance-related social interactions (Miller et al., 1999). In this study, social isolation specifically refers to the deliberate distancing from all social relationships, resulting in significant withdrawal and minimal social engagement.

Previous research documents a strong correlation between social isolation and criminal recidivism in civilian populations (Sung, 2010). Social isolation critically undermines essential relationships and exacerbates maladaptive behaviors, compounding psychosocial challenges. Isolation from key social networks (e.g., family, friends, and work-related interactions) has far-reaching implications for overall psychosocial health and stability.

Veterans reported extensive experiences with social isolation profoundly affecting their critical relationships. One veteran reported, "I'd just sit on my back porch … I wasn't even really involved with my kids." Another noted, "I'm not really friends with anybody," clearly indicating the totality of their withdrawal. A deeper reflection revealed emotional dimensions, with one veteran stating, "I had already isolated myself so badly that, well, I would try not to call my mother." Further insight into the psychological motivations behind isolation was provided by another veteran: "Even then I still don't hang around them [positive influences] too often because, you know, they're always gonna ask how are you doing … I don't have anything positive to ever say, so that's why I tend to just kind of stay by myself."

Social isolation often intensified due to guilt and shame associated with substance use and criminal activities. Veterans acknowledged the direct relationship between their substance use behaviors and increased isolation. One veteran described this clearly: "I couldn't go back to my family. They didn't want me around." Another provided further context, stating, "I'm on the streets … I'm doing geographics … I'm on the run from myself, my house, I'm not at home, I'm guilty … I'm feeling guilty about being out, you know, away from home."

Social isolation also facilitated additional maladaptive behaviors, including reduced participation in recovery programs, increased substance use, and heightened suicide risk. The Department of Veterans Affairs (VA) recognizes connectedness as a vital protective factor against suicide (VA, 2025a, 2025b). One veteran explicitly linked their isolation to suicidal ideation and increased substance use: "I sat almost a whole year in my garage ... I never went out ... I was thinking about suicide ... That's when I started doing the other drugs."

Veterans identified social isolation as a primary factor contributing to relapse into alcohol and drug misuse. One veteran stated succinctly, "The moment I'm alone, that's when it's game on and that's usually when I drink excessively." Another highlighted isolation as inherently linked to their alcohol use: "I've always kind of been by myself and I always associate that with drinking." Another narrative detailed more extreme isolation experiences: "Extreme isolation ... I wasn't seeing anybody, nobody would hear from me for days ... She [wife] would often have to try and get a hold of my family to figure out where I'm at ... I was already drunk at that point, passed out." Similarly, isolation influenced drug use behaviors, with one veteran explaining, "If I did drugs it was away from everybody ... Nobody knew what I was doing." Another reinforced this pattern by stating, "When I was actively involved in my drug use ... I didn't go around ... I was too embarrassed, so therefore, I didn't have much of a relationship then."

Veterans viewed social isolation as a "red flag" signaling a trajectory toward incarceration. One participant bluntly characterized their isolation, stating, "isolation, no doubt ... that's probably the biggest [red flag]." Another summarized succinctly, "I isolated myself ... I just didn't socialize at all." Another described their isolation metaphorically as being "a leaf in the wind," highlighting profound emotional detachment and instability.

Other veterans provided additional context to the complexity and pervasive nature of their isolation. One detailed the extent of withdrawal: "I did a tremendous amount of isolating ... I pushed away from people ... I didn't have very many friends." Another clarified the severity of their isolation: "I didn't have any [relationships] ... The isolation is a big ... I think that would be a huge one." Another veteran explained the isolating behavior: "I would say the biggest red flag of the isolation was I would never hold true to plans ... If I told my sister, hey, I'm going to go visit you all tomorrow ... Then the last minute something would always come up, or I just wouldn't reach out to them at all ... I was already passed out drunk."

Isolation profoundly shaped veterans' perceptions, decision-making processes, and behavioral patterns. For example, one veteran explained their withdrawal due to embarrassment and stigma: "I was so depressed ... I didn't want to see my daughter, see my daughter looking at me the way I was ... So I just left, took off." Another described pervasive isolation stating, "I wasn't interacting with any family members." These accounts indicate that social isolation represents not only withdrawal from social interactions but also withdrawal from meaningful roles and responsibilities within the community and family structures.

Veterans contextualized their experiences of social isolation within the challenging transition from structured military life to less regulated civilian environments, highlighting how their veteran identity profoundly shaped their responses. One veteran's straightforward reflection, "I isolated myself … I just didn't socialize at all," emerged specifically in the context of their discharge from military service and the subsequent loss of camaraderie, cohesion, and structured social interaction characteristic of military environments. The absence of formalized peer relationships, routine check-ins, and clear expectations in civilian life intensified their withdrawal. Similarly, another veteran's observation, "Nobody knew what I was doing," underscores the contrast between civilian life's relative anonymity and the constant supervision and accountability they had previously experienced in military settings. The increased autonomy in civilian life inadvertently opened pathways to secretive behaviors and intensified feelings of isolation. Moreover, the statement, "The moment I'm alone … that's when it's game on," further reveals how frequent solitary periods inherent in civilian life starkly differed from the continuous social presence and structured schedules integral to military culture. The shift from a structured military environment to the informal, less predictable civilian context amplified veterans' experiences of social isolation, significantly increasing their susceptibility to behaviors associated with incarceration risks.

Social isolation emerges as a powerful turning point that disrupts the continuity of veterans' lives, dramatically altering their pathways toward incarceration. Isolation acts as a critical juncture that exacerbates vulnerability, undermines resilience, and amplifies the likelihood of negative outcomes. Recognizing the profound impacts of isolation emphasizes the importance of targeted interventions designed to strengthen social bonds, promote community integration, and address underlying factors contributing to withdrawal. Addressing isolation thus requires comprehensive, community-based, and relationship-centered interventions to effectively interrupt harmful patterns and improve veterans' psychosocial well-being and long-term outcomes.

Unemployment and Economic Motivation

According to the US Bureau of Labor Statistics (BLS, 2015), unemployment refers to individuals who lack employment but are actively available and seeking work. Unemployment is notably prevalent among formerly incarcerated individuals, with rates estimated at 27%, significantly higher than the 6% found within the general population (Couloute & Kopf, 2018). Six months postrelease, only about half (52.6%) of formerly incarcerated individuals find employment (Western et al., 2015). Additionally, incarceration severely impacts economic stability, reducing hourly wages by approximately 11%, annual employment by nine weeks, and annual earnings by around 40% (Pew Charitable Trusts, 2010). Specific to veteran populations, unemployment rates just prior to arrest are alarmingly high: approximately 28% in federal prisons and local jails, and 23% in state jails (Mumola, 2000). Veterans who have never been incarcerated have nearly five times the likelihood of securing employment compared to previously incarcerated veterans (LePage et al., 2005).

In this study, unemployment is operationally defined as the absence of stable and legitimate employment or financial income. Unemployment intersects with other economic stability factors, such as housing and substance misuse. Veterans provided insights into these interconnections through their lived experiences. One veteran succinctly illustrated the linkage between unemployment, housing instability, and incarceration, questioning, "Once you get a felony you can't get an apartment… And what kind of job you going to get out here?" Another veteran described their lived reality explicitly: "I was on the streets … I was sleeping outside … I didn't have a job … I'm an alcoholic and that's how I ended up out there." Additionally, a participant detailed how substance misuse directly undermined their capacity for sustained employment: "I was so absorbed into my addiction … wasn't holding down a job." Further illustrating the damaging impact of alcohol, another veteran shared, "I had started drinking more heavily again … Part of my job entailed operating heavy equipment … I never went back to that job and just kept drinking," later adding, "Got a job in the shipyard … Started drinking … Lost that job."

Closely linked to unemployment is the broader concept of economic motivation, which include the financial pressures or incentives that drive criminal behaviors, particularly those undertaken to support substance use. Economic theory frequently connects drug dependence to criminal activity, asserting that economic desperation significantly drives individuals to commit property crimes and engage in illegal activities (Bennett & Holloway, 2005; Klee & Morris, 2009; Sutherland et al., 2015). Veterans in this study predominantly reported involvement in property crimes or financial fraud as a direct response to economic hardship exacerbated by substance dependency.

One participant candidly summarized their motivations: "Panhandling, boosting, selling dope, whatever … Whatever makes money." Another veteran described the psychological shift under economic desperation stating, "When I use drugs … Then use to the point where financially I'm getting towards the end … My brain automatically thinks, oh, going to the store [to steal]." This sentiment was echoed by another participant who explained, "Once my legitimate financial means have been depleted, my outlet is the stores … To go in the stores and take items to sell, for resale." Reflecting deeper desperation, another veteran stated, "It was the only way I could think of maybe to get off the streets, and certainly make a little money [forge checks] … Yeah, I cashed the checks with the chance of going to jail and maybe even prison … But that was a better, that was the best of the bad choices confronting me." Additionally, one participant recounted turning informal, illicit activities into routine employment: "I was in a semi-boosting ring … I made it into like a job … going into these stores and boosting."

Unemployment and economic motivations emerge clearly as interconnected turning points, each exacerbating the impact of the other, creating compounded vulnerabilities and increasing risks for sustained criminal behavior and incarceration. Veterans' narratives explicitly highlight how unemployment directly fuels economic desperation, significantly influencing the decision-making processes and behavioral patterns leading to criminal activities. Targeted interventions designed to enhance veterans' economic stability through employment support, vocational training, and substance abuse treatment programs are essential to effectively disrupt the intertwined cycles of unemployment, economic desperation, substance misuse, and incarceration. Acknowledging and addressing these interconnected economic challenges provides a practical foundation for preventing veteran incarceration and facilitating long-term reintegration into community and workforce.

Veterans link their experiences of unemployment and economic desperation to their veteran identity, emphasizing the profound challenges of transitioning from structured, stable military employment to civilian labor market uncertainty. Some veterans recount: "Once you get a felony you can't get an apartment … And what kind of job you going to get out here?" underscore veterans' struggles in navigating civilian employment systems, ("out here") which sharply contrast the clear career pathways, consistent pay, and structured daily routines of military life. Additionally, descriptions like "I had started drinking more heavily again … Part of my job entailed operating heavy equipment … I never went back to that job and just kept drinking" highlight how veterans struggled without the rigid discipline and accountability structures inherent to military settings, leading directly to unemployment and subsequent substance misuse. Furthermore, veterans' explanations of economic desperation (e.g., "Panhandling, boosting, selling dope, whatever … Whatever makes money" and "My brain automatically thinks, oh, going to the store (to steal)") contrast markedly with their military identity values of honor, self-sufficiency, and structured economic support. Their recourse to illicit activities as informal employment, expressed explicitly in "I was in a semi-boosting ring … I made it into like a job," starkly contrasts with the structured, legitimate, and respected professional identity provided by military service. Collectively, these accounts illustrate how the disjunction between military-formed identity expectations of stability, structured roles, and consistent employment, and the unpredictable realities of civilian economic life, profoundly shapes veterans' perceptions, responses, and vulnerability to unemployment and economic hardship, significantly heightening their risks for substance misuse, criminal behavior, and subsequent incarceration.

Mental Health, Fatigue, and Impulsivity

Impulsivity, as defined by the American Psychological Association (APA, 2020b), refers to actions characterized by minimal forethought, reflection, or consideration of consequences, particularly when involving risky behaviors. Research on juvenile delinquency operationalizes impulsivity as lacking inhibition, difficulty adapting to cognitive shifts, and rapid decision-making without considering long-term outcomes (White et al., 1994). Impulsive behaviors have been consistently associated with delinquency and criminal offenses in both juveniles and adults, correlating with higher arrest rates (Carroll et al., 2006; Morgan & Lilienfeld, 2000; Ogilvie et al., 2011; Loeber et al., 2012).

In this study, impulsivity specifically refers to an individual's lack of concern for consequences, responsibility, or emotional engagement with their actions. Veterans frequently described impulsivity through their experiences of reaching a point of extreme emotional and psychological exhaustion, often described as "rock bottom." At this stage, veterans demonstrated an attitude of indifference toward the outcomes of their behaviors. One veteran explicitly stated, "It's not my problem … I'll keep drinking, who cares anymore." Another veteran similarly conveyed this disregard: "I went back to doing business as usual … I kept drinking and driving." A further participant acknowledged the risk involved but accepted it due to desperation, saying, "Yeah, I cashed the checks with the chance of going to jail and maybe prison, but that was the best of bad choices confronting me."

Mental health was explicitly linked to impulsivity among many veterans, revealing a profound emotional detachment and disregard for personal wellbeing. One veteran succinctly described their mental state, stating, "I was homeless, depressed, and I didn't care really." Another expressed their emotional numbness clearly: "I was completely apathetic … I didn't really care about consequences." Similarly, a veteran provided insight into their mental health condition by acknowledging, "I'm not a sociopath, but at the time I was almost on the verge of not caring about any form of consequence whatsoever."

The veterans also conveyed how repeated incarcerations intensified their impulsive behaviors and attitudes. One participant plainly described their mindset after repeated arrests: "I didn't care … Because if you get locked up so many times, who cares?" Another veteran echoed this sentiment, stating bluntly, "I really didn't care that I was in jail … I didn't care." Reflecting on interactions with the judicial system, one veteran clearly conveyed their deep apathy: "I don't care what they do to me, I don't give a crap what happens." Another vividly illustrated the persistence of impulsivity despite incarceration: "None of my arrests had any impact on changing behavior in any way shape or form." Similarly, one veteran recounted their immediate return to impulsive behavior postrelease: "I just sat there in my black and white striped trustee overalls and waited my time out until they said I could go home … First thing I did was light a cigarette and buy a beer."

Overall, veterans described impulsivity as a profound indifference toward their own lives and futures, reinforcing harmful behaviors and diminishing the likelihood of behavioral change. One veteran clearly stated their lack of investment in life, asserting, "I didn't give a damn about anything in life." Another described their indifference at the moment of arrest: "I didn't give a rat's ass … didn't have any care at all … I got out of the car and lit a cigarette … I'm going to jail." A different veteran noted how avoiding immediate consequences encouraged their ongoing impulsivity: "I kept getting away with stuff now so I kept pushing it."

Impulsivity functions as an emergent behavioral response to transition to civilian life, which impacted decision-making capabilities and perpetuated cycles of risky behavior and incarceration. This behavior represents not only an immediate behavioral risk but a broader psychological and emotional crisis that necessitates targeted interventions. Veterans said their impulsivity was tied to the emotional fatigue that comes from extended, difficult transition from structured military life to the less predictable civilian environment. In our interviews, veterans presented these statements specifically within the context of no longer being in the military, now navigating civilian life. Veteran reflections such as "It's not my problem … I'll keep drinking, who cares anymore" and "I was homeless, depressed, and I didn't care really" signal emotional fatigue tied directly to veterans' loss of structure ("who care anymore?"), meaning, and identity previously sustained through military service. Their sense of exhaustion and resulting impulsivity emerge from confronting ongoing stressors without the organized support, clear expectations, and communal accountability inherent to military contexts. Another veteran described reaching an emotional breaking point, noting, "I really didn't care that I was in jail … I didn't care," highlighting how repeated disappointments and struggles in civilian life gradually eroded their previously internalized military ideals of discipline, foresight, and consequence awareness. Furthermore, the statement, "I kept getting away with stuff now," illustrates how the absence of immediate accountability, which is typical of military structures, allowed impulsivity to escalate unchecked in civilian settings. A new "now" for our veterans was a less structured and accountable environment. Likewise, the narrative of returning immediately to impulsive behaviors after incarceration ("First thing I did was light a cigarette and buy a beer") emphasizes the stark contrast between the structured rehabilitation and consistent accountability in the military and the perceived emptiness of civilian alternatives. Collectively, these accounts illustrate vividly how the prolonged strain of transitioning from a structured military environment to an uncertain and demanding civilian context led to deep emotional fatigue, significantly reducing veterans' capacity for deliberate, thoughtful decision-making. This directly heightened impulsivity and related risky behaviors, intensifying their vulnerabilities to incarceration and reinforcing the critical need for identity-informed support systems that address transition fatigue and provide structured emotional and behavioral interventions.

This chapter provided an in-depth exploration of critical turning points (homelessness, poor prosocial networks, social isolation, unemployment and economic motivation, and impulsivity) each connected to veteran identity and influencing pathways toward incarceration. The analysis emphasized that these turning points do not occur in isolation but rather dynamically interact and compound one another, collectively intensifying vulnerabilities and shaping veterans' trajectories.

Veterans' narratives illuminated how housing instability profoundly disrupted their expectations of stability and self-sufficiency, rooted in their military identities, leading directly to economic and psychological distress. Similarly, the erosion of supportive social relationships and subsequent isolation starkly contrasted veterans' previous experiences of structured camaraderie and collective accountability within military life, exacerbating emotional distress and susceptibility to maladaptive behaviors.

Economic motivations driven by unemployment and financial desperation further highlighted veterans' struggles transitioning from predictable military employment to civilian economic uncertainties. Financial pressures escalated into criminal behaviors motivated by substance dependence, intensifying their engagement with the criminal justice system. Additionally, impulsivity, stemming from cumulative emotional and psychological fatigue associated with this challenging transition, revealed how veterans' disciplined decision-making, which was once shaped by military service, was progressively undermined, amplifying risks of repeated incarceration.

This chapter underscores the necessity of comprehensive, identity-informed interventions addressing stable housing, meaningful economic opportunities, robust social reintegration programs, and targeted mental health support. Recognizing the interconnectedness of these factors provides a nuanced foundation for understanding veteran incarceration, setting the stage for the subsequent chapter, which further explores additional veteran-specific turning points. This deeper examination promises to expand opportunities for effective, targeted interventions tailored explicitly to the unique challenges veterans face.

References

Andrews, D. A., & Bonta, J. (2024). *The psychology of criminal conduct* (7th ed.). Routledge.

American Psychological Association (APA). (2020a). *APA dictionary of psychology: Social isolation.* https://dictionary.apa.org/social-isolation

American Psychological Association (APA). (2020b). *APA dictionary of psychology: Impulsive*. https://dictionary.apa.org/impulsive

Bennett, T., & Holloway, K. (2005). The association between multiple drug misuse and crime. *International Journal of Offender Therapy and Comparative Criminology, 49*(1), 63–81. https://doi.org/10.1177/0306624X04269003

Blonigen, D. M., Bui, L., Elbogen, E. B., Blodgett, J. C., Maisel, N. C., Midboe, A. M., Asch, S. M., McGuire, J. F., & Timko, C. (2014). Risk of recidivism among justice-involved veterans: A systematic review of the literature. *Criminal Justice Policy Review*, *27*(8), 812–837. https://doi.org/10.1177/0887403414562602

Carroll, A., Hemingway, F., Bower, J., Ashman, A., Houghton, S., & Durkin, K. (2006). Impulsivity in juvenile delinquency: Differences among early-onset, late-onset, and non-offenders. *Journal of Youth and Adolescence*, *35*(4), 519–529. https://doi.org/10.1007/s10964-006-9053-6

Couloute, L., & Kopf, D. (2018). *Out of prison & out of work: Unemployment among formerly incarcerated people*. Prison Policy Initiative. www.prisonpolicy.org/reports/outofwork.html

Elbogen, E. B., Johnson, S. C., Wagner, H. R., Newton, V. M., Timko, C., Vasterling, J. J., & Beckham, J. C. (2012). Protective factors and risk modification of violence in Iraq and Afghanistan War veterans. *The Journal of Clinical Psychiatry*, *73*(6), e767–e773. https://doi.org/10.4088/JCP.11m07593

Elder, G. H. (1985). Perspectives on the life course. In G. H. Elder, Jr. (Ed.), *Life course dynamics,* (pp. 23–49). Cornell University Press.

Greenberg, G. A., & Rosenheck, R. A. (2009). Mental health and other risk factors for jail incarceration among male veterans. *Psychiatric Quarterly*, *80*(1), 41–53. https://doi.org/10.1007/s11126-009-9092-8

Henry, M., Watt, R., Mahathey, A., Ouellette, J., & Sitler, A. (2020). The 2019 annual homeless assessment report (AHAR) to Congress: Part 1 point-in-time estimates of homelessness. Housing and Urban Development, Office of Policy Development and Research. www.huduser.gov/portal/datasets/ahar.html

Klee, H., & Morris, J. (2009). Crime and drug misuse: Economic and psychological aspects of the criminal activities of heroin and amphetamine injectors. *Addiction Research, 1*(4), 377–386. https://doi.org/10.3109/16066359409005204

LePage, J., Bluitt, M., House-Hatfield, T., McAdams, H., Burdick, M., Dudley, D., Michaels, S., Merrell, C., Otto, S., Lenger-Gvist, J., Eisworth, J., Newton, J. A., & Gaston, C. (2005). Improving success in a veterans homeless domiciliary vocational program: Model development and evaluation. *Rehabilitation Psychology*, *50*(3), 297–304. https://doi.org/10.1037/0090-5550.50.3.297

Loeber, R., Menting, B., Lynam, D. R., Moffitt, T. E., Stouthamer-Loeber, M., Stallings, R., Farrington, D. P., & Pardini, D. (2012). Findings from the Pittsburgh Youth Study: Cognitive impulsivity and intelligence as predictors of the age-crime curve. *Journal of the American Academy of Child and Adolescent Psychiatry*, *51*(11), 1136–1149. https://doi.org/10.1016/j.jaac.2012.08.019

Meyers, R. J., Roozen, H. G., & Smith, J. E. (2011). The community reinforcement approach: An update of the evidence. *Alcohol Research & Health, 33*(4), 380–388. https://doi.org/10.1007/978-90-313-9756-3

Miller, W. R., Meyers, R. J., & Hiller-Sturmhofel, S. (1999). The community-reinforcement approach. *Alcohol Research & Health*, *23*(2), 116–121.

Morgan, A. B., & Lilienfeld, S. O. (2000). A meta-analytic review of the relation between antisocial behavior and neuropsychological measures of executive function. *Clinical Psychology Review, 20*(1), 113–136. https://doi.org/10.1016/s0272-7358(98)00096-8

Mumola, C. J. (2000). Veterans in prison or jail. (NCJ 178888). US Department of Justice, Office of Justice Programs. https://bjs.ojp.gov/content/pub/pdf/vpj.pdf

Ogilvie, J. M., Stewart, A. L., Chan, R. C. K., & Shum, D. H. K. (2011). Neuropsychological measures of executive function and antisocial behavior: A meta-analysis. *Criminology: An Interdisciplinary Journal, 49*(4), 1063–1107. https://doi.org/10.1111/j.1745-9125.2011.00252.x

Petrovich, J. C., Pollio, D. E., & North, C. S. (2014). Characteristics and service use of homeless veterans and nonveterans residing in a low-demand emergency shelter. *Psychiatric Services, 65*(6), 751–757. https://doi.org/10.1176/appi.ps.201300104

Pew Charitable Trusts (2010). Collateral costs: Incarceration's effect on economic mobility. The Pew Charitable Trusts. www.pew.org/-/media/3975EB366428437FADA60843AA02C2FC.ashx

Roy, L., Crocker, A. G., Nicholls, T. L., Latimer, E. A., & Ayllon, A. R. (2014). Criminal behavior and victimization among homeless individuals with severe mental illness: A systematic review. *Psychiatric Services, 65*(6), 739–750. https://doi.org/10.1176/appi.ps.201200515

Sampson, R., & Laub, J. (1990). Crime and deviance over the life course: The salience of adult social bonds. *American Sociological Review, 55*, 609–627. https://doi.org/10.2307/2095859

Sampson, R., & Laub, J. (1993). *Crime in the making: Pathways and turning points through life*. Harvard University Press.

Sampson, R. J., & Laub, J. H. (2010). Age-graded theory of informal social control. In F.T Cullen & P. Wilcox (Eds.), *Encyclopedia of Criminological Theory* (pp. 806–813). SAGE.

Sung, H-E. (2010). From diversion to reentry: Recidivism risks among graduates of an alternative to incarceration program. *Criminal Justice Policy Review, 22(2),* 219–234. https://doi.org/10.1177/0887403410376588

Sutherland, R., Sindicich, N., Barrett, E., Whittaker, E., Peacock, A., Hicky, S., & Burns, L. (2015). Motivations, substance use and other correlates amongst property and violent offenders who regularly inject drugs. *Addictive Behaviors, 45,* 207–213. http://dx.doi.org/10.1016/j.addbeh.2015.01.034

Tejani, N., Rosenheck, R., Tsai, J., Kasprow, W., & McGuire, J. F. (2013). Incarceration histories of homeless veterans and progression through a national supported housing program. *Community Mental Health Journal, 50*(5), 514–519. https://doi.org/10.1007/s10597-013-9611-9

Tsai, J., & Rosenheck, R. A. (2012). Incarceration among chronically homeless adults: Clinical correlates and outcomes. *Journal of Forensic Psychology Practice, 12*(4), 307–324. https://psycnet.apa.org/doi/10.1080/15228932.2012.695653

Tsai, J., & Rosenheck, R. A. (2015). Risk factors for homelessness among US veterans. *Epidemiologic Reviews, 37*(1), 177–195. https://doi.org/10.1093/epirev/mxu004

Tsai, J., Rosenheck, R. A., Kasprow, W. J., & McGuire, J. F. (2014). Homelessness in a national sample of incarcerated veterans in state and federal prisons. *Administration and Policy in Mental Health and Mental Health Services Research, 41*(3), 360–367. https://doi.org/10.1007/s10488-013-0483-7

US Bureau of Labor Statistics. (2015). *How the government measures unemployment.* www.bls.gov/cps/cps_htgm.htm

US Department of Veterans Affairs. (2021). VA homeless programs: VA homeless FAQs. www.va.gov/HOMELESS/faqs.asp#accordion-definition

US Department of Veterans Affairs. (2025a). National strategy for preventing veteran suicide 2018–2028. Office of Mental Health and Suicide Prevention. www.mentalhealth.va.gov/suicide_prevention/

US Department of Veterans Affairs. (2025b). Mental health suicide prevention. www.mentalhealth.va.gov/suicide_prevention

Western, B., Braga, A. A., Davis, J., & Sirois, C. (2015). Stress and hardship after prison. *American Journal of Sociology, 120*(5), 1512–1547. https://doi.org/10.1086/681301

White, J. L., Moffitt, T. E., Caspi, A., Bartusch, D. J., Needles, D. J., & Stouthamer-Loeber, M. (1994). Measuring impulsivity and examining its relationship to delinquency. *Journal of Abnormal Psychology, 103*(2), 192–205. https://doi.org/10.1037//0021-843x.103.2.192

8

PERCEPTIONS OF CHOICE AND CONTROL AMONG POSTINCARCERATED VETERANS

Introduction and Definition of External Locus of Control

Personal accountability and the impact individuals have on their lives are deeply affected by locus of control, a key concept in psychology. This idea distinguishes between people who believe they control their lives and those who believe external forces of chance or society do (American Psychological Association, 2025). This model offers a crucial understanding of behavioral trends, especially among veterans dealing with the complexities of incarceration and its aftermath.

Those with an internal locus of control attribute their outcomes to personal decisions, effort, and capabilities. Alternatively, people with an external locus of control typically attribute their circumstances to external factors. Periods of transition or instability highlight how external factors significantly shape an individual's emotional resilience, coping methods, and responses.

Studies on perceived control among prisoners have mainly focused on young offenders and their repeat offending (Ollendick & Hersen, 1979; Ollendick et al., 1980). Considering veterans' unique military backgrounds, identities, and postservice transitions adds significant analytical depth to this perspective. The structured routine, identity, and purpose ingrained by their service significantly influence how they perceive personal agency and external circumstances later in their lives.

The shift from military to civilian life profoundly impacts veterans' sense of personal agency and control. The military's clear roles, responsibilities, and hierarchy give veterans stable identities and structured ways to cope. But, postdischarge, veterans often face unpredictable civilian life, lacking clear roles and consistent support, which might shift their perspectives outward.

DOI: 10.4324/9781003522300-8

The psychological burden of this shift is shown in qualitative data from veterans. "I felt like a total failure," one veteran admitted, expressing profound feelings of inadequacy. An external orientation becomes pronounced when veterans face economic instability and housing insecurity. Veterans experiencing these adversities frequently interpret their circumstances as outcomes of broader systemic barriers rather than challenges they can influence. This external attribution reduces their motivation to seek or utilize interventions, deepening their sense of disempowerment and increasing the likelihood of maladaptive coping behaviors, including substance use or disengagement from supportive services.

Veterans' perspectives on substance misuse further underscore the critical impact of external control perceptions. Faced with relentless pressure, one veteran resorted to drugs, stating, "It was a lot easier, he stayed bugging me about calling somebody … I'll go right down there [to buy drugs]." This explanation shows how perceiving one's choices as dictated by external circumstances significantly influences behavioral responses, increasing susceptibility to harmful behaviors. In addition, how involved veterans are with mental health care depends on their sense of control. A belief in outside forces affecting their lives makes veterans less likely to stay in treatment, hindering starting recovery. One veteran, reflecting on their disengagement from substance abuse treatment, stated, "I knew I needed to stop …," highlighting the internal conflict veterans experience when treatment feels externally imposed rather than internally motivated.

By studying control perceptions and veterans' lived experiences together, we gain insight into incarceration risk factors. Veterans' accounts, viewed in this way, illuminate the critical connections between their sense of outside pressures and their reintegration, coping mechanisms, and growing identities after service. A thorough understanding of veterans' unique situations is vital for creating interventions that empower them, build responsibility, and ultimately lower their risk of imprisonment. Subsequent sections will further explore these intersections, detailing how external control perceptions shape veterans' experiences and outlining actionable strategies for meaningful support and effective reintegration.

External Locus of Control and Veteran Identity

Veterans' reactions to postservice challenges are shaped by their sense of personal agency and their strongly held military identity. The discipline, camaraderie, and resilience learned in the military create a firm base for veterans' personal strength and community connections. However, upon reentering civilian life, veterans encounter new societal contexts that can alter their sense of control, agency, and identity coherence.

Veterans' transitions to civilian life are marked by profound disruptions to their sense of self, according to their accounts. This change is characterized by reduced independence and a heightened reliance on external attributions for individual outcomes. One participant highlighted a stark contrast: "I missed the military so much, I wanted to go back .... I missed all my friends, the camaraderie. Civilians in the workforce were lazy." This perception of civilian environments as unpredictable or incompatible often triggers feelings of external dependency and diminished self-efficacy, reflecting a sharp divergence from the sense of competence and agency fostered during military service.

Postservice instability can exacerbate feelings of disempowerment in veterans because of the conflict between their ingrained military values and their new experiences. This emotional state was succinctly described as a sense of "hopelessness." Another participant stated plainly, "I just gave up." These expressions reveal a critical internal conflict wherein veterans grapple with reconciling their ingrained expectations of control and agency with the reality of civilian systems perceived as beyond their influence.

The way veterans interact with civilian life domains (e.g., occupation, social networks, family, health systems) can reveal how perceived outside control negatively affects their postservice adaptation. Veterans accustomed to clear systems may find civilian institutions confusing because of unfamiliar bureaucracy and vague expectations. One participant shared their difficulty in securing civilian employment: "It was really difficult for me to get the job that I always wanted." Another described feeling overwhelmed by external circumstances affecting their personal space: "We had all kinds of drug dealers coming in and out of our home ... Out of my home." These narratives underscore how veterans perceive their civilian challenges as externally imposed, intensifying feelings of frustration and helplessness.

Veterans articulated how their perceptions of reduced personal agency and increased reliance on external factors were deeply connected to the disruption of their military-formed identities after transitioning into civilian life. As one veteran noted earlier, "I missed the military so much, I wanted to go back .... I missed all my friends, the camaraderie. Civilians in the workforce were lazy," demonstrates how their sense of competence, camaraderie, and clear purpose in the military starkly contrasts with their civilian experiences, causing a shift toward perceiving life outcomes as externally driven. Similarly, describing the chaotic nature of civilian housing ("We had all kinds of drug dealers coming in and out of our home ... Out of my home") highlights the loss of structured and predictable environments inherent to military settings, reinforcing feelings of vulnerability and diminished control. These reflections underscore how veterans' experiences of external control and reduced agency are not simply due to challenging circumstances but specifically arise from conflicts between their deeply ingrained military identities and the unpredictability and complexity of civilian life.

Treatment for mental health and substance abuse underscores the conflict between a servicemember's internalized military identity and their need for outside help. The culture of strength and independence among veterans often leads them to see outside help as a personal failing. Simultaneously, when experiencing mental health or substance use challenges, veterans may attribute these struggles to external influences beyond their control, reinforcing feelings of disempowerment and reducing their willingness to engage with supportive services.

Understanding how identity and perceived control interact helps us create support strategies for veterans' specific needs. By using culturally responsive practices in veteran support and employment programs, civilian institutions can help veterans regain their sense of agency and reduce feelings of external dependence. Programs that pair veterans with mentors who share similar backgrounds can help veterans feel more confident and independent, which helps them adjust to civilian life. Grasping how veterans view their control and deeply held identity is key to developing helpful interventions. These interventions must account for veterans' distinct cultural expectations while actively confronting the disempowerment stemming from their civilian transitions. Through targeted efforts to reinforce veterans' autonomy, community integration, and personal agency, support systems can effectively enhance their capacity to navigate postservice challenges and promote successful civilian reintegration.

External Locus of Control and Veteran Treatment-Seeking Behaviors

Veterans' ways of handling personal difficulties are strongly influenced by military culture, which stresses independence, resilience, and self-reliance. Postservice, the same cultural norms beneficial during active duty complicate mental health and substance use challenges for veterans. Specifically, attributing life outcomes to external factors intensifies feelings of helplessness among veterans, thus affecting their receptiveness to treatment and help-seeking behaviors.

The strong stigma against vulnerability in the military, especially in mental health, leads veterans to believe that seeking help shows weakness or incompetence. Healthcare systems, often unfamiliar and unresponsive to veterans' cultural expectations, amplify their pre-existing perceptions. During their transition, veterans may see obstacles to treatment and positive outcomes as external forces beyond their control. If you think things are happening to you outside of your control, it can make you feel powerless and less likely to take charge of your health.

A veteran described how court-mandated treatment affected their engagement, saying, "what got its way with me is this court they put me in." This external framing can significantly undermine intrinsic motivation and long-term commitment to therapeutic processes, highlighting the critical impact of perceived external imposition on veterans' treatment decisions.

How veterans view treatment success depends on their perception of external factors' influence. Setbacks and slow progress lead veterans to attribute their difficulties to external issues, provider shortcomings, inadequate treatment, or systemic flaws, overlooking internal factors. For example, a veteran remarked, "After that first DUI, I felt that nothing happened to me … So, you know, I was immediately drinking again … Maybe there wasn't enough repercussions." This reflection demonstrates how attributing personal behaviors and outcomes primarily to external factors can diminish feelings of responsibility, reduce engagement, and perpetuate cycles of risk.

Veterans' proactiveness in seeking treatment significantly depends on whether they believe external factors control their health and recovery. Veterans, socialized to prioritize strength and self-reliance within the military, often view seeking help as surrendering control to outside forces. From this perspective, proactive engagement may be significantly reduced, especially for veterans encountering bureaucratic complexities or cultural misunderstandings in civilian healthcare. One participant explained this clearly: "It was really difficult for me to get the help I needed … I didn't know where to start, and nobody seemed to understand my situation." This experience emphasizes how perceived external barriers discourage veterans from actively pursuing and maintaining needed care.

Veterans' history of unsuccessful treatment can create a sense of helplessness, reducing their motivation to pursue additional support. If past interventions seemed forced or irrelevant, veterans may hesitate to seek treatment again. This generates a perpetual loop of withdrawal, as externalizing past setbacks diminishes optimism and drive for future treatment. Veteran accounts show the importance of ensuring treatment programs are responsive, culturally attuned, and affirming to veterans' experiences and perspectives. Solutions to these problems must prioritize boosting veterans' belief in their own capabilities and control over their lives. Better engagement and outcomes result from using culturally responsive, transitional, and veteran-specific counseling strategies. Providing veterans with direct, culturally relevant support not only affirms their identity and experiences, but also reinforces their sense of personal capability and motivation.

In addition, structured programs targeting military members and designed to achieve specific goals can help them regain a sense of empowerment. Counseling that helps veterans set their own goals and focuses on what's important to them can help them feel more independent and motivated. Programs providing clear expectations, transparent support, and validation of veterans' experiences can mitigate negative affects from external attributions. More effective veteran healthcare systems need to consider veterans' perspectives on outside influence. Acknowledging veterans' unique cultural perspectives and addressing perceived external barriers directly can significantly enhance their active engagement in treatment processes, ultimately promoting healthier outcomes and successful community reintegration.

External Locus of Control in Veteran Trajectories and Transitions

Veterans highlighted long-term patterns of employment instability, family upheaval, and mental health crises, as well as pivotal events related to military discharge, as major influences on their lives. These events serve as turning points, critically influencing their overall life paths. How veterans perceive these events, particularly through the lens of external factors determining their life outcomes, informs their response strategies to major life changes. As our veterans' note in this chapter, their response to civilian turning points was an important factor in their incarceration.

Outside obstacles of employers' biases, complex hiring systems, and the mismatch between military and civilian skills causes job hunting difficulties among veterans. Blaming outside forces for job search setbacks reduces veterans' self-motivation and engagement, thus complicating their career shifts. Rather than viewing these setbacks as manageable through individual effort, they see them as beyond personal influence, undermining confidence and initiative in seeking sustainable employment.

Housing instability similarly represents a significant life challenge influenced by externalized perceptions of control. Our veterans who experienced severe disruptions (e.g., loss of property or insecure living conditions) perceive these hardships as resulting from systemic inadequacies or insufficient institutional support. As one veteran poignantly described: "I had a 30-acre farm. I lost it." This perspective amplifies the psychological impact of housing instability, intensifying feelings of helplessness, and complicating the pathway toward regaining economic stability and housing security.

Family disruptions, including relationship breakdowns, loss of family members, or intense caregiving responsibilities, further exemplify the influence of externalized perceptions on veterans' coping strategies. For instance, one veteran facing simultaneous personal losses stated, "I had to give up." This illustrates how perceiving family-related crises as externally imposed can lead to emotional paralysis and diminished coping abilities. Instead of approaching family crises with adaptive problem-solving strategies, veterans who view these situations as externally controlled may experience elevated distress and reduced resilience, increasing the likelihood of negative coping behaviors.

Mental health transitions also reveal the critical role that external perceptions play in veterans' treatment engagement and recovery processes. People may attribute significant mental health issues among veterans to external factors (e.g., traumatic military experiences, lack of support, or social stigma) rather than internal factors. This external attribution reduces their likelihood of actively taking part in available mental health treatments, creating barriers to recovery and extending periods of psychological distress.

The qualitative accounts of veterans further clarify how these perceptions affect their mental health experiences. A belief that outside forces, not personal actions, impact mental health creates barriers to care for veterans. This viewpoint discourages active participation and makes recovery feel harder, increasing the chance of negative behaviors and possible contact with the legal system.

Interventions should actively cultivate veterans' self-determination, personal responsibility, and resilience. Personalized approaches like structured employment, housing aid, and mental health support boost veterans' control, engagement, and coping. Developing these intervention strategies requires recognizing veterans' unique experiences and aligning services with their specific cultural and emotional contexts. Structured reintegration programs designed around clear, achievable goals can empower veterans by reinforcing their internal agency and resilience. Veteran-centered counseling and veteran support empower individuals to see their situations as manageable, not externally imposed. Addressing these perceptions directly is vital for equipping veterans with the confidence and resources needed to navigate major life changes effectively, ultimately reducing vulnerabilities to negative outcomes, including incarceration.

Responsive interventions for veterans facing major life events are better developed by understanding how external control perceptions affect their experiences. Addressing these dynamics helps build resilience, enhances veterans' internal perceptions of agency, and equips them with tools to effectively manage life's critical turning points. Practical implications and targeted strategies informed by these insights are necessary to promote veterans' long-term stability and success.

External Locus of Control, Behavioral Turning Points, and Incarceration Risks

Veterans' perceptions regarding external factors significantly shape their behavioral choices and responses, especially concerning substance use, mental health management, and compliance with legal obligations. These behaviors represent critical junctures, each carrying profound implications for potential involvement in the criminal justice system. Examining these behaviors through the lens of external influence perceptions can reveal key opportunities for targeted interventions that effectively reduce veterans' vulnerabilities.

Substance use is frequently influenced by perceptions of external circumstances, which can diminish veterans' perceived control over their behaviors. Veterans who see substance use as an inevitable response to external pressures often find it challenging to start change independently. As one veteran explained: "The pressure from my roommate … he got me out of bed … he had me go right down the street to a known drug area." This perspective highlights how external circumstances, rather than individual choices, can strongly drive substance-related behaviors, decreasing personal motivation to seek support proactively.

Another veteran explicitly connected their substance use to an external sense of inevitability, expressing, "I didn't want to quit at the time … I knew I was an alcoholic, I just didn't care." This statement clearly illustrates how externalized perceptions can undermine personal responsibility and perpetuate harmful behaviors. Viewing substance use as externally determined significantly reduces individuals' belief in their ability to influence or change these behaviors independently.

Meeting legal requirements, like probation or court-ordered treatment, is a major behavioral shift for veterans, shaped by outside influences. Veterans who feel these obligations are imposed upon them rather than self-chosen often experience reduced motivation and engagement. One veteran articulated the nature of imposed legal obligations: "You're out doing well, you've gotten a job, maybe you've gotten a girlfriend and a place to stay, and boom, here comes this warrant and undoes it all." Another individual described avoiding mandatory classes because of emotional distress: "When I went to those classes, I found out the sex offender I was … that was tough, so I didn't go back; it was just too much for me and might have started me drinking again." These accounts underscore how externally imposed obligations can heighten feelings of helplessness and reduce active participation in necessary treatments or legal compliance.

Veterans also explained that their fatigue from ongoing struggles after military discharge exacerbated their impulsivity and reinforced an externalized locus of control, fundamentally contrasting with their prior structured and disciplined military lifestyle. As one veteran noted earlier regarding their inability to remain engaged in court-ordered classes, "When I went to those classes, I found out the sex offender I was … that was tough, so I didn't go back; it was just too much for me and might have started me drinking again." This statement directly highlights how overwhelming civilian expectations and imposed legal requirements, absent the familiar structure and clear expectations of military life, intensified their sense of emotional exhaustion, leading to impulsive disengagement. Veteran's description of complying reluctantly due to external pressures ("what got its way with me is this court they put me in") further illustrates how veterans' agency becomes diminished by external factors they perceive as incompatible with the disciplined autonomy fostered by their military identity. These narratives clearly demonstrate how veterans' impulsivity, transition fatigue, and externalized locus of control significantly derive from disruptions to their sense of identity, purpose, and structured expectations previously reinforced during military service.

Veterans may attribute involvement in unlawful activities to external influences, further reinforcing diminished personal accountability. One veteran reflected on their criminal involvement, stating: "We were kind of subculture … I would say we had some badass breaks." These statements position criminal behaviors as products of external environments rather than personal decisions, which can decrease personal accountability and perpetuate cycles of criminal involvement. To support veterans experiencing these behavioral turning points, it is crucial to cultivate interventions designed specifically to enhance a sense of personal agency. Helping veterans make their own choices can boost their sense of control over their lives. Initiatives incorporating veteran-specific experiences, including culturally responsive and relatable support structures, can enhance motivation and engagement in personal recovery processes.

Easier access to culturally sensitive mental healthcare and substance abuse treatment is crucial for encouraging veterans to seek help. To actively manage their challenges, veterans are empowered by clear, accessible, and relatable treatment options. Supportive legal and social structures, tailored for veterans, can facilitate their compliance with legal obligations and reinforce personal accountability.

Research should explore how veterans' perceived external control affects their substance use, mental health, and legal actions to minimize criminal justice involvement risks. Comprehensive and culturally informed interventions that actively promote personal empowerment, structured decision-making, and accessible support services can significantly mitigate these risks, fostering sustained recovery, resilience, and successful societal reintegration.

Practical Implications and Recommendations

The study's findings, especially regarding external locus of control, veteran identity, and life course, highlight practical steps and strategies to lower veteran incarceration. Understanding this unique interplay allows for targeted, culturally informed, and effective intervention strategies that address veterans' distinct psychosocial contexts and needs.

First, reinforcing veterans' sense of personal agency represents a foundational step in mitigating external locus orientations. Veterans have benefited from programs that build self-esteem, help them set goals, and teach them to solve problems. Structured interventions that highlight personal strengths and resilience cultivated during military service can empower veterans to recognize and reclaim control over life circumstances, reducing external attributions and enhancing their motivation for positive behavioral changes.

Second, culturally tailored interventions and peer support programs boost veterans' feelings of empowerment in their recovery journey. For example, Veteran peer support initiatives, which leverage shared military experiences, build trust and camaraderie, reduce stigma around mental health and substance use, and enhance treatment engagement (Jain et al., 2012; Solomon, 2004). By validating veteran identity and providing relatable role models, these programs help veterans internalize responsibility for their treatment outcomes, shifting from external to internal locus orientations and promoting sustained behavioral change.

Third, interventions designed explicitly around veteran identity and the veteran standpoint offer considerable potential to reduce incarceration risk by addressing veterans' unique transitional challenges. Standpoint theory highlights the importance of recognizing individuals' lived experiences and contextualizing interventions accordingly (Harding, 2004; Smith, 1987). For veterans, this means developing programs addressing the unique difficulties of transitioning from military to civilian life, such as structured reintegration help, employment aid using their skills, and culturally appropriate mental health care. Interventions validate veterans' unique experiences and identities, empowering them to perceive greater control over their life trajectories.

Systemic reforms aimed at addressing structural and institutional barriers faced by veterans are essential. For instance, improving access to stable and affordable housing, meaningful employment opportunities, and comprehensive healthcare significantly reduces external barriers that reinforce external locus orientations (Tsai & Rosenheck, 2015; Montgomery et al., 2013). Programs around veterans' employment initiatives, transitional housing help, and integrated healthcare services represent practical strategies that enhance veterans' agency, enabling engagement with life transitions and reducing risks of incarceration.

Veterans' engagement and retention in mental health treatment are significantly improved by interventions that consider their cultural background, life journey, and self-perception (Tanielian & Jaycox, 2008). Healthcare providers with military, cultural competence, and life course perspectives training can better understand veterans' psychosocial issues, which improves therapeutic relationships and encourages veterans to take responsibility for their mental health. This approach can significantly reduce treatment resistance and enhance long-term adherence, mitigating the associated risks of incarceration.

Specialized veteran treatment courts provide structured environments emphasizing personal accountability, rehabilitation, and community reintegration. These courts effectively reduce recidivism by integrating mental health treatment, substance abuse services, and judicial oversight within a culturally competent framework (Russell, 2009; Slattery et al., 2013). By aligning closely with veterans' cultural values of accountability, discipline, and resilience, veteran treatment courts shift veterans' locus of control orientations toward internal accountability, significantly enhancing their engagement and long-term recovery outcomes.

By increasing awareness of resources, treatment options, and community support, comprehensive veteran outreach and education programs can proactively address external locus of control issues. Programs that actively engage veterans through community partnerships, veteran service organizations, and educational initiatives increase veterans' perceptions of support and control over their circumstances (Burnam et al., 2009; Zinzow et al., 2013). Outreach efforts are critical for empowering veterans to access necessary resources proactively, reducing external locus orientations, and promoting positive trajectories.

Summary

We have explored the interplay between external locus of control and veteran identity to show the implications for incarceration risk among veterans. Key elements of a successful support system include targeted strategies that promote self-sufficiency, peer support, culturally appropriate interventions, systemic reforms, and specialized judicial approaches. Implementing these recommendations, grounded in scholarly literature and informed by veterans' unique standpoints and identities, significantly enhances veterans' resilience, empowerment, and long-term success, ultimately reducing their vulnerability to incarceration.

External locus of control significantly shapes veterans' identities, behaviors, and life-course trajectories, contributing directly to their risk of incarceration. Using a life-course perspective, veteran identity, and standpoint theory, we gain an understanding of veterans' experiences, revealing how external factors shape their responses to key transitions in employment, housing, mental healthcare, substance abuse, and legal compliance.

Findings on external locus of control emphasize the importance of targeted, culturally appropriate interventions here. The recommendations highlight improvements in personal agency, peer support programs, culturally sensitive care, systemic change, and specialized courts for veterans. These strategic recommendations aim to shift veterans' perceptions from external attributions toward a strengthened internal locus of control, promoting resilience, empowerment, and long-term positive outcomes.

Chapter 9 expands the analysis to include another crucial turning point: the lifelong negative experiences and attitudes of veterans. Specifically, it will explore how adverse interactions within military structures, healthcare systems, and social service agencies shape veterans' attitudes and behaviors, further deepening our understanding of incarceration pathways. Our upcoming conversation builds upon the existing body of knowledge about veterans, offering practical solutions to their specific difficulties.

References

American Psychological Association. (2025). *APA dictionary of psychology: Locus of control*. https://dictionary.apa.org/locus-of-control

Burnam, M. A., Meredith, L. S., Tanielian, T., & Jaycox, L. H. (2009). Mental health care for Iraq and Afghanistan war veterans. *Health Affairs, 28*(3), 771–782. https://doi.org/10.1377/hlthaff.28.3.771

Harding, S. (2004). *The feminist standpoint theory reader: Intellectual and political controversies*. Routledge.

Jain, S., McLean, C., & Rosen, C. S. (2012). Is there a role for peer support delivered interventions in the treatment of veterans with post-traumatic stress disorder? *Military Medicine, 177*(5), 481–483. https://doi.org/10.7205/MILMED-D-11-00401

Montgomery, A. E., Hill, L. L., Kane, V., & Culhane, D. P. (2013). Housing chronically homeless veterans: Evaluating the efficacy of a Housing First approach to HUD-VASH. *Journal of Community Psychology*, *41*(4), 505–514. https://doi.org/10.1002/jcop.21554

Ollendick, T. H., Elliot, W., & Matson, J. L. (1980). Locus of control as related to effectiveness in a behavior modification program for juvenile delinquents. *Journal of Behavior Therapy and Experimental Psychiatry, 11*(4), 259–262. https://doi.org/10.1016/0005-7916(80)90067-1

Ollendick, T. H., & Hersen, M. (1979). Social skills training for juvenile delinquents. *Behavior Research and Therapy, 17*(6), 547–554. https://doi.org/10.1016/0005-7967(79)90098-6

Russell, R. T. (2009). Veterans treatment court: A proactive approach. *New England Journal of Criminal and Civil Confinement*, *35*(2), 357–372.

Slattery, M., Dugger, M. T., Lamb, T. A., & Williams, L. M. (2013). Catch, treat, and release: Veteran treatment courts addressing the challenges of returning home. *Substance Use & Misuse, 48*(10), 922–932. https://doi.org/10.3109/10826084.2013.797468

Smith, D. E. (1987). *The everyday world as problematic: A feminist sociology*. University of Toronto Press.

Solomon, P. (2004). Peer support/peer provided services underlying processes, benefits, and critical ingredients. *Psychiatric Rehabilitation Journal*, *27*(4), 392–401. https://doi.org/10.2975/27.2004.392.401

Tanielian, T., & Jaycox, L. H. (Eds.). (2008). *Invisible wounds of war: Psychological and cognitive injuries, their consequences, and services to assist recovery*. RAND Corporation. www.rand.org/pubs/monographs/MG720.html

Tsai, J., & Rosenheck, R. A. (2015). Risk factors for incarceration among homeless veterans: A two-year cohort study. *Psychiatric Services*, *66*(8), 853–859. https://doi.org/10.1093/epirev/mxu004

Zinzow, H. M., Britt, T. W., Pury, C. L., Raymond, M. A., McFadden, A. C., & Burnette, C. M. (2013). Barriers and facilitators of mental health treatment seeking among active-duty army personnel. *Military Psychology*, *25*(5), 514–35. https://doi.org/10.1037/mil0000015

9

NEGATIVE SERVICE EXPERIENCES AND VETERANS' PATHWAYS TO INCARCERATION

Introduction and Conceptualization of Negative Service Experiences

Negative service experiences for veterans involve unsatisfactory interactions with institutions including the military, healthcare, and social services. Trust, personal agency, and psychosocial well-being are altered in veterans. From large-scale organizational factors to individual interactions, negative experiences can manifest in diverse forms. Recognizing these differences is key to understanding how negative service experiences uniquely impact veterans' reintegration and their likelihood of incarceration.

Poor service on a large scale can be due to problems within an organization's systems or culture. The military's organizational culture may contribute to the stigmatization of mental health, injury, and pain management for veterans. As was mentioned in previous chapters, military standards typically stress resilience, toughness, and self-reliance, implying veterans are expected to independently manage their mental and physical health problems. Holding expectations may unintentionally cultivate settings where seeking assistance is stigmatized or perceived as a failing, substantially contributing to negative mental health consequences (Clement et al., 2015). The internalization of these norms by veterans can lead to avoidance of support, thereby increasing their vulnerabilities. A common story for our veterans was the perception of being instructed to persevere through their pain. As one veteran shared, "I was in pain .... I was told to suck it up."

On the other hand, negative encounters at the individual level result from personal interactions, which may involve direct conflicts or difficult exchanges

DOI: 10.4324/9781003522300-9

with healthcare professionals, social workers, or military leaders. Dismissive, unsympathetic, or misunderstanding encounters severely damage veterans' trust in and use of needed services. Personal interactions can have a lasting impact on veterans, influencing their attitudes and behaviors for years to come. The psychological and emotional toll of negative personal interactions on veterans is substantial, resulting in feelings of isolation, distrust, and marginalization.

Individual life trajectories are shaped by timing and context, with key transitions playing a crucial role, as life course theory emphasizes (Elder, 1998; Sampson & Laub, 1993). Negative service encounters can dramatically shift veterans' trajectories toward incarceration when considered within a life course framework. These experiences, while not always immediately preceding incarceration, produce lasting changes in outlook, actions, and ways of handling problems, paving the path toward future involvement with the legal system.

Additionally, the idea of veteran identity offers another crucial theoretical connection to negative service experiences. Veterans' responses to negative institutional encounters are significantly shaped by their strong sense of discipline, self-reliance, and resilience, which are core components of their identity (Demers, 2011). When service experiences don't meet veterans' identity-based expectations, it creates deep internal conflict and undermines their trust in institutions. When trust is broken, people struggle to use authorized support services, develop alternative coping skills, and face a greater risk for incarceration when these behavioral avenues fall outside legal channels.

Incarceration pathways of veterans, therefore, may be better understood by considering their unique social positions and personal histories (Collins, 2019; Harding, 2004). Focusing on veterans' lived experiences and accounts situates negative service experiences in their overall life stories and reveals how these meaningful encounters trigger life transitions toward incarceration. It also highlights the importance of matching institutional support with what veterans need and want.

Consequently, negative service experiences are far more significant than simply isolated incidents of displeasure or conflict. They represent underlying, systemic problems in institutional culture, personal trust, and veterans' feeling of empowerment. Veterans' behaviors and choices after service are significantly shaped by critical transitions stemming from their experiences, thus impacting their risk of imprisonment.

This chapter explores the personal effects of negative customer service on veterans. We'll examine how these experiences specifically manifest interactions with military culture, healthcare, and social services in the following sections. By doing this, we find crucial points to intervene and offer targeted plans to lessen negative service encounters and reduce veterans' chances of incarceration.

Military Culture and Pain Management: Navigating Conflicting Expectations

Resilience, self-reliance, toughness, and personal accountability are hallmarks of military culture. Pain and mental health management for veterans are significantly shaped by cultural factors. These positive expectations, while operationally beneficial, can impede transitions, notably for veterans facing chronic pain, mental health problems, or injuries. Crucial insights into veteran reintegration and potential incarceration are gained by examining the impact of cultural expectations on their perspectives and actions.

Studies show military cultures often discourage individuals from openly discussing physical and mental health problems, creating environments where vulnerability and help-seeking are stigmatized (Acosta et al., 2014; Vogt et al., 2014). A shared belief among veterans in our study was that that they must cope with pain and psychological distress without help, reflecting the internalization of cultural norms. Veterans' accounts show that while they suffered significant physical and emotional distress, they felt compelled to cope alone, revealing an emergent health strategy. One veteran vividly explained this tension: "I was dealing with PTSD … I didn't know how to share my emotions). This statement demonstrates the conflict stemming from a culture that esteems resilience yet does not have established routes to express needs and vulnerabilities.

Negative interactions in pain management add to the core health challenges veterans face. In both military and civilian VA settings, veterans recounted healthcare experiences where medication was the primary treatment, neglecting underlying emotional and psychological needs. These types of interactions bred frustration, mistrust, and a sense of detachment from caregivers and the care received. The effects are clear in this veterans' account: "I'd been fighting PTSD for a long time and was so doped … I couldn't feel anything." Negative emotional association with medical outcomes, such as numbness, led to feelings of dissatisfaction with prescribed care: "I didn't like taking them [mental health medications] because they made me drowsy." Veteran stories show how these experiences are often the precursor to medical noncompliance, misuse of substances, and a pathway to incarceration.

The difficulties veterans face in managing pain and injury with their superiors reveal deeper issues within the military. Veterans described situations where they faced serious personal legal repercussions due to difficulties meeting military demands on pain management and performance. A veteran described his command's detrimental response following his injury, alleging attempts by authority figures to blame him, pursue punitive measures, and direct personal hostility from a senior NCO: "After I got hurt my command was so bad they actually tried to blame me for getting hurt … they tried to actually get higher up to take legal action on me … one particular staff, an NCO, disliked me so much that he was trying to burn me for getting hurt." When injured veterans face negative reactions, particularly blame or hostility, from authority figures who should provide support, it profoundly shapes their perceptions, intensifying mistrust, resentment, and emotional distress, ultimately diminishing their willingness to engage constructively with institutional support systems. Following this encounter, the veteran described reaching a point where "I stopped giving a damn," subsequently adopting self-directed coping mechanisms, notably involving self-medication. This shift toward self-managed approaches, particularly substance use, heightens vulnerability to behavioral risks and increased the likelihood of interactions with the criminal justice system.

Negative service interactions alone are not deterministic factors that inevitably lead to incarceration. Instead, these experiences often serve as pivotal moments in which veterans begin to diverge from institutionally approved pathways for managing pain, mental health, and overall well-being. When veterans encounter hostility, blame, or perceived institutional neglect, particularly from those they expect to provide support and validation, they may gradually lose trust in authorized avenues of care. This diminished trust, coupled with ongoing feelings of resentment and emotional abandonment, can drive veterans to seek alternative coping mechanisms outside established channels. Alternative approaches commonly involve behaviors like self-medication through substance misuse, actively avoiding interactions with healthcare providers or authority figures, and adopting an attitude of disregard for personal well-being and legal compliance. Some veterans described behaviors reflecting a broader disengagement from societal norms, such as reckless driving or disregarding traffic laws (even while driving "I just drank all the damn time"), actions that increase the likelihood of interactions with law enforcement. These behaviors further heighten the risk of discovery or involvement with illegal substances and activities. Over time, reliance on these unauthorized coping strategies amplifies veterans' isolation from legitimate support systems, compounding their vulnerability to legal conflicts and potential involvement with the criminal justice system. In this way, negative interactions within service institutions contribute indirectly to veterans' long-term vulnerability, creating conditions conducive to behavioral patterns associated with increased incarceration risk.

Veteran identity is linked to how veterans perceive, respond to, and internalize negative service experiences, especially those involving military culture, healthcare systems, and interactions with authority figures. Veterans often express deep frustration when their experiences starkly contrast with core military values of resilience, self-reliance, and clear institutional accountability. As reflected in one veteran's experience (e.g., "I was dealing with PTSD ... I didn't know how to share my emotions") the internalization of military expectations to "cope alone" frequently prevents veterans from seeking necessary support, exacerbating emotional distress and feelings of isolation. Similarly, another veteran's painful memory of being told to "suck it up" deepened their sense of internal conflict and mistrust toward institutions. These reflections clearly illustrate how negative encounters become personally significant turning points, profoundly disrupting veterans' expectations of identity-based competence, agency, and self-reliance, and directly shaping subsequent behaviors and coping strategies that increase vulnerability to incarceration.

Negative Interactions with Healthcare Professionals: Erosion of Trust and Engagement

Effective healthcare engagement for incarcerated veterans relies fundamentally on building and maintaining trust during transitional periods. Negative experiences with healthcare providers can profoundly damage this trust, deepening veterans' feelings of helplessness, isolation, and frustration. Veterans often report encounters characterized by perceived inequity, dismissive attitudes, or inadequate cultural understanding on the part of medical and mental health professionals. Veterans emphasized social interactions that involve misunderstandings, insufficient empathy, and treatment plans that do not resonate with or acknowledge veterans' specific lived experiences and needs (Mittal et al., 2013). These problematic healthcare interactions directly shape veterans' perspectives regarding future healthcare utilization, significantly influencing their willingness to participate actively in ongoing medical and mental health interventions. Consequently, compromised trust not only reduces treatment adherence but may also prompt reliance on harmful coping mechanisms, including substance misuse and avoidance of necessary care, thereby exacerbating veterans' vulnerabilities and complicating their long-term psychosocial stability and reintegration outcomes.

One veteran described severe consequences arising from perceived gaps in healthcare, particularly around medication management: "They only gave me a seven-day supply … I wasn't able to get into my doctor … so I ran back to heroin." This scenario illustrates how insufficient healthcare can escalate desperation, driving veterans toward dangerous coping methods, including substance misuse. Research demonstrates that inadequate medical support significantly contributes to increased substance misuse among veterans, thereby raising their risk for legal troubles and potential incarceration (Blonigen et al., 2014; Tsai et al., 2013). Substance misuse not only represents personal health risks but frequently leads veterans toward behaviors directly associated with criminal activity and subsequent incarceration, as seen in cases involving illegal substance possession and related offenses. The veteran's reliance on heroin exemplifies how perceived gaps in institutional healthcare services can lead to choices with severe health and legal consequences.

Other veterans expressed similar dissatisfaction with the handling of mental health medications prescribed without appropriate follow-up or consideration of their broader circumstances. One veteran shared their experience: "I took myself off of it [mental health medication] … it just seemed like every time I'd go in there and be like, hey, I want to get surgery done, I want to get this fixed, they just no, we're gonna give you more pills." This withdrawal from recommended treatments often pushes veterans toward substance dependency or unmanaged mental health conditions, increasing their likelihood of encounters with law enforcement and subsequent incarceration. This type of experience aligns with research highlighting the critical impact of healthcare disconnects, showing that inadequate follow-up or fragmented care can lead to noncompliance, untreated mental health issues, and an elevated risk of engaging in harmful or illegal behaviors (Elbogen et al., 2013; Finlay et al., 2016). These institutional shortcomings can inadvertently propel veterans toward behaviors associated with increased incarceration risk, such as substance abuse or actions stemming from untreated mental health crises.

Veterans' trust and willingness to pursue mental health support can also be negatively affected by healthcare providers' reactions to their disclosures. One veteran recalled a troubling interaction: "I told him I was pulling out my hair and he stepped back and he told me that I was crazy." The resulting isolation and untreated mental health issues further heighten risks of engaging in illegal behaviors or substance use that can lead directly to legal consequences and incarceration. Experiences of stigma, misunderstanding, or insensitive responses from providers reinforce veterans' mistrust and reluctance to engage with mental health care, contributing to untreated psychological conditions and increasing susceptibility to incarceration-related behaviors (Harding, 2004; Collins, 2019; True et al., 2015). This erosion of trust may lead veterans to withdraw entirely from professional support, further exacerbating mental health crises and amplifying their risk for behaviors and decisions that ultimately intersect with the criminal justice system. Veterans' interpretations and narrations of their negative healthcare encounters provide crucial insights into their behaviors and choices, particularly regarding healthcare avoidance or substance misuse. These negative encounters reinforce veterans' feelings of isolation and marginalization, making them reluctant to engage further with healthcare systems.

Enhancing cultural competence training for healthcare professionals, particularly regarding veteran-specific issues, can significantly improve veterans' perceptions of healthcare interactions. This means centering the process of rebuilding trust and improving veterans' healthcare experiences. Evidence-based practices of collaborative treatment planning and patient-centered communication strategies, which actively incorporate veterans' perspectives and preferences, have been shown to improve engagement and adherence (Burnam et al., 2009; Zinzow et al., 2013). Adverse interactions with healthcare professionals can be major turning points influencing veterans' trust, treatment engagement, and broader psychosocial trajectories. These interactions, viewed through the lens of veteran identity, shows critical areas for intervention.

Negative Encounters with Social Service Providers: Implications for Reentry and Reintegration

The successful transition of veterans from prison back into civilian society is significantly influenced by their experiences with social service providers. Negative interactions with critical services (i.e., employment services, HUD, legal aid, and law enforcement) can undermine veterans' trust, willingness to engage with supportive resources, and overall psychological stability. Detrimental encounters not only complicate veterans' attempts at successful community reintegration but also heighten the risk of behaviors and choices that place them on a path toward incarceration (Blonigen et al., 2014; Tsai et al., 2013).

Veterans often perceive interactions with social services as dismissive, overly bureaucratic, impersonal, or adversarial, negatively shaping their attitudes and reducing the likelihood of continued service utilization. According to Keene et al. (2018), these problematic interactions can significantly impair veterans' ability to maintain stable housing, secure employment, and effectively engage with their communities. In particular, adversarial or unresponsive encounters exacerbate feelings of alienation, frustration, and powerlessness, potentially leading veterans to adopt coping mechanisms of substance misuse or behaviors that increase risks of illegal activities. One veteran illustrated a troubling interaction when attempting to access emergency support through a crisis hotline: "I was at the Race Trac and I called the 1-800-VA crisis hotline … them cops came quick, but they roughed me up … I'm asking for help and y'all roughed me up." This veteran's experience highlights how negative interactions with authority figures directly encouraged distrust in institutions, reinforcing withdrawal from legitimate support and pushing them toward behaviors that elevated their risk for involvement with law enforcement.

Housing support services also represent a significant source of frustration for many veterans. One individual explicitly described bureaucratic challenges and insensitive interactions: "I said if I had money to get an apartment I wouldn't be sitting in your office [VA Housing] … They ask redundant questions." This perceived indifference and bureaucratic complexity discouraged sustained pursuit of essential housing resources, indirectly guiding this veteran toward precarious living situations. Unstable conditions often coincide with higher exposure to environments and activities that carry increased legal risks, creating pathways toward the criminal justice system (Blonigen et al., 2014; Tsai et al., 2013).

Similarly, experiences with legal aid services can deepen veterans' frustration and contribute to feelings of disenfranchisement. A veteran articulated their discouragement clearly: "I haven't been able to get help from the legal aid from here through the VA … I'm very angry about that." For this veteran, the inadequacy of institutional legal support not only intensified existing frustrations but also diminished trust in the legitimacy and responsiveness of available services. Consequently, this veteran became more susceptible to behaviors involving non-compliance with legal requirements, substance use, or risky decisions that ultimately contributed to their pathway into incarceration (Elbogen et al., 2013; Finlay et al., 2016).

Overcoming these specific challenges requires targeted, responsive improvements in social service provision and institutional practices. Clear communication, streamlined procedures, culturally sensitive interactions, and comprehensive support mechanisms tailored explicitly for veterans can enhance their trust and engagement, thereby reducing vulnerability to high-risk behaviors and subsequent legal complications. Understanding and actively mitigating these negative service encounters are essential steps toward fostering veterans' long-term stability, promoting successful reintegration, and reducing the risk of future incarceration.

Negative encounters with social service providers, though seemingly isolated events, often set the stage for long-term trajectories characterized by mistrust, disengagement, and vulnerability. These experiences may indirectly contribute to increased likelihood of incarceration by influencing veterans' subsequent interactions and choices. By prioritizing veterans' perspectives, a standpoint emerges of how veterans interpret and respond to negative service encounters, highlighting their profound impact on trust, agency, and reintegration potential (Harding, 2004; Collins, 2019). Veterans' narratives clearly indicate that negative interactions with social service providers significantly affect their perceptions and willingness to utilize crucial reintegration resources.

Veterans' sense of disillusionment with civilian institutions, particularly healthcare and social services, can arise from perceived violations of the structured, responsive environments ingrained during their military service. For instance, a veteran's description of frustration with institutional inefficiency ("I said if I had money to get an apartment I wouldn't be sitting in your office [VA Housing] … They ask redundant questions") reflects a critical divergence between their structured military experience and the perceived chaotic, indifferent civilian bureaucracy. Another veteran's recollection ("Nobody even at HUD was answering phones, and where am I supposed to go?") demonstrates how unmet expectations for clear, timely, and decisive institutional responses, consistent with their military service experiences, fuel intense frustration and withdrawal from supportive services. Our veterans' reported feelings of helplessness and eroded trust. Ultimately, this often drove them toward alternative coping strategies outside legitimate support channels, including substance misuse and disengagement from critical care, behaviors directly associated with increased risk for incarceration.

Research shows the critical role social service systems play in shaping individuals' post-incarceration transitions (Western, 2018; Keene et al., 2018). When these interactions are perceived negatively, they can substantially impede veterans' ability to navigate essential aspects of reintegration, including housing, employment, mental health care, and community integration. Negative experiences can create cyclical patterns of mistrust and disengagement, further limiting veterans' access to necessary resources and services. A focus on improving the quality and sensitivity of veterans' interactions with social service providers is needed. Specialized training for providers on veterans' unique needs, trauma-informed care practices, and streamlined bureaucratic processes can significantly enhance veterans' service experiences (LePage & Garcia-Rea, 2012). Furthermore, veteran-centered care models emphasizing empathy, responsiveness, and active listening have shown promise in reducing barriers to service engagement and promoting trust in institutional providers (Russell, 2009; Tanielian & Jaycox, 2008). Negative encounters with social service providers represent critical turning points impacting veterans' reintegration processes and trajectories toward incarceration. This suggests the need for deliberate, veteran-focused reforms that can significantly enhance reintegration outcomes and reduce vulnerabilities to incarceration among veterans.

Interconnectedness of Service-Related Adverse Experiences with Other Risk Behaviors

Veterans' adverse interactions with military, healthcare, and social service providers do not occur in isolation; instead, these encounters create cumulative effects that interact dynamically with other known risk behaviors associated with incarceration, including substance misuse, disengagement from mental healthcare, and mistrust of authority. Examining this interconnectedness is crucial for understanding the compounded disadvantages that veterans experience across their lifespan and identifying precise intervention points to mitigate incarceration risks effectively.

Service-related adverse experiences deeply influence veterans' attitudes toward substance use, particularly in contexts where they perceive inadequate healthcare or institutional support. Veterans who experience dismissive or inadequate responses from healthcare providers may resort to substance misuse as a coping mechanism. For instance, one veteran articulated a direct causal relationship between insufficient medical support and relapse into heroin use: [T]hree or four days without suboxone … so I ran back to heroin." This account highlights how unsatisfactory healthcare interactions intensify veterans' vulnerabilities, driving them toward substance misuse as an alternative to perceived institutional neglect.

Veterans' firsthand accounts provide critical insights into how institutional interactions influence their attitudes and decision-making behaviors, significantly shaping their life trajectories. This epistemological approach reveals how veterans interpret and respond to these encounters, illustrating clearly that the erosion of trust stemming from institutional interactions shapes their behaviors in ways that increase incarceration vulnerability. The cumulative impact of these interactions creates substantial barriers to successful reintegration, reinforcing maladaptive behaviors related to substance misuse, mental health treatment disengagement, and mistrust of authorities.

As has been shown, veteran identity provides valuable insights into the interconnectedness of these risk behaviors. Veterans' deeply internalized values of self-reliance, resilience, and personal accountability often clash with negative institutional encounters, leading to intensified internal conflicts and feelings of disillusionment (Demers, 2011). These conflicts not only reduce veterans' willingness to seek help but also exacerbate their susceptibility to maladaptive coping strategies, reinforcing their overall vulnerability to incarceration.

Effective interventions should prioritize rebuilding trust between veterans and institutional providers through improved responsiveness, cultural sensitivity, trauma-informed care practices, and transparent communication (Tanielian & Jaycox, 2008). Peer support programs that validate veterans' experiences and perspectives can also play a crucial role in mitigating feelings of alienation and mistrust (Russell, 2009; Zinzow et al., 2013). Systemic reforms to reduce bureaucratic barriers, streamline service delivery, and enhance institutional accountability can significantly improve veterans' experiences, ultimately reducing risky behaviors and improving reintegration outcomes.

Understanding the interconnectedness between service-related adverse experiences and other risk behaviors is essential for effectively supporting veterans' reintegration. By explicitly addressing these compounded effects through targeted, culturally informed interventions and institutional reforms, stakeholders can significantly reduce incarceration vulnerabilities and promote veterans' successful transition back into civilian life.

Practical Implications and Recommendations for Reducing Negative Service Experiences

Informed by qualitative research and academic models, these practical strategies are designed to help veterans reintegrate successfully and avoid re-incarceration. Recommendations highlight culturally competent training, increased institutional transparency, peer-led program development, and integrative theory for strong, practical interventions.

Enhancing Cultural Competence among Healthcare and Social Service Providers

Veterans report a major problem: a huge gap between what they expect from healthcare and social services and what they receive. Research demonstrates that improving cultural competence can substantially improve provider-veteran relationships, trust, and overall engagement with services (Tanielian & Jaycox, 2008; Zinzow et al., 2013). Culturally competent training should explicitly focus on understanding military culture, values, norms, and the unique transition challenges veterans face. Providers trained in cultural competence demonstrate increased empathy and sensitivity, reducing incidents of perceived dismissiveness and enhancing veterans' engagement and trust (Koblinsky et al., 2006).

Providers should be educated on the warrior ethos, resilience expectations, mental health stigma, and other cultural aspects shaping veterans' experiences. This training enables providers to better align their communication, service delivery methods, and overall interactions with veterans' expectations, significantly reducing adverse encounters. By explicitly addressing veterans' cultural values and expectations, providers can facilitate more effective, respectful, and trust-building interactions.

Increasing Institutional Transparency and Accountability

Institutional transparency and accountability play crucial roles in addressing veterans' negative service experiences. Veterans in our study consistently described frustration with opaque and bureaucratic procedures, creating substantial barriers to accessing essential services. As highlighted in the narratives, frustration and mistrust frequently stemmed from institutions perceived as indifferent, overly bureaucratic, or unresponsive to veterans' immediate and practical needs. One veteran expressed difficulty accessing housing support, highlighting the lack of institutional responsiveness: "Nobody even at HUD was answering phones, and where am I supposed to go?"

Clear, transparent, and accountable institutional processes can mitigate frustrations significantly. Steps should include simplifying service procedures, clearly communicating expectations and timelines, and establishing straightforward mechanisms for veterans to voice concerns and receive timely responses (Keene et al., 2018). Institutions providing services to veterans through the VA and HUD, for example, can adopt explicit accountability measures, including regular evaluations of responsiveness, efficiency, and veteran satisfaction. These accountability practices enhance trust, promote proactive engagement, and support veterans' successful reintegration into civilian life.

Strengthening Peer-Led Programs and Veteran-Specific Support

Peer-led programs offer unique opportunities to validate and support veterans' experiences, facilitating trust-building, increased engagement, and effective reintegration (Russell, 2009; Solomon, 2004). Veterans frequently express greater comfort and trust when interacting with peers who share similar lived experiences, such as military service or incarceration histories. Peer support programs can effectively mitigate negative service encounters by providing empathetic, culturally relevant support and validation. These programs enable veterans to navigate bureaucratic hurdles, manage treatment engagement, and access social resources more effectively.

Peer-led programs should be expanded within VA and community-based organizations, emphasizing mentorship, mutual support, and shared experiential knowledge. Veteran peer leaders should receive comprehensive training to ensure effective advocacy and support, addressing veterans' multifaceted reintegration challenges, including housing, employment, mental health, and substance use management. Peer-led initiatives create community contexts where veterans feel validated, understood, and supported, significantly improving their reintegration outcomes and reducing vulnerabilities to negative experiences.

Situating Veteran Insights in Life Turning Points

To best connect veterans with resources, we must prioritize their direct experiences in program design and delivery. Relevant, responsive, and respectful interventions addressing veterans' negative experiences require their crucial input. Interventions grounded in veterans' perspectives should focus explicitly on identifying and addressing critical turning points and cumulative disadvantages veterans experience throughout their transitions (Elder, 1998; Sampson & Laub, 1993). This approach enables focused aid during major life changes, acknowledging that negative experiences can affect veterans long-term, not just before imprisonment.

Likewise, studies on veteran identity emphasize the need to acknowledge and honor the cultural values, norms, and expectations veterans hold (Demers, 2011). Interventions that work well will respect the identities of veterans and create programs that support veterans' values of resilience, self-reliance, and accountability. This alignment encourages veterans to actively use social, healthcare, and community resources, building trust and reducing negative experiences.

Veterans' qualitative accounts, scholarly work, and critical and relevant issues within theoretical frameworks are practical recommendations for action. Improved cultural competence for providers, greater institutional transparency and accountability, more peer programs, and clearer theoretical integration will greatly reduce negative veteran service experiences. Together, these wide-ranging strategies enhance veterans' reintegration success, improve their mental health, and lower their risk of returning to prison. Institutions and providers can improve veteran support and successful reintegration into civilian life by implementing these recommendations to foster trust and respect.

Summary

This chapter explored how negative service experiences significantly affect veterans' reintegration and increase their risk of imprisonment. This chapter uses veterans' stories and theories like standpoint epistemology, life course theory, and veteran identity theory to show how bad experiences in the military, healthcare, and social services create major problems that affect veterans' trust, involvement, and how they cope. Veterans' perceptions of treatment, service use, substance misuse, and authority interactions are heavily shaped by their past experiences, making them more prone to incarceration.

Veterans' stories highlight the need for focused, culturally sensitive help to deal with the difficulties they face after serving. Enhancing provider training, promoting transparency, and strengthening peer support are promising strategies to address negative experiences. Stakeholders can improve veteran reintegration and reduce incarceration by directly tackling the cultural and institutional issues behind negative service experiences.

Chapter 10 examines the link between self-care, incarceration risk, and self-medication as a coping strategy, building upon important discoveries. This discussion will explore the link between veterans' independent health management (and self-medication) and their reintegration challenges and incarceration vulnerability. To better understand veteran reintegration and incarceration, Chapter 10 focuses on the interconnected roles of self-care and coping behaviors.

References

Acosta, J. D., Becker, A., Cerully, J. L., Fisher, M. P., Martin, L. T., Vardavas, R., Slaughter, M. E., & Schell, T. L. (2014). *Mental health stigma in the military.* RAND Corporation. https://doi.org/10.7249/RR426

Blonigen, D. M., Bui, L., Harris, A. H. S., Hepner, K. A., & Kivlahan, D. R. (2014). Perceptions of behavioral health care among veterans with substance use disorders: Results from a national evaluation of mental health services in the Veterans Health Administration. *Journal of Substance Abuse Treatment, 47*(2), 122–129. https://doi.org/10.1016/j.jsat.2014.03.005

Burnam, M. A., Meredith, L. S., Tanielian, T., & Jaycox, L. H. (2009). Mental health care for Iraq and Afghanistan war veterans. *Health Affairs, 28*(3), 771–782. https://doi.org/10.1377/hlthaff.28.3.771

Clement, S., Schauman, O., Graham, T., Maggioni, F., Evans-Lacko, S., Bezborodovs, N., Morgan, C., Rüsch, N., Brown, J. S., & Thornicroft, G. (2015). What is the impact of mental health-related stigma on help-seeking? A systematic review of quantitative and qualitative studies. *Psychological Medicine, 45*(1), 11–27. https://doi.org/10.1017/S0033291714000129

Collins, P. H. (2019). *Intersectionality as critical social theory*. Duke University Press.

Demers, A. (2011). When veterans return: The role of community in reintegration. *Journal of Loss and Trauma, 16*(2), 160–179. https://doi.org/10.1080/15325024.2010.519281

Elbogen, E. B., Wagner, H. R., Johnson, S. C., Kinneer, P., Kang, H., Vasterling, J. J., Timko, C., & Beckham, J. C. (2013). Are Iraq and Afghanistan veterans using mental health services? New data from a national random-sample survey. *Psychiatric Services, 64*(2), 134–141. https://doi.org/10.1176/appi.ps.004792011

Elder, G. H., Jr. (1998). The life course as developmental theory. *Child Development, 69*(1), 1–12. https://doi.org/10.1111/j.1467-8624.1998.tb06128.x

Finlay, A. K., Harris, A. H., Rosenthal, J., Blue-Howells, J., Clark, S., McGuire, J., Timko, C., Frayne, S. M., Smelson, D., Oliva, E., & Binswanger, I. (2016). Receipt of pharmacotherapy for opioid use disorder by justice-involved U.S. Veterans Health Administration patients. *Drug and Alcohol Dependence, 160*, 222–226. https://doi.org/10.1016/j.drugalcdep.2016.01.013

Harding, S. (2004). *The feminist standpoint theory reader: Intellectual and political controversies*. Routledge.

Keene, D. E., Rosenberg, A., Schlesinger, P., Guo, M., & Blankenship, K. M. (2018). Navigating limited and uncertain access to subsidized housing after prison. *Housing Policy Debate, 28*(2), 199–214. https://doi.org/10.1080/10511482.2017.1336638

Koblinsky, M., Matthews, Z., Hussein, J., Mavalankar, D., Mridha, M. K., Anwar, I., Achadi, E., Adjei, S., Padmanabhan, P., Marchal, B., De Brouwere, V., & van Lerberghe, W. (2006). Maternal survival series steering group: Going to scale with professional skilled care. *Lancet, 368*(9544), 1377–1386. https://doi.org/10.1016/S0140-6736(06)69382-3

LePage, J. P., & Garcia-Rea, E. A. (2012). Lifestyle coaching's effect on 6-month follow-up in recently homeless substance dependent veterans: A randomized study. *Psychiatric Rehabilitation Journal, 35*(5), 396–402. https://doi.org/10.1037/h0094500

Mittal, D., Drummond, K. L., Blevins, D., Curran, G., Corrigan, P., & Sullivan, G. (2013). Stigma associated with PTSD: Perceptions of treatment seeking combat veterans. *Psychiatric Rehabilitation Journal, 36*(2), 86–92. https://doi.org/10.1037/h0094976

Russell, R. T. (2009). Veterans treatment court: A proactive approach. *New England Journal of Criminal and Civil Confinement, 35*(2), 357–372.

Sampson, R., & Laub, J. (1993). *Crime in the making: Pathways and turning points through life*. Harvard University Press.

Solomon, P. (2004). Peer support/peer provided services underlying processes, benefits, and critical ingredients. *Psychiatric Rehabilitation Journal, 27*(4), 392–401. https://doi.org/10.2975/27.2004.392.401

Tanielian, T., & Jaycox, L. H. (Eds.). (2008). Invisible wounds of war: Psychological and cognitive injuries, their consequences, and services to assist recovery. RAND Corporation. www.rand.org/pubs/monographs/MG720.html

True, G., Rigg, K. K., & Butler, A. (2015). Understanding barriers to mental health care for recent war veterans through photovoice. *Qualitative Health Research, 25*(10), 1443–1455. https://doi.org/10.1177/1049732314562894

Tsai, J., Rosenheck, R. A., Kasprow, W. J., & McGuire, J. F. (2013). Risk of incarceration and other characteristics of Iraq and Afghanistan era veterans in state and federal prisons. *Psychiatric Services, 64*(1), 36–43. https://doi.org/10.1176/appi.ps.201200188

Vogt, D., Fox, A. B., & Di Leone, B. A. L. (2014). Mental health beliefs and their relationship with treatment seeking among U.S. OEF/OIF veterans. *Journal of Traumatic Stress*, *27*(3), 307–313. https://doi.org/10.1002/jts.21919

Western, B. (2018). *Homeward: Life in the year after prison*. Russell Sage Foundation.

Zinzow, H. M., Britt, T. W., Pury, C. L., Raymond, M. A., McFadden, A. C., & Burnette, C. M. (2013). Barriers and facilitators of mental health treatment seeking among active-duty army personnel. *Military Psychology*, *25*(5), 514–35. https://doi.org/10.1037/mil0000015

10

SELF-CARE CONCEPT FORMATION AND INCARCERATION RISKS

Self-Medicating as Coping Behavior

Introduction and Conceptualization of Self-Care and Self-Medication

Self-care, broadly conceptualized, encompasses deliberate and self-initiated actions that individuals engage in to maintain physical, mental, and emotional well-being. According to the World Health Organization (WHO, 2024), self-care involves activities individuals undertake on their own behalf, such as lifestyle behaviors, self-medication, and managing chronic conditions. While typically viewed positively, self-care strategies can manifest negatively when individuals engage in harmful or maladaptive behaviors. Among veterans, negative self-care practices often include the use of substances as a method of coping with unresolved physical pain, emotional distress, and psychological trauma.

Self-medication specifically refers to the use of substances (licit or illicit) to manage psychological distress, physical pain, or emotional discomfort without the explicit direction or oversight of healthcare professionals (Khantzian, 1997; Harris & Edlund, 2005). In this context, self-medication becomes an unhealthy coping mechanism through which veterans address perceived inadequacies or dissatisfaction with formal medical care or psychosocial support systems. This practice, although initially intended to manage immediate symptoms, often exacerbates veterans' underlying health and psychosocial conditions, thereby increasing vulnerability to a variety of negative outcomes, including incarceration.

Interviewed veterans provided complex understandings of their self-medication behaviors and the rationales behind them for this study. Their substance use was often framed as a preferable coping strategy to prescribed

DOI: 10.4324/9781003522300-10

medical or psychiatric care. For instance, one veteran clearly articulated this preference: "Using alcohol and drugs just as a remedy … Instead of using the prescribed medicine, I'm using that." Another veteran explained the rationale behind self-medicating: "It made me feel better … temporarily." These quotes illustrate how self-medication is directly connected to veterans' dissatisfaction with formal medical treatments, leading them to pursue alternative coping mechanisms that ultimately have profound implications for their overall well-being.

The significance of comprehending self-medication as a coping mechanism stems from its ability to create cycles of inadequate mental healthcare, isolation, distrust in formal support, and heavier reliance on substances (Abraham et al., 2017; Pietrzak et al., 2009). Our study's veterans frequently attributed their self-medication to negative healthcare interactions or ineffective treatments. Because of these experiences, they were less trusting of and less willing to engage with the formal healthcare system, which resulted in limited access to beneficial treatments and interventions.

Individual trajectories are influenced by cumulative experiences and critical life transitions, which can produce enduring changes in behavior patterns and coping strategies (Elder, 1998; Sampson & Laub, 1993). Self-medication, viewed through a life course lens, represents a critical coping strategy developed over time in response to cumulative dissatisfaction and mistrust stemming from earlier negative service experiences or unresolved trauma. This coping mechanism, though initially intended as temporary relief, becomes entrenched as a habitual response, significantly increasing veterans' long-term risks for adverse outcomes, including incarceration.

Veterans' own accounts (Harding, 2004; Collins, 2019) provide critical insights into how and why they choose self-medication as a coping strategy. Veterans' narratives reveal that self-medication often emerges from a sense of agency in managing their symptoms when formal healthcare systems seem inadequate or ineffective. Veteran identity clarifies these dynamics by highlighting the internalized cultural expectations of resilience, toughness, and independence that shape veterans' self-care practices (Demers, 2011). Veterans' deep-seated beliefs in self-reliance can discourage them from openly seeking professional help, leading them toward self-medication as a more culturally congruent coping method. This alignment with veteran identity can inadvertently reinforce substance misuse behaviors, particularly when formal healthcare interactions do not meet veterans' identity-based expectations for effective support and care.

This chapter delves deeply into the relationship between self-care concept formation, self-medication coping behaviors, and veterans' pathways toward incarceration. We will continue to explore veteran life stories to bring to light key incarceration turning points and transitions, specifically, their stories of self-medication illuminate pathways of incarceration. Later sections of this chapter will delve deeper into these intricate relationships, examining specific behaviors, attitudes, and institutional interactions influencing veterans' self-medication, and providing practical solutions to lessen these risks and aid veterans' successful transition back to civilian life.

Veteran Identity, Self-care Expectations, and Post-Military Realities

Veterans' self-care and health expectations after service are shaped by shared values ingrained during military training and service. Veterans' adjustment to civilian life is hindered by a disconnect between their perceived self-care needs and practical challenges, potentially leading to unhealthy coping methods. The self-care concepts developed by veterans are rooted in the military training that stresses physical fitness, mental fortitude, and personal responsibility (Demers, 2011). Upon transitioning to civilian life, veterans frequently expect to independently manage their health, emotions, and psychosocial stressors, reflecting ingrained expectations. But civilian life contrasts sharply with military life, lacking the structure, clear support, and straightforward processes that veterans are used to, often feeling impersonal and insufficient.

As with negative service experiences, gaps between expectations and reality strongly impact veterans' coping and adaptation post-military discharge (Ahern et al., 2015). Veterans' narratives illustrate how gaps manifest, highlighting the complexities and challenges of transitioning from military self-care paradigms to civilian contexts. One veteran articulated this struggle when describing reliance on substances: "I drank because I just, I was self-medicating." Unmet expectations and frustrations with healthcare systems often lead veterans to turn toward self-medication as an alternative form of self-care.

Self-Medication as Coping: Legal Substance Use and Prescription Misuse

Veterans frequently highlight inadequacies in medical or psychiatric care as primary factors driving them toward self-medication practices. They express considerable dissatisfaction with treatments prescribed, often describing these interventions as ineffective, debilitating, or incompatible with their daily functionality. For instance, one veteran explicitly recounted the prescriber "would give me some medicine, it made me slobber on myself, I couldn't function or nothing … that's why I self-medicate." Illustrated is not just a frustration with treatment quality but a profound disruption of personal autonomy and dignity, prompting veterans to seek alternative, unauthorized solutions. These narratives reveal how discrepancies between veterans' expectations for healthcare, rooted deeply in military experiences, and the realities encountered in civilian contexts shape their perceptions and coping strategies. Through self-medication, veterans often attempt to regain control and functionality that they perceive institutional care has diminished or neglected. Consequently, their engagement in substance misuse emerges not merely as harmful behavior but as a conscious, albeit risky, response to unresolved healthcare issues and institutional shortcomings.

The internalized identity of veterans further intensifies these healthcare challenges, generating significant emotional and psychological conflicts. Military training instills strong values of strength, resilience, and self-sufficiency, which become deeply embedded aspects of veteran identity. When healthcare systems fail to align with these internal standards, veterans often internalize blame, viewing their unmet needs as personal failures rather than systemic shortcomings. Veterans repeatedly illustrated this tension by describing heroin use as a coping mechanism for unresolved physical pain and psychological distress. One veteran specifically connected their heroin use to unmanaged physical pain: "I was using heroin for pain in my back … I was always hurting, so I did heroin for the pain." Veteran accounts underscore the profound internal struggle that occurs when veterans' lived realities diverge sharply from their internalized expectations of effective healthcare and self-management. This internal dissonance significantly impacts their decision-making, pushing them toward alternative, unauthorized coping strategies, including substance misuse, in a deliberate effort to reconcile internal standards with external healthcare realities.

Transitions from structured military environments to civilian contexts represent critical turning points for veterans, particularly when it comes to managing chronic pain and health issues. Veterans often describe the significant strain experienced when moving from a military setting, where individual resilience and self-reliance were primary strategies for managing pain, to civilian life, where extended or ongoing medical care becomes necessary. This shift was described by veterans in statements such as, 'I couldn't function,' and 'I was always hurting.' These words reveal veterans' increasing difficulty in independently managing prolonged pain, highlighting their growing need for sustained, external healthcare support. Facing what they perceive as impersonal or inadequate care from civilian institutions, formerly incarcerated veterans may feel compelled toward alternative, unauthorized methods of pain relief, including self-medication or engagement in activities that eventually place them at risk of incarceration. For these individuals, the inability to secure appropriate healthcare and effective pain management marked a crucial point where reliance on illegal behaviors became a coping mechanism, inadvertently increasing their vulnerability to the criminal justice system.

The adoption of illicit substances coping mechanisms is intertwined with veterans' experiences of ineffective medical and psychiatric care. Veterans consistently expressed dissatisfaction with prescribed treatments, citing adverse side effects, lack of holistic consideration, and inadequate management of their symptoms. A veteran described illicit drug use as preferable to prescribed psychiatric medications: "I prefer that feeling [from crack cocaine] more than the dull feeling of the chemicals I was prescribed. Crack cocaine made me feel more lively; it helped me cope with certain feelings."

There exists a critical imperative to effectively bridge the divide between the self-care expectations veterans internalize during military service and the realities they face in healthcare settings. The transition from military to civilian life introduces unique challenges, particularly in healthcare interactions, which often lead to misunderstandings and unmet expectations. Providing specialized training in military cultural competence to healthcare providers and social service professionals can align their practices more closely with veterans' expectations and needs (Tanielian & Jaycox, 2008; Zinzow et al., 2013). Healthcare providers equipped with an understanding of military culture can offer empathetic validation and culturally attuned guidance, significantly reducing veterans' reliance on substance misuse by offering credible and relatable alternatives grounded in shared experiences and mutual understanding (Solomon, 2004).

Moreover, veterans' patterns of self-medication highlight systemic shortcomings and institutional barriers that need urgent attention. Veterans repeatedly articulate frustrations with bureaucratic complexity, impersonal interactions, and perceived dismissiveness from institutional systems, contributing to their reluctance to seek or sustain necessary care. Institutional accountability, transparency, and responsiveness within healthcare and social services must be substantially strengthened to address these concerns. Implementing broader systemic reforms aimed at reducing bureaucratic barriers and enhancing providers' responsiveness and accountability can greatly restore veterans' trust, thus decreasing their inclination toward maladaptive coping mechanisms and self-medication behaviors (Keene et al., 2018; Russell, 2009).

The observed discrepancies between veterans' ingrained expectations of self-reliance developed during military service and healthcare realities create vulnerabilities that significantly influence their behavioral responses. The life course framework highlights how veterans' accounts provide essential insights into these discrepancies, underscoring the need for culturally competent, veteran-centered interventions. By explicitly acknowledging and addressing veterans' unique lived experiences and internalized self-care expectations, healthcare and social services can offer more effective support, reducing reliance on harmful coping mechanisms. These targeted approaches hold substantial promise for improving veterans' psychosocial stability, enhancing their overall mental health outcomes, and ultimately mitigating their vulnerability to incarceration and related adverse outcomes.

Veterans encounter physical, psychological, and emotional challenges following military service, which lead complex medical and psychological needs that must be managed in civilian contexts. The concept of self-medication, defined as the intentional use of substances (legal, prescription, or illicit) to relieve physical or emotional distress without appropriate medical supervision, emerges prominently among veterans during reintegration periods (Harris & Edlund, 2005; Khantzian, 1997). Self-medication strategies, particularly involving legal substances and prescription medication misuse, serve as a way to manage unresolved trauma, chronic pain, and psychological distress, influencing veterans' incarceration trajectories.

Alcohol Use and Coping Among Veterans

Veterans frequently encounter significant challenges upon transitioning from military service to civilian life, including psychological trauma, chronic physical pain, and difficulties managing mental health symptoms. Many veterans cope with these unmet psychological and physical needs through self-medication practices involving illicit substances and alcohol. These behaviors often originate from veterans' efforts to alleviate emotional distress, physical discomfort, and psychological symptoms in response to perceived inadequacies within formal healthcare systems. Understanding the motivations, experiences, and consequences associated with these self-medicating behaviors provides essential insights into veterans' pathways toward incarceration and broader psychosocial outcomes.

Legal substances, including prescribed medications and alcohol, often represent veterans' initial self-medication attempts, especially in contexts where medical or psychiatric care does not adequately address their needs. Veterans express dissatisfaction with prescribed treatments, citing inefficacy, negative side effects, or lack of holistic consideration as primary factors driving their self-medication choices. For instance, one veteran described their dissatisfaction with prescribed medications, noting, "I took myself off of it. The medications made me feel numb, disconnected … that wasn't me." Of note is the frustration and dissatisfaction when formal medical approaches prioritize medication without sufficiently addressing underlying concerns or individualized treatment preferences. These experiences emphasize a critical gap between the expectations veterans have for healthcare efficacy and their actual experiences, leading to alternative coping mechanisms they perceive as more effective.

Alcohol serves as an easily accessible coping strategies for veterans seeking immediate relief from unresolved trauma, chronic pain, and mental health challenges. Veterans' narratives consistently illustrate these practices, demonstrating a clear, intentional rationale for substance use as a coping mechanism. Veterans frame these coping strategies as necessary responses to manage intense psychological and physical symptoms. One veteran explained, "It just made none of the stuff come up. It was like my brain was somewhere else, and it just wiped that stuff off. It's easy, easier to use." These powerful firsthand accounts illustrate how veterans view substance use as both practical and essential coping mechanisms in response to unmet psychological and emotional needs.

Alcohol was cited by veterans as an accessible, socially acceptable form of self-medication. Veterans described using alcohol explicitly to manage emotional distress or mental health symptoms. One veteran described using alcohol to cope with loss, noting: "When my mother died, and somebody close, I drink sometimes to numb the effect." Another veteran reinforced the intentionality of alcohol use for coping purposes, stating, "Prescriptions made me drool. I didn't feel like myself." Alcohol was adopted by our veterans' as a coping strategy, particularly when formal mental healthcare is perceived as inappropriate.

Alcohol holds unique significance for veterans as a coping mechanism, particularly when considered in the context of military culture and its deeply ingrained emphasis on self-reliance, discipline, and personal autonomy. Veterans frequently note that alcohol's accessibility and social acceptability set it apart from other substances, including prescription medications or illicit drugs. Alcohol's ease of procurement, coupled with its cultural integration as a socially acceptable substance, provides veterans with a readily available means to manage psychological and physical distress discreetly. Veterans describe alcohol use as aligned with their internalized values of independence and control; it enables them to maintain autonomy over their coping practices. Unlike prescription medications, which typically require medical supervision and often induce significant side effects that compromise daily functioning, alcohol allows veterans to self-regulate, preserving a sense of personal agency and autonomy over their pain and emotional management. This distinction aligns closely with veterans' military-instilled expectations of independence and self-management, making alcohol a particularly appealing option for coping with unresolved trauma or chronic physical discomfort.

Moreover, veterans often emphasize alcohol's specific psychological effects as preferable to prescribed psychiatric medications, which many describe as overly sedating or depersonalizing. Prescription medications, according to veterans, frequently produce a sense of being disconnected, overly impaired, or emotionally detached, undermining their ability to maintain control and autonomy over daily life. In contrast, alcohol is often described as providing a controlled, functional form of relief, offering a moderated numbness that reduces pain and emotional distress without fully removing their sense of self. Veterans highlight this key distinction clearly, indicating that alcohol use maintains a degree of personal control and identity coherence consistent with their internalized military values of strength and emotional self-regulation. This nuanced perspective sheds important light on why alcohol becomes a preferred coping method, allowing veterans to manage distress while preserving their internal sense of resilience, control, and self-reliance, which are core components of military identity.

Research indicates that alcohol's social acceptability and ease of access significantly contribute to its prevalence among veterans as a coping mechanism. Studies emphasize that veterans often gravitate toward substances perceived as socially normalized and culturally integrated, making alcohol a logical choice given its societal ubiquity (Bray & Hourani, 2007; Timko et al., 2017). Additionally, research underscores that veterans' use of alcohol frequently relates to their desire to maintain control over their coping strategies, reflecting their culturally ingrained values of independence and strength (Burnett-Zeigler et al., 2011). Consequently, interventions aiming to address alcohol misuse among veterans must explicitly recognize and integrate the nuanced cultural and psychological factors that underpin veterans' preferences for alcohol as a self-managed coping method. Effective support strategies must consider these distinctive elements, providing accessible, culturally responsive interventions that align closely with veterans' deeply held values and expectations.

Critical transitions and accumulated experiences significantly shape long-term behaviors and attitudes, influencing veterans' vulnerability to incarceration (Elder, 1998; Sampson & Laub, 1993). Self-medication behaviors often do not directly precede incarceration events but create significant cumulative disadvantages over time, influencing veterans' long-term coping strategies and vulnerability to adverse outcomes. Veterans' narratives demonstrate how these behaviors accumulate, leading to progressive disengagement from formal medical care and increased reliance on substances, ultimately heightening incarceration risks. Not surprisingly, veterans frequently interpret reliance on medications or treatments perceived as ineffective or impairing as contrary to a military identity built on self-reliance and resiliency. This conflict often results in veterans rejecting formal medical treatments, favoring alternative coping strategies they perceive as more congruent with their internalized self-concepts.

From a veteran standpoint, their firsthand experiences offer insights into understanding the motivations behind their self-medication behaviors. Veterans' accounts of self-medicating clearly illustrate how perceived inadequacies in formal care shape their coping behaviors, decisions, and attitudes toward healthcare systems. Individuals' experiences during critical life transitions significantly shape long-term behaviors and outcomes (Elder, 1998; Sampson & Laub, 1993). Veterans' decisions to self-medicate with illicit substances and alcohol represent significant coping strategies adopted during critical transitional periods. Although these behaviors may initially provide temporary relief, over time, they accumulate and exacerbate vulnerabilities to substance dependence, healthcare disengagement, and increased risk of incarceration.

Veterans internalize military values of self-reliance, resilience, and toughness, often viewing the need for external support or reliance on prescribed medications as conflicting with their identity (Demers, 2011). Internalized expectations can lead veterans to interpret their struggles with prescribed medications as personal weaknesses or failures, reinforcing reliance on substances perceived as providing more effective immediate relief. This dynamic creates a significant barrier to effective healthcare engagement, perpetuating cycles of maladaptive coping behaviors and increasing incarceration vulnerability.

Veterans' reliance on alcohol as coping strategies means culturally competent interventions are those that meet veterans' holistic needs. Effective interventions should emphasize comprehensive, trauma-informed, and culturally tailored healthcare practices, aligning closely with veterans' expectations and lived experiences (Tanielian & Jaycox, 2008). Integrated substance use and mental health treatment programs, enhanced provider training in military cultural competence, and expanded peer-led support initiatives offer significant promise for effectively addressing veterans' self-medication behaviors (Zinzow et al., 2013).

Peer support programs hold substantial potential for effectively mitigating veterans' reliance on substance use coping mechanisms. These programs, emphasizing shared military and life experiences, provide veterans with culturally relevant, empathetic, and responsive support, significantly reducing stigma and barriers to healthcare engagement (Russell, 2009; Solomon, 2004). By validating veterans' experiences and offering practical coping strategies, peer support programs can effectively reduce reliance on maladaptive coping behaviors.

Institutional responsiveness, accountability, and effectiveness are also critical for reducing veterans' self-medication behaviors. Improving veterans' access to timely, responsive, and effective medical and psychiatric care significantly reduces their reliance on alternative coping strategies. Institutional reforms, including streamlining bureaucratic processes, enhancing provider responsiveness, and incorporating veterans' perspectives directly into healthcare planning, can substantially improve veterans' healthcare experiences and reduce self-medication behaviors (Keene et al., 2018). Veterans' intentional use of illicit substances and alcohol as coping mechanisms reflects deeper institutional and identity-based conflicts encountered during civilian reintegration.

In all, these stories point to a need for interventions explicitly focused on aligning medical and psychological care with veterans' lived experiences and coping preferences. Providers must be equipped with specialized training in military cultural competence, recognizing and respecting veterans' identity-informed self-care expectations (Tanielian & Jaycox, 2008). Collaborative, patient-centered treatment approaches, emphasizing active veteran involvement in healthcare planning, are critical in effectively addressing veterans' self-medication behaviors (Zinzow et al., 2013). Streamlining medication management, improving follow-up procedures, and clearly communicating treatment expectations can build trust and encourage sustained engagement with formal healthcare services (LePage & Garcia-Rea, 2012; Russell, 2009).

Impact of Self-Medicating Behaviors on Treatment Engagement and Institutional Trust

Veterans' self-medicating behaviors, including the intentional use of alcohol and illicit drugs, significantly influence their relationship with formal healthcare systems and social service providers. These behaviors emerge as coping strategies to manage unmet psychological, emotional, and physical needs, often rooted in dissatisfaction and mistrust toward institutional treatment approaches. Understanding the impact of self-medication practices on treatment engagement and institutional trust is crucial, as these behaviors profoundly affect veterans' willingness to participate in formal healthcare and support systems, further shaping their incarceration trajectories.

Veterans who self-medicate typically express explicit dissatisfaction with formal healthcare services and treatments provided to them. This dissatisfaction directly influences their trust and engagement with healthcare institutions, leading to avoidance behaviors and subsequent reliance on substances as alternative coping strategies. For instance, one veteran clearly articulated their disengagement from formal healthcare due to perceived inefficacy: "I took myself off therapy. It wasn't working for me. I was like, 'I'll just self-medicate.'" Here again, there is an association between dissatisfaction with formal medical treatment and the adoption of self-medicating behaviors, which further reinforces veterans' withdrawal from healthcare services.

The concept of institutional trust is particularly relevant in veterans' disengagement from formal treatment. Trust, defined as the belief that institutions and providers will act competently, ethically, and responsively in meeting individuals' needs, is foundational to effective healthcare engagement (Armstrong et al., 2006). Veterans who perceive healthcare interactions as ineffective, dismissive, or impersonal often develop deep-seated mistrust toward these institutions, exacerbating their vulnerability and reliance on self-medication practices.

Veterans' negative healthcare experiences and subsequent reliance on self-medication represent significant turning points in their reintegration trajectories (Elder, 1998; Sampson & Laub, 1993). Cumulative experiences significantly influence long-term behavioral patterns and psychosocial outcomes. Negative interactions with healthcare providers, coupled with reliance on self-medication, create a cumulative cycle of mistrust, healthcare avoidance, and increased vulnerability to negative outcomes, including reincarceration.

Psychosocial Dimensions of Veteran Self-Medication

Self-medication behaviors among veterans often emerge from complex psychosocial challenges extending beyond physical pain management. Veterans frequently encounter psychological distress rooted in trauma, social isolation, homelessness, and persistent fears, conditions that differ fundamentally from acute physical injuries. Research indicates that individuals facing sustained psychological stressors, including unresolved trauma or significant social isolation, often adopt substance use as a proactive coping strategy aimed at emotional regulation, social integration, and alleviating persistent psychological symptoms (Khantzian, 1997; Leeies et al., 2010). Unlike self-medication strictly related to acute physical conditions, psychosocial self-medication typically serves broader functions, integrating deeply into individuals' daily life strategies over extended periods. Veterans facing homelessness or prolonged isolation, for example, may adopt substances as consistent tools not merely for temporary relief but as enduring methods to manage daily emotional and social functioning. This form of self-medication evolves into a normalized aspect of their daily routines, serving as a dependable coping mechanism that addresses ongoing psychological pressures and existential challenges. Thus, psychosocial self-medication embodies a complex, integrated response to sustained psychological and social adversity rather than solely a reactive measure to discrete physical discomfort.

Veterans' experiences of trauma frequently result in chronic psychological symptoms, notably vivid nightmares, anxiety, and other distressing emotional manifestations. Persistent trauma-related symptoms profoundly disrupt their daily lives, often motivating veterans to seek immediate relief through self-medication practices. The decision to self-medicate is not arbitrary; rather, it emerges as a deliberate coping strategy aimed at managing specific trauma-induced symptoms that traditional medical interventions may fail to address adequately.

One veteran tied his use of illicit substances to trauma-related nightmares, explaining, "I was trying to self-medicate … because when I was on the drug [illegal], I didn't have the nightmares, I didn't have the shakes." Another veteran similarly perceived his self-medicating as helping with "anxiety and depression". These statements illustrate the targeted and intentional nature of veterans' self-medication behaviors, emphasizing their efforts to manage specific symptoms which severely impede their quality of life. Nightmares, particularly those associated with traumatic military experiences, significantly disrupt sleep patterns, emotional stability, and overall psychological well-being, compelling veterans toward substances that offer immediate, albeit temporary, relief.

Other veterans shared a similar rationale for substance use as a trauma-coping mechanism: "Mine was all trying to feel better and forget, not think about the trauma." This perspective highlights how substance use serves as a method to temporarily suppress or manage overwhelming trauma-related emotions and memories. Our veterans who face persistent psychological distress perceive traditional treatments, such as prescription medications or counseling, as insufficiently responsive or slow to provide relief, making self-medication a practical and immediate alternative.

The self-directed nature of substance use as a coping strategy reflects veterans' attempt to reclaim a sense of agency and control in managing their psychological trauma. By selecting substances that are seen as alleviating specific trauma symptoms (e.g., nightmares or anxiety), veterans can momentarily regain functionality and emotional balance, despite the significant long-term risks associated with these behaviors. This deliberate choice highlights the complexity of veterans' experiences, demonstrating how self-medication becomes a critical, albeit risky, component of their trauma management repertoire.

Confronting these challenges effectively requires healthcare interventions that recognize and directly respond to the specific trauma-related symptoms veterans experience. Interventions emphasizing trauma-informed care, including evidence-based therapies specifically targeting nightmares and trauma-related symptoms, could significantly reduce reliance on self-medication practices. Developing and implementing comprehensive treatment strategies that provide immediate symptom relief, emotional validation, and practical coping skills will be essential in addressing veterans' psychological needs and reducing their vulnerabilities associated with self-medication. Ultimately, recognizing the deliberate and symptom-specific nature of veterans' self-medication behaviors provides crucial insights for developing effective, targeted treatments. Enhancing trauma-responsive healthcare services that directly address veterans' core psychological symptoms may foster improved treatment engagement, better emotional regulation, and significantly reduce reliance on harmful coping mechanisms.

The experience of homelessness introduces a unique set of stressors that profoundly impacts veterans' psychosocial stability, compelling many toward self-medication as a primary coping mechanism. Homeless veterans often face intense emotional strain, marked by social isolation, uncertainty, and a pervasive sense of vulnerability. These conditions can significantly amplify pre-existing psychological distress, driving individuals to seek immediate relief through accessible substances. One veteran explicitly linked their homelessness and emotional struggles to substance use, stating, "When you're on the street homeless, you know, you don't know what to do, and you get depressed and stuff, so I self-medicate." This narrative underscores the specific intersection between homelessness-induced emotional distress and the deliberate choice to use substances as a coping strategy.

Moreover, veterans' homelessness not only intensifies existing mental health issues but also creates a reinforcing cycle of social disengagement and mistrust toward formal institutions. Research highlights that homelessness significantly reduces veterans' access to essential services and support networks, pushing them toward self-managed coping methods that inadvertently escalate their vulnerability to interactions with the criminal justice system (Tsai et al., 2015;

Finlay et al., 2019). Without stable housing and reliable healthcare access, self-medication becomes a practical and immediate means of emotional and psychological relief. Effective interventions must directly address the root causes of homelessness, providing stable housing solutions combined with comprehensive mental health and substance use services tailored explicitly for veterans, thus breaking this cycle of vulnerability and self-medication.

Veterans' use of self-medication strategies often extends beyond responses to acute events or immediate crises, evolving instead into lifelong coping mechanisms deeply embedded within their broader psychosocial contexts. Veterans' identification with military culture and values sets strong cultural expectations that influence veterans' coping strategies over extended periods. However, the chronic realities of unresolved trauma, persistent physical pain, and prolonged institutional mistrust often conflict with these deeply ingrained expectations. Research indicates that veterans frequently turn to self-medication to manage ongoing psychosocial stressors and emotional burdens resulting from unresolved military trauma and ineffective institutional support (Heward et al., 2024). Consequently, substance misuse and avoidance behaviors become consistent, long-term approaches for managing enduring psychological and emotional discomfort rather than isolated responses to transient difficulties.

One veteran articulated this ongoing struggle, stating, "I've been self-medicating for most of my adult life … I started with alcohol … I continued with other things, hashish, and speed." This perspective highlights how self-medication evolves into a sustained coping method, integral to managing continuous psychosocial pressures and internal conflicts. Rather than being temporary or event-driven, these coping behaviors represent adaptive responses deeply connected to veterans' identities, cultural values, and lived experiences. To address this sustained reliance on self-medication, healthcare interventions must move beyond addressing isolated symptoms and instead provide comprehensive, culturally attuned support systems that acknowledge the enduring nature of veterans' psychosocial needs. Recent studies underscore the importance of holistic, trauma-informed, and culturally sensitive interventions in effectively reducing long-term substance reliance and promoting sustained engagement with institutional support (Moledina et al., 2021).

Practical Implications and Recommendations for Addressing Self-Medicating Behaviors

The following practical recommendations outline targeted interventions aimed at enhancing veteran-specific substance use treatment programs, developing integrated healthcare and mental health services, strengthening peer-led initiatives, and emphasizing institutional accountability and transparency.

Enhancing Veteran-Specific Substance Use Treatment Programs with Culturally Competent Approaches

A crucial step toward effectively addressing veterans' self-medicating behaviors involves improving the cultural competence of substance use treatment programs specifically tailored to veterans. Cultural competence refers to providers' capacity to recognize and appropriately respond to the cultural contexts, values, and experiences of their patient populations (Betancourt, Green, Carrillo, & Ananeh-Firempong, 2003). For veterans, this involves a deep understanding of military cultural norms, veteran identity expectations, and the unique challenges faced during reintegration into civilian life.

Research demonstrates that culturally competent substance use programs improve veterans' trust, engagement, and treatment outcomes by aligning care more closely with their lived experiences (Tanielian & Jaycox, 2008; Zinzow et al., 2013). Providers within these programs should receive specialized training on military cultural competence, including recognition of common veteran experiences, including trauma, stigma surrounding help-seeking, and resilience-oriented coping mechanisms (Acosta et al., 2014). Providers who understand the veteran-specific context of substance use can deliver interventions that resonate meaningfully with veterans' internalized expectations and lived realities (Tanielian & Jaycox, 2008; Zinzow et al., 2013).

By actively incorporating veterans' lived experiences and preferences into healthcare planning, institutions can foster greater trust and more sustained engagement. Peer-led initiatives provide significant opportunities to rebuild institutional trust among veterans. Peer support programs validate veterans' experiences, promote shared understanding, and offer empathetic, culturally sensitive support (Russell, 2009; Solomon, 2004). These programs directly address the root causes of mistrust and treatment disengagement, creating supportive contexts where veterans feel respected, understood, and validated. Responsiveness, accountability, and transparency within healthcare institutions are necessary for improving veterans' healthcare experiences and reducing reliance on self-medication coping strategies. Streamlined bureaucratic procedures, clearly communicated treatment expectations, and responsive institutional feedback mechanisms significantly enhance veterans' trust and willingness to engage proactively with formal healthcare systems (Keene et al., 2018).

Developing Integrated Healthcare and Mental Health Services Focused on Self-Care and Coping Behaviors

Integrated healthcare services that explicitly address veterans' self-care concepts and coping behaviors offer significant potential for mitigating self-medication behaviors. Integrated care models provide comprehensive and coordinated healthcare services addressing veterans' physical health, mental health, and substance use issues simultaneously (Leung et al., 2022). These approaches enhance the efficacy of healthcare delivery by reducing fragmentation, improving communication between providers, and offering veterans more holistic support.

In developing integrated healthcare services, healthcare providers should explicitly incorporate veterans' self-care expectations and coping strategies into treatment planning and implementation. Standpoint epistemology highlights that incorporating veterans' lived experiences into healthcare decision-making processes significantly enhances their engagement and trust (Harding, 2004; Collins, 2019). Veterans' qualitative narratives reveal their strong preferences for treatments aligned with their internalized self-care expectations, emphasizing individualized, patient-centered care approaches that respect their lived experiences.

Strengthening Peer-led and Community-Based Initiatives to Support Veterans' Coping Strategies

Peer-led programs represent powerful resources for addressing veterans' self-medicating behaviors by providing empathetic, culturally relevant support grounded in shared experiences. Peer support involves veterans with similar lived experiences helping fellow veterans navigate healthcare systems, manage coping behaviors, and access essential resources (Solomon, 2004). These initiatives enhance veterans' social connectedness, reduce stigma surrounding substance use and mental health, and provide meaningful alternatives to maladaptive coping strategies.

One veteran described peer support's effectiveness clearly, noting the value of shared understanding: "Talking with someone who's been there makes a huge difference. They get it, and they help me feel less isolated." Our qualitative data again underscore peer support programs' critical role in addressing veterans' substance use behaviors. Expanding these initiatives within veteran healthcare and community-based programs significantly improves veterans' self-care practices and mental health engagement, reducing vulnerabilities to maladaptive coping behaviors and reincarceration.

Emphasizing Institutional Accountability and Transparency to Rebuild Veterans' Trust

Institutional accountability and transparency significantly influence veterans' trust in healthcare and social services, directly affecting their coping behaviors. Veterans consistently describe institutional unresponsiveness, bureaucratic barriers, and perceived provider indifference as primary motivators for their reliance on self-medication (Keene et al., 2018). Enhancing institutional accountability and transparency involves clearly communicating treatment options, processes, and expectations; ensuring responsive and empathetic interactions; and actively involving veterans in healthcare planning and decision-making.

Summary

This chapter provided an exploration of veterans' self-care concept formation and self-medication behaviors as coping mechanisms. Through analyzing detailed personal narratives, the chapter clearly outlined how veterans' internalized expectations around self-care, deeply influenced by military culture, often clash with post-military realities. Veterans frequently articulated dissatisfaction with formal medical and psychiatric treatments, describing their reliance on legal substances, prescription misuse, and illicit substance use as more effective strategies for managing physical pain, psychological distress, and emotional trauma. Coping behaviors, though initially intended as practical solutions to unmet needs, often lead veterans toward increased vulnerabilities, including heightened risks for incarceration.

The analysis emphasized how veterans' self-medicating behaviors significantly impact their perceptions of institutional effectiveness and trustworthiness, resulting in decreased treatment engagement and increased avoidance of healthcare services. This erosion of institutional trust, stemming from perceived inadequacies in healthcare delivery, bureaucratic barriers, and impersonal interactions, underscores a critical intersection between veterans' self-care practices, coping strategies, and their broader psychosocial outcomes.

Targeted strategies should include recognition of how veteran identity intersects with self-medication coping behaviors, so that culturally competent substance use treatment programs, integrated healthcare approaches, peer-led initiatives, and enhanced institutional accountability are promoted. By explicitly acknowledging and addressing veterans' lived experiences, institutional inadequacies, and cultural expectations, these strategies aim to rebuild trust, promote proactive healthcare engagement, and mitigate incarceration risks effectively.

Building upon these foundational insights, Chapter 11 will further explore veterans' adaptation strategies to negative life events, emphasizing the role of trauma as a fundamental turning point behavior influencing incarceration pathways. Chapter 11 will provide an in-depth analysis of how traumatic experiences, compounded with other identified turning point behaviors, including self-medication, negative service interactions, and coping strategies, interact to shape veterans' psychosocial trajectories. This forthcoming exploration will deepen our understanding of trauma's critical role in influencing veterans' behaviors and will offer additional insights into targeted interventions for successful reintegration and reduced incarceration vulnerabilities.

References

Abraham, T., Cheney, A. M., & Curran, G. M. (2017). A Bourdieusian analysis of U.S. military culture ground in the mental help-seeking literature. *American Journal of Men's Health, 11*(5), 1358–1365. https://doi.org/10.1177/1557988315596037

Acosta, J. D., Becker, A., Cerully, J. L., Fisher, M. P., Martin, L. T., Vardavas, R., Slaughter, M. E., & Schell, T. L. (2014). *Mental health stigma in the military.* RAND Corporation. https://doi.org/10.7249/RR426

Ahern, J., Worthen, M., Masters, J., Lippman, S. A., Ozer, E. J., & Moos, R. (2015). The challenges of Afghanistan and Iraq veterans' transition from military to civilian life and approaches to reconnection. *PLoS ONE, 10*(7), e0128599. https://doi.org/10.1371/journal.pone.0128599

Armstrong, K., Rose, A., Peters, N., Long, J. A., McMurphy, S., & Shea, J. A. (2006). Distrust of the health care system and self-reported health in the United States. *Journal of General Internal Medicine*, *21*(4), 292–297. https://doi.org/10.1111/j.1525-1497.2006.00396.x

Betancourt, J. R., Green, A. R., Carrillo, J. E., & Ananeh-Firempong, O. II. (2003). Defining cultural competence: A practical framework for addressing racial/ethnic disparities in health and health care. *Public Health Reports*, *118*(4), 293–302. https://doi.org/10.1093/phr/118.4.293

Bray, R. M., & Hourani, L. L. (2007). Substance use trends among active duty military personnel: Findings from the United States Department of Defense Health Related Behavior Surveys, 1980–2005. *Addiction*, *102*(7), 1092–1101. https://doi.org/10.1111/j.1360-0443.2007.01841.x

Burnett-Zeigler, I., Ilgen, M., Valenstein, M., Zivin, K., Gorman, L., Blow, A., Duffy, S., & Chermack, S. (2011). Prevalence and correlates of alcohol misuse among returning Afghanistan and Iraq veterans. *Addictive Behaviors*, *36*(8), 801–806. https://doi.org/10.1016/j.addbeh.2010.12.032

Collins, P. H. (2019). *Intersectionality as critical social theory*. Duke University Press.

Demers, A. (2011). When veterans return: The role of community in reintegration. *Journal of Loss and Trauma*, *16*(2), 160–179. https://doi.org/10.1080/15325024.2010.519281

Elder, G. H., Jr. (1998). The life course as developmental theory. *Child Development, 69*(1), 1–12. https://doi.org/10.1111/j.1467-8624.1998.tb06128.x

Finlay, A. K., Owens, M. D., Taylor, E., Nash, A., Capdarest-Arest, N., Rosenthal, J., Blue-Howells, J., Clark, S., & Timko, C. (2019). A scoping review of military veterans involved in the criminal justice system and their health and healthcare. *Health & Justice*, *7*(1), 6. https://doi.org/10.1186/s40352-019-0086-9

Harding, S. (2004). *The feminist standpoint theory reader: Intellectual and political controversies*. Routledge.

Harris, K. M., & Edlund, M. J. (2005). Self-medication of mental health problems: New evidence from a national survey. *Health Services Research, 40*(1), 117–134. https://doi.org/10.1111/j.1475-6773.2005.00345.x

Heward, C., Li, W., Chun Tie, Y., & Waterworth, P. (2024). A scoping review of military culture, military identity, and mental health outcomes in military personnel. *Military Medicine, 189*(11–12), e2382–e2393. https://doi.org/10.1093/milmed/usae276

Keene, D. E., Rosenberg, A., Schlesinger, P., Guo, M., & Blankenship, K. M. (2018). Navigating limited and uncertain access to subsidized housing after prison. *Housing Policy Debate*, *28*(2), 199–214. https://doi.org/10.1080/10511482.2017.1336638

Khantzian, E. J. (1997). The self-medication hypothesis of substance use disorders: A reconsideration and recent applications. *Harvard Review of Psychiatry*, *4*(5), 231–244. https://doi.org/10.3109/10673229709030550

Leeies, M., Pagura, J., Sareen, J., & Bolton, J. M. (2010). The use of alcohol and drugs to self-medicate symptoms of posttraumatic stress disorder. *Depression and Anxiety*, *27*(8), 731–736. https://doi.org/10.1002/da.20677

LePage, J. P., & Garcia-Rea, E. A. (2012). Lifestyle coaching's effect on 6-month follow-up in recently homeless substance dependent veterans: A randomized study. *Psychiatric Rehabilitation Journal, 35*(5), 396–402. https://doi.org/10.1037/h0094500

Leung, L. B., Rubenstein, L. V., Jaske, E., Taylor, L., Post, E. P., Nelson, K. M., & Rosland, A. M. (2022). Association of integrated mental health services with physical health quality among VA primary care patients. *Journal of General Internal Medicine*, *37*(13), 3331–3337. https://doi.org/10.1007/s11606-021-07287-2

Moledina, A., Magwood, O., Agbata, E., Hung, J. H., Saad, A., Thavorn, K., & Pottie, K. (2021). A comprehensive review of prioritized interventions to improve the health and wellbeing of persons with lived experience of homelessness. *Campbell Systematic Reviews, 17*(2), e1154. https://doi.org/10.1002/cl2.1154

Pietrzak, R. H., Johnson, D. C., Goldstein, M. B., Malley, J. C., & Southwick, S. M. (2009). Psychological resilience and postdeployment social support protect against traumatic stress and depressive symptoms in soldiers returning from Operations Enduring Freedom and Iraqi Freedom. *Depression and Anxiety*, *26*(8), 745–751. https://doi.org/10.1002/da.20558

Russell, R. T. (2009). Veterans treatment court: A proactive approach. *New England Journal of Criminal and Civil Confinement*, *35*(2), 357–372.

Sampson, R., & Laub, J. (1993). *Crime in the making: Pathways and turning points through life*. Harvard University Press.

Solomon, P. (2004). Peer support/peer provided services underlying processes, benefits, and critical ingredients. *Psychiatric Rehabilitation Journal*, *27*(4), 392–401. https://doi.org/10.2975/27.2004.392.401

Tanielian, T., & Jaycox, L. H. (Eds.). (2008). *Invisible wounds of war: Psychological and cognitive injuries, their consequences, and services to assist recovery*. RAND Corporation. www.rand.org/pubs/monographs/MG720.html

Timko, C., Hoggatt, K. J., Wu, F. M., Tjemsland, A., Cucciare, M., Rubin, A., & Simpson, T. L. (2017). Substance use disorder treatment services for women in the Veterans Health Administration. *Women's Health Issues*, *27*(6), 639–645. https://doi.org/10.1016/j.whi.2017.04.001

Tsai, J., & Rosenheck, R. A. (2015). Risk factors for homelessness among U.S. veterans. *Epidemiologic Reviews*, *37*(1), 177–195. https://doi.org/10.1093/epirev/mxu004

World Health Organization. (2024). *Self-care for health and well-being*. www.who.int/news-room/fact-sheets/detail/self-care-health-interventions

Zinzow, H. M., Britt, T. W., Pury, C. L., Raymond, M. A., McFadden, A. C., & Burnette, C. M. (2013). Barriers and facilitators of mental health treatment seeking among active-duty army personnel. *Military Psychology*, *25*(5), 514–535. https://doi.org/10.1037/mil0000015

11

NEGATIVE LIFE EVENTS AS INCARCERATION TURNING POINTS

Introduction and Conceptualization of Negative Life Events as Incarceration Turning Points

Key life experiences leave a lasting mark on an individual's mental, emotional, and social well-being, fundamentally affecting how they behave, cope, and ultimately live their lives. The cumulative impact of familial bereavement, relationship failures, financial struggles, combat trauma, and difficult reintegration into civilian life significantly affects veterans, potentially influencing their encounters with the legal system. The nuanced paths leading some veterans to prison can be understood by exploring important life events, their impact, and veterans' adaptive strategies. This chapter investigates veteran adaptation to and influence by significant life hardships, revealing individual and systemic factors.

The impact of negative life events on veterans can be analyzed in the context of their wider social, economic, and institutional circumstances. Qualitative stories are especially valuable because they reveal how personal resilience, support systems, and societal contexts uniquely affect each veteran. Through detailed, firsthand accounts, veterans articulate how key life events impact their sense of identity, psychological resilience, and ability to navigate transitions effectively. These narratives provide critical insights into how veterans understand, interpret, and respond to significant adversity, contributing depth and context beyond quantitative analyses alone.

Studies show that overcoming significant adversity is not a solitary process, but is intertwined with broader social and community networks (Rafferty et al., 2020). The helpfulness or hindrance of social relationships, community, and institutions strongly influences veterans' capacity for adaptation. Social

DOI: 10.4324/9781003522300-11

connections, as depicted in this chapter's qualitative narratives, can protect veterans from negative consequences or intensify their difficulties. The importance of supportive relationships and communities in successfully adapting to significant life challenges is underscored by these qualitative insights.

Examining veterans' stories reveals how their military experiences, relationships with family, and community connections intertwine to either strengthen or weaken their ability to cope. Qualitative research offers valuable insights into veterans' experiences with adversity, emotional responses, and utilization of support resources (Reid et al., 2024). Veterans' lived experiences offer essential perspectives absent from purely quantitative studies, showing pathways to incarceration and informing the design of culturally sensitive and targeted interventions. This chapter examines veteran adaptation to significant life difficulties, highlighting the link between personal journeys and societal impact. Ultimately, recognizing and addressing these interconnected life events and adaptations is essential for effectively supporting veterans' successful reintegration into civilian society and reducing vulnerabilities to adverse outcomes.

The Impact of Death and Grief on Veteran Pathways

Grief and significant personal losses profoundly impact individuals facing major life transitions, shaping their emotional health, coping mechanisms, and behavioral outcomes. For veterans, losing close loved ones is not merely an emotional setback; it serves as a critical turning point, deeply influencing their long-term emotional stability and decision-making processes. Veterans who subsequently experienced incarceration identified these moments of grief and loss as critical junctures that significantly influenced their trajectories toward behaviors associated with criminal justice involvement. When directly asked about the role that family loss and grief played in their paths toward incarceration, veterans explicitly connected their experiences of emotional exhaustion and instability to subsequent risky decisions. They described how overwhelming grief diminished their ability to maintain clear judgment and increased impulsive decision-making, which heightened their engagement in activities leading to legal troubles.

Veterans consistently describe the profound disruptions that accompany significant personal losses. One veteran articulated the immediate emotional impact clearly: "I couldn't function man, my mother's death … it really affected me." Candid statements reveal how grief undermines veterans' basic daily functioning and emotional equilibrium, creating vulnerabilities that disrupt their coping mechanisms and interpersonal relationships. These disruptions can lead veterans to seek immediate and accessible coping methods, frequently involving substance use, which in turn elevates their risk for encounters with law enforcement and subsequent incarceration. Veterans explicitly noted that persistent emotional distress resulting from significant personal losses directly impacted their decision-making capacities. Emotional turmoil associated with unresolved grief often led to impaired judgment, increased reliance on substances, and decreased ability to navigate stressful situations, thus creating conditions ripe for behaviors linked to incarceration.

Compounding losses further amplify emotional instability and social isolation among veterans. One veteran described experiencing multiple consecutive family deaths, underscoring the severe cumulative emotional burden: "My mom died … my husband died, same year … my sister died, same year … all of a sudden I was without anybody, without anything." This layered grief intensifies veterans' sense of isolation and loss of social support, severely affecting their emotional stability and their ability to maintain healthy, supportive relationships. Isolation resulting from compounded losses frequently propels veterans toward harmful coping strategies, including reliance on substances or behaviors that ultimately increase their vulnerability to criminal justice involvement. Veterans described grief as a pivotal emotional event that reshaped their coping strategies, pushing them toward substance use and social withdrawal. These coping mechanisms, initially adopted to manage profound emotional pain and isolation, progressively isolated them further from supportive social networks and institutional resources, thereby significantly increasing their vulnerability to legal problems and eventual incarceration.

Traumatic experiences associated with grief can also trigger or exacerbate underlying mental health challenges, further complicating veterans' coping processes. A veteran vividly detailed the lasting psychological effects of traumatic losses: "My friend died in my arms, in the back of my uncle's house … My other friend got stabbed … I had some hard times man." Another veteran explicitly connected their substance use to grief, noting, "When my mother died and you know somebody close I drink sometimes to numb the effect." Firsthand accounts underscore how grief-related trauma drives veterans toward substance use as a deliberate coping mechanism. While initially employed to manage immediate emotional distress, these behaviors often lead to long-term negative consequences, including substance dependence and incarceration. Several veterans highlighted that the emotional fatigue and diminished coping capabilities stemming from unresolved family losses and grief directly influenced their risk assessment and decision-making. They explained how their compromised emotional states and increased impulsivity led them to decisions and behaviors they recognized in hindsight as pathways toward criminal justice involvement.

Kaplow et al. (2013) research on grief shows how it impacts reintegration by weakening crucial social connections and undermining emotional resilience. The diminished social support and heightened emotional distress that accompany unresolved grief notably increase veterans' susceptibility to behaviors and choices linked with incarceration. Additionally, unresolved grief can significantly strain familial relationships, which often provide critical emotional and social stability during transitional periods. A veteran illustrated the disruptive impact of compounded familial losses clearly: "My mom died Christmas Eve … My dad died six months later on his birthday … I'm like great, Mom six months ago and now dad." Relational instability deepens veterans' emotional distress and isolation, increasing their likelihood of turning toward harmful coping behaviors that heighten their risk of involvement with the criminal justice system.

Furthermore, the traumatic context in which some losses occur further complicates veterans' emotional recovery. One veteran described the lasting emotional toll of witnessing traumatic deaths firsthand: "I had people die in my arms … He had an aneurysm … My other friend got stabbed … I had a friend got electrocuted." The intensity and prolonged nature of traumatic experiences can significantly impair veterans' emotional processing, leading to prolonged grief and trauma responses. These conditions exacerbate emotional dysregulation, further influencing behaviors associated with heightened incarceration risk, including substance misuse and social disengagement.

To help veterans through grief and loss, we need specifically designed, trauma-informed support. Veteran-focused grief counseling combined with mental health and substance use treatment, and strong peer support can help mitigate the negative effects of grief. Robust support systems acknowledging and addressing veterans' trauma can significantly reduce harmful coping mechanisms, incarceration rates, and promote better long-term health. Losses do not occur in isolation but interact deeply with veterans' existing vulnerabilities, life histories, and social contexts. Underlying mental health issues may worsen due to grief, reducing coping skills and increasing the risk of unhealthy coping methods like substance misuse. Understanding these interconnected effects is crucial to giving grieving veterans effective, focused help, building emotional strength, and encouraging healthy coping skills to reduce incarceration risks.

Marital Breakdown and Its Role in Veterans' Pathways to Incarceration

Marital and relationship breakdowns profoundly shape veterans' emotional well-being and influence critical decision-making processes, significantly affecting their life trajectories post-service. For veterans, relationships serve as foundational sources of emotional stability and social support; thus, their disruption can lead to considerable psychological strain. Veterans who subsequently experienced incarceration frequently identified relationship dissolution, such as divorce, separation, or interpersonal conflicts, as critical turning points that contributed substantially to their vulnerability and risk behaviors associated with incarceration.

Veterans pointed to relational disruptions as intensifying existing emotional distress and amplified psychological instability, significantly influencing their coping mechanisms. One participant described the direct emotional impact clearly: "Basically, the reason why I'm all messed up is because I'm heartbroken over my ex-wife, I still love her … I just couldn't deal with it … since then, I've been hospitalized like five other times." This narrative highlights the immediate and ongoing emotional turmoil caused by relationship breakdowns, which disrupt veterans' emotional equilibrium and push them toward increased reliance on substance misuse or withdrawal from formal support systems.

The interplay between marital distress and personal psychological challenges, including mental health disorders or substance misuse, may exacerbate veterans' vulnerabilities. Another veteran shared, "I was going through a marriage that was like on the down spin … She was kind of tired of my behavior, and I was tired of my behavior also … So that contributed to me just doing what I did." This insight underscores how relationship breakdown can create conditions that foster negative coping behaviors and impair decision-making processes, ultimately increasing the likelihood of engaging in activities that lead toward legal consequences.

Substance abuse emerges prominently as both a coping response and contributing factor in the narratives veterans provided about marital dissolution. One veteran explicitly connected their addiction issues to the deterioration of their marriage, noting: "I just went through a divorce … When I hurt her and went through this divorce … It just opened my eyes really to the person that I really respected … My addiction made me treat her the way I treated her … Which wasn't right." Self-reflection reveals how relational instability and substance use mutually reinforce one another, creating conditions that push veterans further into risk behaviors associated with incarceration.

Veterans' cultural and identity expectations, deeply influenced by their military training, compound the emotional and psychological impact of relationship dissolution. Another veteran expressed profound disappointment, stating, "I always thought I would be happily married and never be divorced … I don't want to be divorced … She cheated on me … I just have really deep feelings for her." This internal conflict between ingrained expectations of relational stability and harsh realities amplifies emotional distress, further compromising veterans' coping capabilities and increasing susceptibility to behaviors leading to criminal justice interactions.

Relational breakdowns also serve as pivotal moments of crisis, intensifying emotional turmoil and propelling veterans toward behaviors that heighten their risk of incarceration. A veteran clearly described this turning point: "I finally hit a bottom when me and my wife separated." This realization illustrates how critical relationship events not only influence immediate emotional responses but also profoundly shape veterans' longer-term trajectories, often setting the stage for increased vulnerability to maladaptive behaviors and subsequent legal complications.

Veterans explicitly connected relationship dissolution to increased substance use, demonstrating how coping strategies adopted during relational crises significantly contribute to their incarceration risks. One participant explained, "After my divorce I started drinking." Another recounted a similar escalation, linking marital instability directly to substance use and legal issues: "My vows didn't last long after my second DUI ... got chaptered out of the military ... I was going to have a dead-end job anyway ... might as well drink was my rationale." These statements clearly indicate how relational instability directly fosters conditions conducive to substance misuse, thereby heightening risks of incarceration.

The compounded emotional burden arising from relationship disruptions combined with other significant life events, which include family loss, further exacerbates veterans' vulnerabilities. One veteran described the overwhelming emotional strain clearly: "After I caught my ex-wife cheating, it was during that whole week of my mother's death ... I just snapped ... had a mental breakdown." Interconnected emotional crises can severely impair veterans' emotional resilience, leading them to adopt risky coping behaviors that ultimately increase their vulnerability to criminal justice involvement.

Scholarship has demonstrated a link between marital breakdowns, heightened psychological distress, increased substance misuse, and involvement in behaviors leading to incarceration (Wang et al., 2015). Structured relationship support programs, emphasizing culturally sensitive counseling and practical coping strategies, can effectively mitigate these risks and promote emotional resilience, relational stability, and successful community reintegration (Fogle et al., 2020). Recognizing and addressing the profound impact of marital and relationship dissolution on veterans' emotional stability and behavior provides essential pathways for reducing their vulnerability to incarceration, enhancing their coping capacities, and supporting long-term psychosocial well-being.

Economic Instability and Symbolic Loss

Economic stability fundamentally influences veterans' emotional resilience, psychological health, and successful integration into civilian society. However, veterans frequently encounter significant financial instability upon transitioning from military service, posing serious challenges to their psychosocial stability and adaptive coping capabilities. Economic hardship often intersects with substantial symbolic losses (e.g., loss of property, personal possessions, and valued memorabilia) intensifying emotional distress and reinforcing behaviors linked to incarceration risks.

Veterans consistently identified economic disruptions as critical turning points shaping their emotional and behavioral responses. One veteran vividly described the severe disruption of economic stability: "I had a 30-acre farm … lost it … ended up living under a bridge." This significant financial setback not only jeopardized basic living conditions but also deeply impacted the veteran's sense of self-worth and emotional security. Profound economic loss creates feelings of isolation, hopelessness, and diminished control, significantly elevating the risk of adopting harmful coping behaviors, including substance use or illegal activities, which subsequently heightens incarceration vulnerability. From an identity theory perspective, such losses undermine the structured sense of purpose and competence established during military service (Joseph et al., 2023). The inability to maintain economic stability challenges veterans' self-concept as capable and self-reliant, leading to identity dissonance that can trigger high-risk coping mechanisms. Life course research underscores that these moments function as negative turning points, redirecting trajectories toward instability and, potentially, justice involvement. While previous studies have linked poverty to recidivism, few have examined how veterans interpret financial collapse as a direct violation of their military-shaped identity, making this a critical contribution to the literature.

This account reflects more than the loss of shelter or income. It illustrates how a dramatic shift from stability to deprivation can erode the identity veterans develop through service. Military life reinforces expectations of order, role clarity, and reliability of resources; when these expectations collapse, the dissonance can make civilian environments feel unpredictable and unsafe. As explored in earlier chapters, the timing of such events during transition periods can intensify their destabilizing effects, redirecting veterans toward coping strategies that may feel self-preserving in the moment but heighten long-term legal risk. We asked veterans how they interpret these moments as a violation of the self-concept forged in service to understand incarceration pathways.

Symbolic losses, involving emotionally significant items connected to veterans' identities and personal histories, amplify these financial hardships. Veterans articulated the powerful emotional toll of losing personal artifacts tied to their military identity. One veteran recounted, "I lost all my military records, all my medals, my dad's flag … I lost a lot in a five-year period … I just kept pushing them down [emotions]." The emotional burden of symbolic loss intensifies veterans' psychological vulnerability and can lead to maladaptive coping mechanisms, including substance abuse and isolation. When veterans are unable to effectively manage this emotional burden through formal support systems, their reliance on unhealthy coping strategies significantly increases their risks for behaviors leading toward incarceration.

Symbolic items such as medals, flags, and service records carry meaning far beyond their physical presence. They anchor veterans' sense of continuity between their service and civilian lives. Losing these items can feel like a rupture in personal history and serve as proof and recognition of their contributions. Earlier discussion on identity underscores that when these tangible affirmations are gone, veterans may feel less grounded in their place within civilian society. This can fuel withdrawal from formal supports, not because of indifference, but because those systems are perceived as unable to protect what matters most. Such meaning-making is rarely visible in large-scale studies but is central to understanding veterans' post-service decision-making.

Standpoint theory helps explain why the loss of military records, medals, and family heirlooms is experienced not just as property loss but as the erasure of status, history, and belonging. These items function as tangible affirmations of service and sacrifice; losing them disrupts veterans' narrative continuity and sense of legitimacy in civilian life. Such symbolic losses are largely invisible in quantitative research, yet qualitative accounts reveal their role as catalysts for disengagement from institutional supports. By making these meanings explicit, the present findings expand the understanding of non-material factors in incarceration pathways.

Incarceration experiences further exacerbate economic hardship by stripping veterans of critical personal belongings and economic resources. One veteran clearly linked the loss of property due to incarceration with profound emotional destabilization: "I'm arrested, so my truck was towed, all my belongings gone … So when I got out it was like I had nothing." These direct experiences underline how economic instability, coupled with institutional encounters, severely disrupt veterans' capacity to regain stability, prompting continued engagement in behaviors that elevate their incarceration risk. This account also highlights how justice system contact itself can deepen structural disadvantage. From a life course perspective, the arrest not only marked a formal turning point but also accelerated cumulative disadvantage by removing critical resources and disrupting routines. For veterans, the effect is magnified by the sudden loss of both mobility and possessions, which undermines their perceived agency. The absence of institutional safeguards to protect personal property during incarceration reflects a policy gap that can exacerbate reentry challenges.

Encounters with the justice system that result in the loss of property can further entrench instability by stripping away resources necessary for reintegration. For veterans, the effect is compounded by the military-conditioned value placed on self-sufficiency and preparedness. Having little to nothing on release can feel like a personal and institutional failure. The absence of protective measures to safeguard possessions during incarceration reflects a structural gap in reentry planning, one that disproportionately impacts those already navigating the challenges of transition from service.

Economic challenges intertwined with identity crises arising from transitions to civilian life further complicate veterans' coping strategies. Veterans accustomed to structured military environments often find themselves unprepared for economic self-management in civilian contexts, leading to psychological distress and substance reliance as coping strategies. One veteran described this clearly: "Once I EAS'd [End of Active Service] I didn't know what to do ... That was my, that was the only life that I knew ... I didn't know how to do anything else ... So I picked up the bottle ... That's when that started." This narrative underscores how economic instability during the critical transition period significantly contributes to ongoing substance misuse, deepening the cycle of vulnerability and increasing the likelihood of interactions with the criminal justice system. The transition from a structured military environment to unstructured civilian life is a classic identity rupture, particularly when coupled with economic strain. Veterans' accounts here demonstrate how the absence of clear expectations, role clarity, and stable income undermines the behavioral self-regulation learned in service. This aligns with theories of role exit, where the loss of a valued identity without a viable replacement increases vulnerability to maladaptive behaviors. The finding reinforces the importance of early, identity-informed interventions during the separation process.

The above veteran's words highlight the challenge of role exit without adequate role replacement. Military life provides a defined purpose, clear routines, and recognition; when these are removed without a viable civilian counterpart, the resulting void can lead to coping through substance use. This is not simply about personal choice, but about navigating a loss of structure and identity at a time when financial instability makes recovery even more difficult. Addressing this dynamic requires interventions that preserve or recreate aspects of structure and purpose during transition.

Economic hardship increases veterans' susceptibility to mental health conditions, substance misuse, and legal difficulties, exacerbating their overall psychosocial vulnerabilities (Shue et al., 2021). Symbolic losses further amplify emotional distress, complicating veterans' adaptation to civilian life and increasing their reliance on maladaptive coping behaviors (Heward, 2024). Veterans' economic and symbolic losses require comprehensive intervention strategies explicitly tailored to their unique experiences. Effective interventions include targeted employment programs that leverage military-acquired skills, robust financial counseling services, and structured economic support mechanisms. Implementing these tailored programs significantly reduces financial stress, enhances emotional stability, and fosters successful reintegration. Institutional approaches must also emphasize the preservation or respectful replacement of symbolic items, integrating emotional validation with practical support, thus significantly reducing veterans' reliance on maladaptive coping behaviors associated with increased incarceration risks.

Efforts to address the profound impacts of economic and symbolic losses on veterans' psychosocial stability and coping strategies are essential. By providing comprehensive and culturally responsive economic and emotional support systems, policymakers, healthcare providers, and social service professionals can meaningfully reduce veterans' vulnerabilities, enhancing their prospects for successful long-term reintegration and reducing their likelihood of incarceration.

Recognition and validation of the profound emotional significance of symbolic losses are essential. Programs that facilitate the preservation, recovery, or respectful replacement of personal memorabilia can significantly support veterans' emotional processing and recovery. Integrating emotional support with practical assistance in managing symbolic losses can mitigate emotional distress, enhancing veterans' adaptive coping mechanisms and emotional resilience.

Supporting the economic and symbolic dimensions of veterans' post-service experiences, policymakers, healthcare providers, and social service professionals can significantly improve veterans' emotional stability, adaptive coping capacities, and successful reintegration outcomes. Recognizing the interconnected nature of economic stability, symbolic meaning, and psychological well-being provides essential insights for effectively reducing veterans' vulnerabilities and enhancing their overall life outcomes.

Compound Traumas and Overlapping Adversities

The interplay of multiple adverse life events significantly influences veterans' psychological and emotional stability by creating cumulative burdens that amplify each other's effects. Individual experiences (e.g., marital dissolution or economic distress) may independently cause substantial distress; however, when multiple adversities overlap or occur in quick succession, they compound by intensifying emotional turmoil beyond the sum of each event individually. This compounding effect complicates veterans' coping mechanisms, potentially impairing emotional regulation and rational decision-making, thereby increasing their susceptibility to involvement in the criminal justice system.

Complex emotional distress arises when veterans experience multiple concurrent or successive negative life events. Unlike isolated incidents, compounded adversities involve relational losses, traumatic incidents, familial disruptions, and parental conflicts occurring simultaneously or rapidly following one another. These adversities magnify each other's emotional impact, intensifying psychological burdens. One participant described the amplified emotional toll resulting from simultaneous relational and familial disruption, noting, "Not seeing my son, he was getting older, I missed out when he was turning into a teenager … I missed out on him growing up." Narratives illustrate how the combination of disrupted family relationships with other stressors heightens feelings of isolation, regret, and emotional vulnerability, undermining protective social and emotional resources. These experiences can be understood as compounded losses, where multiple domains of life (e.g., family, emotional connection, and social support) are simultaneously destabilized. The clustering of adverse events intensifies their impact, not merely through additive stress but by limiting the capacity to recover from any single loss. For veterans, whose identity is often anchored in loyalty, duty, and maintaining bonds, family separation represents both an emotional and moral injury, further eroding resilience. Relationships with family members often hold symbolic weight as evidence of stability and personal responsibility. Losing contact during formative periods in a child's life can evoke a sense of moral injury, or a belief that they have failed to meet obligations central to their identity. This deepens the emotional toll of family separation and can reinforce disengagement from prosocial roles and networks, increasing vulnerability to justice involvement.

Veterans also highlighted acute traumatic events occurring alongside broader emotional and relational difficulties, significantly compounding their psychological distress. A particularly striking account highlighted the emotional complexity surrounding a traumatic event involving an ex-spouse's overdose: "My ex-wife overdosed on Xanax … foam was coming out of her mouth when she was laying down … I was holding her baby, her son, not mine … It was really a traumatic event." This personal experience demonstrates how a traumatic event combines with relationship stressors (e.g., carrying the responsibility of someone else's child), which compound pressures. From a standpoint perspective, such events are interpreted not only as personal crises but as moments that test veterans' ingrained sense of responsibility and protective roles. The inability to prevent harm or stabilize the situation can create profound dissonance with their self-image as capable protectors, leading to guilt and self-blame. This description illustrates the weight of dual responsibilities during a crisis: managing an acute trauma while simultaneously caring for a dependent in a non-parental role. For veterans, who are trained to respond decisively in emergencies, such moments can heighten feelings of helplessness when outcomes are beyond their control. This dissonance between expectation and reality can intensify stress responses and contribute to long-term emotional strain. Research on civilian trauma may seek to further explore these identity-specific dynamics, underscoring the need for veteran-centered qualitative research to inform trauma-informed reentry support.

The emotional impact of multiple simultaneous traumatic experiences becomes particularly evident in narratives involving significant personal loss and difficult decisions. One veteran recounted the severe psychological burden associated with a family crisis: "They had me pull the life support … I had to sign the paper because I'm the oldest … I thought I killed my mother for pulling the life support … I didn't cry or nothing, I just was in a … numb, I was numb." This example highlights that compounded emotional experiences (loss, responsibility, and guilt) do not merely add up; they amplify one another, creating overwhelming emotional strain. Amplified emotional overload can severely impair emotional processing and effective coping strategies, pushing veterans toward behaviors with long-term negative outcomes, including criminal activities. The layering of grief, perceived responsibility, and irreversible decision-making can destabilize even those with strong coping frameworks. Veterans' service experience often reinforces a belief in the importance of protecting life and maintaining control in critical moments. When the outcome conflicts with these deeply held values, the emotional impact can be enduring, shaping self-perception and influencing future choices.

Overlapping adversities involving domestic instability and relational disruption further amplify veterans' vulnerabilities. Domestic violence and relational abandonment often intersect, intensifying psychological distress beyond their individual impacts. One participant explicitly described this amplified adversity: "I was a single mother … I had a very, very bad also experience though with domestic violence … It was just horrible." The coexistence of relational instability, violence, and single parenthood generates compounded psychological distress, isolation, and emotional exhaustion that is multiplicatively greater than any single adversity. This amplified emotional burden can severely impair decision-making and coping abilities, increasing veterans' likelihood of criminal involvement.

Similarly, compounded familial disruptions and parental conflicts experienced during formative years have a lasting, amplifying impact into adulthood. Participants consistently highlighted familial conflicts and parental decisions that drastically intensified their emotional vulnerability: "My mother had an affair … She moved to Alaska with the man … She left me … I was angry." Compounded familial adversities significantly disrupt emotional stability and familial support systems, intensifying residual anger, resentment, and feelings of abandonment. These heightened emotions not only impair immediate emotional well-being but also exacerbate long-term coping difficulties, significantly heightening the risk of behaviors associated with criminal justice involvement. Experiences of abandonment in formative years can interact with later service experiences, creating complex emotional legacies. The trust and interdependence cultivated in military units may contrast sharply with early-life instability, making betrayals or perceived rejections in civilian life especially difficult to navigate. This context can help explain why some veterans respond to relational stress with withdrawal or high-risk behaviors.

Adversities are strongly correlated with intensified mental health struggles, maladaptive coping behaviors, and increased vulnerability to negative outcomes. Rafferty et al. (2020) specifically underscore how veterans' compounded life adversities significantly elevate risks for psychological distress, emotional instability, and maladaptive coping strategies. These compounded adversities often lead to chronic emotional challenges, heightened stress responses, and increased susceptibility to involvement with the criminal justice system. Notably, compound traumatic experiences can create profound psychological effects that extend well beyond singular traumatic incidents. Cumulative trauma exposure is consistently associated with increased symptoms of PTSD, depression, anxiety, and substance use disorders, significantly complicating individuals' psychological stability and adaptation processes (Center for Substance Abuse Treatment, 2014). Veterans who experience multiple overlapping adversities report greater difficulties in emotional regulation, relationship stability, and occupational functioning, indicating that compound adversity significantly influences their broader psychosocial outcomes.

The interaction of relational instability, personal loss, and trauma creates a uniquely challenging emotional environment for veterans. Relational and emotional adversities impacted how our veterans decided to cope with adversity, often choosing substance misuse and social withdrawal as a way to manage distress (Kirkham et al., 2025). These behaviors further isolate veterans from supportive social networks and increase their risk of involvement with the criminal justice system.

Shining a light on the cumulative nature of veterans' overlapping adversities provides essential guidance for effective intervention strategies. Comprehensive interventions must explicitly address these compounded challenges, recognizing their interconnected emotional, relational, and psychological impacts. Integrated intervention approaches that include trauma-informed care, comprehensive mental health support, family counseling, and community-based social integration are essential. Targeted support designed to address overlapping adversities directly mitigates veterans' emotional burdens, enhancing their resilience, coping capacity, and overall reintegration success. By explicitly recognizing the cumulative impact of compounded adversities through qualitative insights, targeted interventions can more effectively support veterans' emotional stability, psychological well-being, and successful community reintegration. Comprehensive strategies addressing multiple overlapping adversities offer substantial promise for reducing veterans' vulnerabilities to negative coping behaviors and adverse outcomes, providing meaningful pathways for emotional recovery, relational stability, and overall psychosocial resilience.

The Impact of Military Discharge and Associated Life Challenges

Leaving the military is a life-changing moment for veterans, altering their identity, role, and how others see them. Post-service life for veterans varies drastically depending on their discharge type (honorable, general, or dishonorable), affecting access to vital resources, social support, and economic opportunities. Veteran's post-discharge well-being is shaped by their discharge conditions, impacting their reintegration into civilian life and potentially increasing their risk of negative outcomes with criminal justice system (Reid et al., 2024).

Separation from military service presents substantial challenges to one's sense of self. The shift from military to civilian life often leaves veterans with intense feelings of loss, uncertainty, and emotional distress. Difficulties with self-perception and social integration can arise from a change in identity, thus intensifying pre-existing emotional sensitivities. New studies highlight the frequent identity crises among transitioning veterans, marked by low self-esteem and uncertainty about their place in society after leaving the military (Kleykamp et al., 2021). This disruption to deeply held military roles and responsibilities results in disorientation, negatively affecting emotional health and coping abilities. As shown, our veterans described how major life events were key turning points toward incarceration.

The combination of these challenges may worsen anxiety, depression, and trauma-related disorders. Veterans lacking sufficient institutional support and mental healthcare during their transition are especially prone to emotional decline. Post-discharge reintegration stress increases mental health risks and the adoption of drug usage and social withdrawal (Brooks Holliday & Pedersen 2017). These coping mechanisms hinder veterans' successful reintegration, leading to more interactions with law enforcement.

Social isolation following discharge, particularly when associated with stigmatized or dishonorable conditions, further exacerbates veterans' emotional and psychological distress. Veterans' feelings of alienation and social exclusion are tied to discharge-related stigma. These experiences shape their willingness and capacity to engage with social support networks or community-based resources, reinforcing isolation and compounding vulnerability (McGuffin et al., 2021). To work on the challenges associated with military discharge suggests a multifaceted, culturally sensitive approach. Comprehensive discharge planning, inclusive policies, and tailored transitional programs specifically addressing veterans' distinct post-discharge challenges are essential. Improving access to healthcare, providing effective employment transition programs, and offering dedicated social and psychological support can significantly mitigate the adverse impacts of discharge-related transitions. There is a place for holistic interventions that consider the broader social context, foster community awareness, reduce stigma, and promote supportive networks to facilitate veterans' successful reintegration and emotional well-being.

The implications of military discharge extend well beyond the administrative or procedural event, deeply influencing veterans' psychosocial trajectories and life outcomes. Recognizing and effectively addressing these interconnected challenges through comprehensive policy and targeted interventions provides critical opportunities to enhance veterans' resilience, stability, and successful integration into civilian life, ultimately reducing their vulnerability to negative coping strategies and involvement with the criminal justice system.

Practical and Policy Recommendations

Based on the qualitative insights detailed in Chapter 11 regarding veterans' adaptations to negative life events and their associated risks for incarceration, several focused practical and policy recommendations emerge. These recommendations aim to address the unique and compounded challenges identified through veterans' narratives and are intended to enhance existing support frameworks with innovative and targeted interventions.

Implementing Comprehensive Grief and Loss Counseling Programs

Given the profound emotional toll associated with losses of family members or close friends, specialized grief and loss counseling tailored explicitly for veterans should be developed. These programs should incorporate culturally informed therapeutic interventions to address compounded grief experiences effectively. Offering individualized counseling as well as group sessions can help veterans process their grief constructively, mitigating associated emotional distress and reducing reliance on substance misuse. Recent research underscores the efficacy of targeted grief interventions in reducing prolonged emotional distress and improving veterans' psychological outcomes following significant losses (Kaplow et al., 2013).

Enhancing Family Support Through Relational Stability Initiatives

Veterans in Chapter 11 repeatedly highlighted the critical role familial relationships play in their post-service stability. Policies should facilitate and expand access to relational counseling programs that specifically address the needs of veterans and their families. These initiatives could include family education, communication skill development, and strategies for managing relational stress during reintegration. Strengthening familial support structures has been consistently shown to significantly reduce isolation, emotional distress, and associated negative coping strategies among transitioning veterans (Creech, Hadley, & Borsari, 2014). Policymakers should allocate resources to expand these specialized family support programs, integrating them into broader veteran healthcare and social services frameworks.

Economic Stabilization through Targeted Financial and Employment Support

Economic instability and the symbolic loss of personal assets significantly increase veterans' vulnerability to negative outcomes. Therefore, comprehensive economic stabilization programs should be established, incorporating financial counseling, employment transition assistance, and targeted economic incentives for employers who hire veterans. Policy measures should include job-training initiatives specifically designed to translate military-acquired skills into civilian employment, enhancing veterans' economic security and reducing financial-related stressors. Integrated employment and economic stability interventions substantially improve veterans' mental health outcomes, decrease reliance on maladaptive behaviors, and reduce criminal justice system interactions (Shue et al., 2021).

Comprehensive Transition Programs Addressing Military Discharge Conditions

Given the influence military discharge conditions exert on veterans' reintegration, policies must address the unique challenges faced by veterans discharged under conditions other than honorable. Legislative changes should be enacted to expand eligibility for essential services, including mental health care, housing assistance, and employment programs, regardless of discharge status. Specialized transition support programs must include dedicated psychological and economic resources explicitly addressing the stigma and barriers faced by veterans discharged under less favorable conditions. Recent research confirms that expanding service eligibility and providing tailored transition support significantly mitigates adverse psychological outcomes and enhances successful reintegration among affected veterans (Reid et al., 2024).

Expanding Community Integration and Veteran-specific Social Networks

Finally, building robust community integration frameworks and supportive veteran-specific social networks is critical. Policies should promote and fund community initiatives that facilitate meaningful veteran participation and connection, including veteran-specific community centers, mentorship programs, and volunteer opportunities that validate and utilize veterans' unique skills and experiences. By fostering robust, community-based social connections, initiatives enhance veterans' social integration, emotional resilience, and psychological stability, directly mitigating risks associated with social isolation and maladaptive coping behaviors (Chinchilla et al., 2019). By implementing these targeted, evidence-based policies and practical strategies, stakeholders can effectively address veterans' cumulative vulnerabilities, enhancing their successful reintegration and significantly reducing their susceptibility to incarceration and related adverse outcomes.

References

Brooks Holliday, S., & Pedersen, E. R. (2017). The association between discharge status, mental health, and substance misuse among young adult veterans. *Psychiatry Research, 256*, 428–434. https://doi.org/10.1016/j.psychres.2017.07.011

Center for Substance Abuse Treatment. (2014). *Trauma-informed care in behavioral health services* (Treatment Improvement Protocol [TIP] Series No. 57). Substance Abuse and Mental Health Services Administration. www.ncbi.nlm.nih.gov/books/NBK207191/

Chinchilla, M., Gabrielian, S., Hellemann, G., Glasmeier, A., & Green, M. (2019). Determinants of community integration among formerly homeless veterans who received supportive housing. *Frontiers in Psychiatry, 10*, 472. https://doi.org/10.3389/fpsyt.2019.00472

Creech, S. K., Hadley, W., & Borsari, B. (2014). The impact of military deployment and reintegration on children and parenting: A systematic review. *Professional Psychology: Research and Practice, 45*(6), 452–464. https://doi.org/10.1037/a0035055

Fogle, B. M., Tsai, J., Mota, N., Harpaz-Rotem, I., Krystal, J. H., Southwick, S. M., & Pietrzak, R. H. (2020). The National Health and Resilience in Veterans Study: A narrative review and future directions. *Frontiers in Psychiatry, 11*, Article 538218. https://doi.org/10.3389/fpsyt.2020.538218

Heward, C., Li, W., Chun Tie, Y., & Waterworth, P. (2024). A scoping review of military culture, military identity, and mental health outcomes in military personnel. *Military Medicine, 189*(11–12), e2382–e2393. https://doi.org/10.1093/milmed/usae276

Joseph, J. S., Smith-MacDonald, L., Filice, M. C., & Smith, M. S. (2023). Reculturation: A new perspective on military-civilian transition stress. *Military Psychology, 35*(3), 193–203. https://doi.org/10.1080/08995605.2022.2094175

Kaplow, J. B., Layne, C. M., Saltzman, W. R., Cozza, S. J., & Pynoos, R. S. (2013). Using multidimensional grief theory to explore the effects of deployment, reintegration, and death on military youth and families. *Clinical Child and Family Psychology Review, 16*(3), 322–340. https://doi.org/10.1007/s10567-013-0143-1

Kirkham, R., Liu, C., Wulundari, T., Aidman, E., Yucel, M., Wiley, J., & Albertella, L. (2025). Emotion regulation and coping in active military personnel: A systematic review. *Stress and Health, 41*(3), e70036. https://doi.org/10.1002/smi.70036

Kleykamp, M., Montgomery, S., Pang, A., & Schrader, K. (2021). Military identity and planning for the transition out of the military. *Military Psychology, 33*(6), 372–391. https://doi.org/10.1080/08995605.2021.1962176

McGuffin, J. J., Riggs, S. A., Raiche, E. M., & Romero, D. H. (2021). Military and veteran help- seeking behaviors: Role of mental health stigma and leadership. *Military Psychology, 33*(5), 332–340. https://doi.org/10.1080/08995605.2021.1962181

Rafferty, L. A., Wessely, S., Stevelink, S. A. M., & Greenberg, N. (2020). The journey to professional mental health support: A qualitative exploration of the barriers and facilitators impacting military veterans' engagement with mental health treatment. *European Journal of Psychotraumatology, 10*(1), Article 1700613. https://doi.org/10.1080/20008198.2019.1700613

Reid, T., & Sims, K. M. (2024). (Dis)honorably discharged: Identifying policy gaps in military civilian reintegration. *Health Affairs Scholar, 2*(2). https://doi.org/10.1093/haschl/qxae021

Shue, S., Matthias, M. S., Watson, D. P., Miller, K. K., & Munk, N. (2021). The career transition experiences of military veterans: A qualitative study. *Military Psychology, 33*(6), 359–371. https://doi.org/10.1080/08995605.2021.1962175

Wang, L., Seelig, A., Wadsworth, S. M., McMaster, H., Alcaraz, J. E., & Crum-Cianflone, N. F. (2015). Associations of military divorce with mental, behavioral, and physical health outcomes. *BMC Psychiatry, 15*, Article 128. https://doi.org/10.1186/s12888-015-0517-7

12

VETERAN IDENTITY, INCARCERATION PATHWAYS, AND IMPLICATIONS FOR POLICY, PRACTICE, AND EVALUATION

Reframing Pathways Through a Veteran Standpoint

The preceding chapters have shown that understanding veteran incarceration pathways benefits from drawing on multiple, complementary forms of evidence. This book contributes to that broader knowledge base by bringing veteran perspectives and identity frameworks into direct conversation with established theories and empirical patterns. Veteran identity, which is rooted in the structured norms, values, and expectations of military life, interacts in complex ways with postservice experiences, personal circumstances, and institutional settings (Heward et al., 2024; Lancaster & Hart, 2015).

The life course perspective reminds us that these encounters are rarely discrete, one-time events; instead, they are connected turning points that unfold over time, where timing, sequence, and individual interpretation shape longer trajectories (Elder, 1998; Sampson & Laub, 1993). The qualitative approach in this study complements existing large-scale and administrative data by providing insight into how veterans interpret events, how these interpretations influence subsequent decisions, and how identity informs responses to opportunities and challenges. In this way, the findings add depth and nuance to the broader field, supporting both theoretical development and practical program design.

Interpreting Turning Points Through a Veteran Identity Lens

Findings from Chapters 8 through 11 demonstrate how veterans interpret and make sense of the experiences that shape their reintegration. These accounts extend beyond a simple catalog of circumstances. These stories preserve

DOI: 10.4324/9781003522300-12

meanings veterans attach to pivotal moments and how those meanings inform decisions, coping strategies, and relationships with institutions. Viewed through the lens of veteran identity, these turning points are not merely chronological markers. These junctures are where identity, personal history, and situational context converge to shape pathways toward incarceration.

For many participants, the period following military service was marked by forms of dislocation that directly challenged their sense of self. Homelessness, unemployment, or the loss of military-connected possessions were not experienced as isolated hardships, but as fundamental disruptions to a self-concept built on stability, competence, and contribution. As discussed in Chapter 4, veteran identity is not fixed; it is continually renegotiated in response to shifting roles, changing relationships, and encounters with institutions (Joseph et al., 2023; Tajfel & Turner, 1979). When postservice life failed to provide spaces where that identity could be affirmed or valued, trust in civilian systems eroded. In these circumstances, self-reliance was a strength in military contexts but also became a strategy for maintaining agency that could manifest in choices carrying legal risk, such as avoiding formal support systems or turning to informal, and sometimes unlawful, means of meeting basic needs.

Some veterans described cascading challenges that compounded the strain of transition. The life course perspective (Elder, 1998; Sampson & Laub, 2010) offers a framework for understanding why challenges that occur in quick succession (e.g., bereavement coinciding with relationship breakdown, or economic hardship coupled with untreated injury) can intensify vulnerability and narrow perceived options. Participants often explained these collisions in terms that revealed the emotional and cognitive shifts they triggered: a sense that viable paths forward had closed, leading to coping strategies like substance use or withdrawal from social supports. These accounts highlight not only the sequence of stressors but also the interpretive lens veterans applied. This helps us see these events as signals of diminished control and belonging, which in turn shaped their willingness or ability to engage with stabilizing resources.

For others, the most decisive turning points were crossroads created by interactions with institutions. Engagements with healthcare providers, housing agencies, or benefits systems were described as moments that could either reinforce a veteran's sense of dignity and belonging or confirm feelings of alienation. Where veterans encountered respectful treatment, acknowledgment of their military background, and opportunities for shared decision-making, they tended to remain engaged and saw these institutions as viable partners in their postservice lives. Conversely, experiences marked by indifference, bureaucratic barriers, or a lack of cultural understanding deepened mistrust and sometimes prompted complete disengagement. As the interviews made clear, these were not simply administrative exchanges; they functioned as tests of whether institutions could be trusted to uphold the values and mutual accountability veterans associated with their service (Koenig et al., 2014; Meyer & Wynn, 2018).

The link between these turning points and pathways toward incarceration becomes clearer when veteran identity is considered as the interpretive anchor. Veterans frequently contrasted the structure, discipline, and predictability of military life with the perceived instability, ambiguous norms, and absence of collective accountability in civilian contexts. For instance, a participant's description of remaining in a living situation where drug use was prevalent, despite recognizing its risks, reflected both a lack of alternative structured environments and the absence of the clear behavioral boundaries they were accustomed to in service. Another veteran's account of reconnecting with peers engaged in criminal activity illustrated the pull of familiarity and camaraderie in contexts where structured, prosocial peer networks were unavailable. In these cases, identity-driven expectations for order, mutual responsibility, and predictable consequences were unmet, increasing the likelihood of choices that carried legal repercussions.

Taken together, these narratives underscore that veteran identity is not simply a background characteristic, but an active interpretive framework through which experiences are understood and acted upon. The turning points described in Chapters 8 through 11 suggest how identity-based expectations, which are shaped by structured routines, mutual accountability, and clearly defined roles in military service, profoundly influence veterans' appraisals of civilian contexts. The life course perspective helps situate these moments within broader trajectories, showing how the timing, sequence, and accumulation of events can either reinforce or destabilize the alignment between a veteran's self-concept and the environments they inhabit (Elder, 1998; Sampson & Laub, 2010). Standpoint theory further clarifies that these interpretations are not interchangeable with those of non-veterans; they are grounded in a distinct social position that carries its own norms, values, and criteria for trust and legitimacy (Harding, 2004; Smith, 1987).

This theoretical framing reveals that incarceration pathways for veterans cannot be fully understood through structural or situational variables alone. Decisions at key junctures, whether to seek help, disengage from services, or associate with certain peers, are filtered through identity-informed perceptions of order, fairness, and belonging. When civilian institutions fail to meet these expectations, the resulting dissonance can amplify withdrawal, heighten reliance on self-managed coping strategies, and increase exposure to risky or unlawful activities. Conversely, when environments and relationships affirm veteran identity, they can anchor stability and support positive adaptations. Recognizing this interpretive process is crucial for designing interventions that move beyond generic risk reduction to actively engage with veterans' own frameworks of meaning. Such an approach not only strengthens theoretical accounts of turning points and life trajectories but also offers a new basis for targeted, identity-informed policy and practice.

Why Veteran Voice Matters in Understanding Pathways

The qualitative interview approach used in this study was intended to complement quantitative and administrative data, offering additional layers of understanding. While large-scale datasets can describe broad patterns in unemployment and justice involvement, they cannot fully capture how veterans themselves interpret these experiences, or how such interpretations influence their next steps. Veterans in this study often reframed common "risk factors" in terms of relational or moral expectations. For example, losing a job was described not only as a financial loss but also as a signal that their skills and service were undervalued in civilian society. Similarly, negative medical encounters were interpreted as a lack of recognition for their sacrifices. Standpoint theory (Harding, 2004; Smith, 1987) helps position these narratives as situated knowledge, offering insights that enrich and expand existing theoretical models.

Listening to veterans' reasoning in their own words provides more understanding of decision-making processes that might appear puzzling from an outside perspective. By situating those decisions within the context of military conditioning and postservice realities, practitioners and policymakers can better align interventions with veterans' own frameworks of meaning, making such efforts more relevant and sustainable.

From Identity Theory to Practice: The Bridge to Program Design

Linking these findings back to the theoretical foundations in Chapters 4 and 5 underscores the value of aligning interventions with identity-informed expectations and life course positioning. Resilience, structure, and self-reliance are core aspects of veteran identity. They can serve as powerful protective resources in some contexts while unintentionally creating barriers to help-seeking in others (Lancaster & Hart, 2015; Currier et al., 2017). The same discipline and independence that foster adaptability in high-pressure environments can, in postservice life, contribute to reluctance in accessing support, particularly if services are perceived as undermining autonomy or competence.

Translating these insights into program design requires more than simply offering services; it involves creating conditions in which veterans can engage without feeling that their core identity is compromised. Programs that are perceived as paternalistic, overly directive, or disconnected from military culture risk reinforcing disengagement. In contrast, supports that invite active participation, draw on veterans' leadership abilities, and recognize the value of their lived experience can transform service use from an act of dependency into one of agency and contribution. Peer-led models are a strong example of this alignment: they provide relational credibility, cultural understanding, and an opportunity for veterans to see themselves not only as recipients of aid but as partners in shaping outcomes (Chinman et al., 2010).

The life course perspective adds an additional layer by emphasizing timing and trajectory. Interventions are most effective when they occur at moments of openness to change, before cycles of avoidance, mistrust, or maladaptive coping have become entrenched. The findings in Chapters 8 through 11 suggest several possible early indicators: subtle social withdrawal, visible frustration with bureaucratic processes, or the compounding of stressors such as housing instability and health challenges. Programs that are attuned to these signals can respond proactively, offering supports before veterans reach a crisis point.

In practical terms, bridging identity theory and life course principles means designing interventions that are both culturally congruent and timely. This may involve embedding services in familiar or trusted spaces, integrating veteran voices into program governance, and ensuring that pathways into assistance are flexible enough to meet veterans where they are geographically, psychologically, and socially. It also means recognizing that reintegration is not a single event but a dynamic process. Just as identity is renegotiated across different stages of the life course, interventions must be adaptable, able to shift focus as veterans' needs, priorities, and self-perceptions evolve.

When programs align with veterans' identity-based values and respond to the rhythms of their life trajectories, they are more likely to foster trust, sustain engagement, and ultimately support lasting reintegration outcomes. In this way, theoretical insights into identity and life course development are not abstract; rather, they are practical tools for shaping supports that veterans recognize as relevant, respectful, and worth embracing.

Veterans' stories throughout this book reveal how postservice experiences are interpreted through the values, expectations, and sense of order formed in military service. Across economic instability, symbolic loss, compounded traumas, and institutional encounters, these are not simply stories of hardship. They are stories of identity, belonging, and the struggle to preserve a sense of self in changing and often unsupportive environments. Earlier chapters explored how the timing of events, the accumulation of challenges, and the vantage point shaped by service experiences influence the choices veterans make, the supports they engage with or avoid, and the paths they follow over time. By centering veteran stories, this book shows that incarceration and reintegration cannot be fully understood without considering the meanings veterans attach to the events in their lives. This understanding points to the importance of policies and programs that address not only external challenges, but also the ways veterans make sense of and respond to them.

Why the Nature of the Data Matters

Quantitative data from recent large-scale studies continue to deepen our understanding of veterans' incarceration risks. A meta-analysis of 79 samples representing over 1.2 million veterans found that among those with any criminal-legal involvement, approximately 80% reported a mental health condition, 70% a substance use disorder, and 40% experienced homelessness (Edwards et al., 2025). In a recent scoping review, researchers documented elevated rates of housing instability, unemployment, suicide, and overdose among justice-involved veterans, while also noting gaps in representation across sociodemographic groups (Singh et al., 2024).

While such quantitative work is invaluable for mapping prevalence and identifying broad risk factors, including mental health diagnoses, substance use histories, and socioeconomic instability, reliance on quantitative data alone carries inherent limitations. Wide-ranging risk factors, when not grounded in the lived experiences of veterans themselves, can miss the nuanced ways these factors operate in context. For veterans, the interpretation of these risk factors is often filtered through military norms and values that shape perceptions of both problems and solutions. Without capturing these interpretive layers, evaluation metrics and program measures risk overlooking the very factors that inform whether an intervention will be perceived as credible, relevant, and worth engaging with at all.

These issues have been recognized in recent scholarship, with researchers calling for greater integration of veterans' lived experiences into both research and program development (Knight et al., 2022; Peppard et al., 2023; St. Cyr et al., 2022). This call reflects not just a desire for narrative richness, but a recognition that standpoint-informed accounts can reveal mechanisms of risk and resilience that aggregate data cannot.

The dataset developed in this study seeks to address these gaps. Guided by both the life course perspective and a veteran standpoint framework, the interviews elicited detailed narratives that contextualize broad risk factors within individual biographies. This approach produced insights that are hard to see in big data. For example, understanding self-medicating not only as a symptom of substance use disorder but as an intentional, if maladaptive, form of self-care makes sense when viewed through the lens of veteran identity. The discipline, self-reliance, and problem-solving orientation cultivated in military service can lead some veterans to frame managing symptoms independently as a sign of competence, even when it carries long-term risks. Similarly, unresolved grief can erode emotional resilience and increase vulnerability to justice involvement, particularly when loss disrupts key relationships or symbolic anchors tied to service. In both cases, self-medicating as a form of self-care and grief from the loss of loved ones can diminish emotional resilience and influence later decisions, including those linked to justice involvement. The values and beliefs cultivated in military service can shape how veterans respond to these challenges, sometimes reinforcing a preference to manage difficulties alone. These patterns are important for theoretical refinement because they show how turning points are understood and acted upon within the values, expectations, and social context of military experience.

These analytic insights from a veteran standpoint extend to practice. At the micro level, qualitative accounts revealed behavioral "red flags" identified by veterans themselves, such as social isolation, abrupt disengagement from prescribed psychiatric care, and substitution of licit or illicit substances for prescribed treatments. These signals offer practitioners across disciplines (e.g., from primary care providers to mental health specialists) concrete indicators for early intervention. At the macro level, the findings underscore the need for interventions that are tailored not only to veterans' material needs but also to the ways they define autonomy, competence, and trust.

Speaking of trust, the qualitative research process itself can serve as an important mechanism for building trust between veterans and those conducting the research. Many veterans in this study described feeling overlooked or misunderstood in prior interactions with service providers and institutions. The one-on-one, conversational nature of qualitative interviews offers a counterpoint, providing space for their experiences to be heard without judgment and on their own terms. This kind of respectful, culturally attuned engagement is consistent with prior research showing that trust is a prerequisite for meaningful veteran participation in both healthcare and research settings (Hibler et al., 2023). We suggest that engendering an environment where veterans feel their perspectives are valued models the kind of reciprocal interaction that can lay the groundwork for future service use. In research contexts, this trust-building can improve the quality and authenticity of the data collected; in practice settings, it can open pathways for veterans to re-engage with supports they might otherwise avoid. Viewing qualitative engagement as both a method of inquiry and a potential intervention underscores its value in the broader continuum of veteran-focused work.

Centering veterans' interpretive processes in our dataset serves as a methodological and conceptual bridge between descriptive epidemiology and individualized intervention design. It demonstrates that qualitative research can generate both theoretical advancements and actionable insights. These same insights can also be translated into measurable indicators for evaluating program impact that include tracking reductions in "red flag" behaviors or increases in trust toward service providers. This approach can help ensure that evaluation criteria reflect what matters most to veterans themselves. The following section builds on this foundation, detailing how such evidence can guide program evaluation, design, and assessment for veterans transitioning from incarceration.

Policy: Designing Programs Around Veteran Identity

Effective policy for justice-involved veterans requires more than funding individual programs. It demands system-wide strategies that address where and how veterans encounter the justice system, and how institutions can respond in ways that reflect their identity and lived experience. The following section examines how existing VA and community programs operate, and outlines design principles that policymakers and administrators can use to guide resource allocation, program standards, and equity goals.

Developing programs for such a complicated domain as incarceration can feel overwhelming. The scale of the needs, including reducing homelessness, unemployment, substance use, mental illness, and reincarceration can make efforts seem hopelessness. Though many state and non-profit organizations assist those leaving prison, the VA has been on the forefront in coordinating services for these vulnerable veterans with its Veterans Justice Programs (VJP) (Blue-Howells et al., 2013). The VJP intervenes at two specific time points in veterans' involvement in the criminal justice system, specifically those just entering the system, and those leaving prison. The VJP oversees two programs, focused on veterans involved in the legal system.

The first is Veterans Justice Outreach (VJO) (Finlay et al., 2016; Tsai et al., 2017; US Department of Veterans Affairs, 2025a). There are over 700 veterans justice outreach staff, known as VJO specialists, working closely with veterans treatment courts when veterans are in earlier stages of their involvement in the criminal justice system. These specialists serve as members of the treatment court teams, assessing the veterans' treatment and psychosocial needs, and working to help veterans access VA services.

The second program overseen by the Veterans Justice Programs is the Health Care for Reentry Veterans (HCRV) (VA, 2025b). Staffed in all states, HCRV staff work with prison pre-release veterans providing referrals and connections to VA services including employment, medical, social, and mental health. Veterans enrolled in HCRV services are veterans with the most severe difficulties with high rates of mental illness, substance use and homelessness, then those not using services. Veterans enrolled in services have demonstrated quicker access to healthcare services and higher use of mental health services than veterans not using HCRV services (Hwong et al., 2024).

Veteran identity-informed programming should start with a clear intervention logic (Hyde et al., 2022). Veteran identity can meet friction in civilian systems through unclear processes, perceived indifference, or cultural misunderstandings. These mismatches frequently emerge at life-course turning points (e.g., bereavement, marital dissolution, discharge complications, job loss, health crises) where coping choices such as self-medication or withdrawal can escalate risk for justice involvement. Programs that (a) affirm identity through predictable structure, clear role tasks, and peer credibility, (b) reduce friction with transparent steps and warm handoffs, and (c) buffer turning points with targeted supports, are more likely to prevent escalation. Mapping these elements onto the Sequential Intercept Model (SIM) for veterans clarifies where in the justice continuum (pre-arrest through community supervision) each can be delivered for maximum effect.

Recent evaluations show that Veterans Treatment Courts (VTCs) significantly reduce recidivism and improve outcomes by focusing on veterans' unique needs through coordinated support (Hartley & Baldwin, 2019; Tsai et al., 2017). Similarly, the Postincarceration Engagement (PIE) program, which adds peer support specialists to the VA's HCRV framework, has demonstrated promising results, including higher rates of substance use and mental health treatment engagement, greater housing stability, and notably low re-arrest rates (Hyde et al., 2022). These findings underscore how integrating peer-led, identity-aware strategies into reentry services can enhance program effectiveness for justice-involved veterans.

Practice: Translating Insight into Action

Turning policy concepts into real-world change requires actionable strategies that can be delivered by practitioners in diverse justice, healthcare, and community settings. This section focuses on interventions and tools, such as specialized courts, coordinated discharge planning, housing-first models, and peer-support reentry programs, that translate veteran identity research into direct practice.

Recent evaluations underscore the potential of existing VA and community programs when they integrate identity-responsive features (Hartley & Baldwin, 2019; Finlay et al., 2016). VA's Health Care for Reentry Veterans (HCRV) and Veterans Justice Programs (VJP/VJO) have demonstrated improved linkage to care and coordinated discharge planning, especially when peers are embedded at release. Veterans Treatment Courts continue to show reductions in recidivism, failure-to-appear rates, and probation violations, with recent studies noting greater effects when courts provide integrated treatment navigation and peer mentorship (Hartley & Baldwin, 2019). Housing-first approaches through HUD-VASH and SSVF, combined with identity-attuned case management, are associated with higher housing stability and lower acute-care utilization. Peer-support reentry models, such as PIE program, have been associated with improved linkage to healthcare, greater housing stability, and increased treatment engagement for justice-involved veterans (Hyde et al., 2022).

As seen in our research on turning points, Veterans leaving incarceration face many barriers that are not currently reflected in traditional large-scale databases. It also may not be pragmatic for comprehensive collection of information about all turning points for all veterans involved in reintegration programs as assessments can be time consuming and therefore expensive related to resources needed. As has been demonstrated, active interactive qualitative methods can provide key insights into the complex lives of veterans leaving incarceration and provide information on the overall systems and services they are engaged in. There are several methods where qualitative data collection can be beneficial in the assessment of veterans.

Traditional Test Development

The first way qualitative data can be used is in the creation of traditional testing instruments. For example, programs can develop assessment tools, such as self-report surveys, which can be used to assess the turning points for their importance and relevance for individual veterans (Cecil et al., 2020; Kline, 2005). At the early stages of test development, the domain, or construct, targeted must be defined through the input of experts and the literature. However, though experts and the scientific literature are very informative, without the inclusion of lived experiences in the understanding of the construct, a test risks lacking relevancy to the targeted audience as well as potentially missing important facets. Data presented in this book showed that veterans have unique insights into the processes affecting them and the course of their lives.

Applying Qualitative Insights to Assessment Design

One way to translate qualitative findings on veterans' life-course turning points into practice is to incorporate these insights into existing risk/needs assessments and reentry planning protocols. By systematically including questions on recent losses, changes in health status, and disruptions in housing or employment, practitioners can better identify moments of heightened vulnerability and respond with timely, targeted supports. Prior research emphasizes that such targeted assessment domains can help match veterans to appropriate services earlier in the justice process.

The detailed information can be obtained through flexible interviews that explore the range of veteran experiences. Using the methods presented in earlier chapters, the information obtained will be analyzed and coded into broad components and themes. After understanding the themes, the information obtained through qualitative methods can be incorporated into the actual items. Items can be written that incorporate the language used by issue holders, allowing for more meaningful and natural phrasing. For example, in Chapter 7, a veteran reported "I didn't hang around the good people … I had people using me … I thought they were my friends … Every one of them were drug addicts." This statement provides rich examples of the language used by veterans to describe their feelings and experiences related to poor prosocial networks. These statements can be used to develop questions such as "I hang around good people – true or false" or "I feel people are using me – not true, somewhat true, very true," allowing the exploration of poor prosocial networks as a criminal trajectory; other domains can be explored in the same ways. Once items are created, scale development can then proceed to testing items, assessing psychometric properties, and refining the scale through traditional methods.

Mixed Methods

A second use of qualitative data is as primary evidence in a mixed method design (Noyes et al., 2019). Though a comprehensive description of mixed methods is outside of the scope of this chapter, mixed methods include qualitative and quantitative research questions and designs, collection of both qualitative and quantitative data, and the incorporation of qualitative and quantitative data into the results. Mixed methods approaches are valued for the breadth of topics that can be assessed, the ability to evaluate very complex and/or novel topics, and the comprehensive nature of the data collected.

Mixed methods are an important tool in the development of new programs and interventions. For example, a program may be designed to reduce reincarceration. That program may want to target a specific domain, in the case of our work focusing on mediating or ameliorating the effects of a turning point on criminal trajectories. As an example, let us consider a program working to address the poor prosocial networks that predict criminal behavior. As an early step, interviews with veterans and clinicians would be beneficial to conceptualize the individual and program needs. These interviews with issue holders could focus on precursors to engaging in negative relationships, specific behaviors associated with the negative relationships, how the veterans built more appropriate relationships, and what skills they used to avoid negative relationships. These interviews can help the program determine how to identify at-risk veterans that would benefit from the program. Additionally, the information obtained can create the foundation for a program where the program can improve the skills or resources that have been more tailored to the lived experiences of veterans to avoid or reduce negative interactions.

One example of translating these research insights into a targeted, high-impact intervention is facilitated service connections at the point of release (Hyde et al., 2022). For veterans with substance use disorders or high trauma exposure, the period immediately after release presents heightened risks for relapse, housing instability, and justice re-involvement. Reentry research highlights the importance of facilitated service connections at the point of release, ensuring veterans are immediately linked, in person, to healthcare, housing, and benefit supports. This may include pre-arranged appointments within the first week of release, transportation, benefit reinstatement, and accompaniment by a peer specialist or case manager to early service contacts. While most empirical studies come from broader justice-involved or behavioral health populations, these approaches are consistent with identity-attuned, veteran-focused reentry strategies.

Evaluation: Building for Scale and Lasting Impact

Effective evaluation determines not only whether programs achieve their intended outcomes, but also whether they do so equitably and in alignment with veteran identity and lived experience. This section describes how to measure success beyond recidivism, integrate mixed methods to capture complex outcomes, and apply implementation frameworks to scale and sustain effective approaches.

Mixed methods also create advantages in the domains of program evaluation, specifically but not limited to work with formerly incarcerated veterans. As has been discussed, large databases are important for tracking large easy to categorize variables, providing important information related to the large goals of the program, e.g. housing, employment, reincarceration, etc. Additionally, traditional surveys are rapid and relatively cheap ways to assess preselected domains of interest. However, both levels of data collection are limited as they cannot flexibly identify what makes a program successful or what is needed to improve the program, as they lack the granularity to provide insight into barriers, facilitators, attitudes, and challenges.

Evaluations should extend beyond recidivism and service utilization to capture proximal outcomes tied to veteran identity. Measures can include trust in providers, perceived cultural competence (drawn from VA patient experience surveys), clarity of next steps, time-to-first-kept appointment, adherence to turning-point care pathways, and frequency of peer contact. These indicators are sensitive to change within 60–180 days, offering early feedback on whether a program aligns with veteran expectations. Implementation frameworks can help interpret these findings and guide broader application. The Consolidated Framework for Implementation Research (CFIR) provides a structured way to identify barriers and facilitators to implementation (e.g., organizational culture, leadership engagement, and external policy influences) so that successful elements can be sustained or scaled. The RE-AIM framework (Reach, Effectiveness, Adoption, Implementation, and Maintenance) complements CFIR by focusing on whether programs are reaching the intended population, producing meaningful outcomes, being adopted by sites, implemented as intended, and sustained over time. Together, CFIR and RE-AIM are examples of how evaluation results are not only about whether a program works, but also about how to maintain and replicate it in different settings serving justice-involved veterans (Glasgow et al., 2019).

Results from detailed interviews can guide program managers on progress that is being made and emergent unpredictable issues that arise. These interviews do not have to cover all participants engaged in the program but can be conducted on a relatively small representative sample. This approach minimizes the cost to the program while providing broad valuable, detailed, and actionable information to improve program functioning.

There are limitations related to mixed methods that should be noted. Mixed method approaches, especially related to interviews, are time consuming, even with a small representative sample, so this must be considered; however, the importance of mixed method approaches should be considered when conceptualizing the support for programs. Also, though mixed method approaches are more comprehensive, not every program needs these approaches to be effective. Finally, mixed methods approaches require an additional level of scientific and analytic expertise to successfully accomplish, expertise which may not be available; however, even basic interview information may be useful to program managers.

Ensuring Programs Work for All Veterans

Justice-involved veterans are not a monolith (Eichler, 2021). Program design and evaluation should stratify and adapt services for women veterans, racial and ethnic minority veterans, rural veterans, and those from different service eras. For example, women veterans with MST histories may benefit from gender-specific peer support and trauma-informed housing; rural veterans may require telehealth-enabled reentry planning. Reporting outcomes by subgroup ensures that gains are equitably distributed and helps identify where targeted adjustments are needed.

Equity in program design is not only a matter of fairness but a practical necessity for ensuring effectiveness. Ignoring subgroup-specific needs risks reinforcing disparities, undermining trust, and wasting resources on interventions that fail to resonate with the people they are intended to serve. When tailored approaches are built in from the start, programs better reflect the realities of veterans' lives, leading to higher engagement, improved outcomes, and stronger policy impact.

Overall, the use of mixed methods in a system as complicated as the factors affecting those related to incarceration will allow programs to obtain a more complete understanding. It's inclusion is recommended for expanding the number of programs and their effectiveness. Mixed methods make it possible to identify both what works across populations and what must be adapted for specific groups, which lays the groundwork for more responsive, equitable, and sustainable systems of care.

Conclusion

The Human Dimension

At its heart, this book is about listening. It is about listening in a way that resists quick fixes and easy generalizations. It has meant hearing the voices of veterans whose lives have crossed into the criminal justice system and recognizing in their accounts both the fractures in the institutions meant to serve them and the need for deliberate efforts to help them build and sustain resilience. These voices are not data points alone; they are living narratives that challenge us to see the human stakes behind statistics. They remind us that policies and programs cannot be abstractions crafted from a distance. They must emerge from the realities veterans live every day, from the nuanced ways they navigate identity, loss, and trust. In the language of veterans themselves and in the moments where identity is lost and reclaimed, where trust is broken and painstakingly rebuilt, we find not just testimony, but the raw material from which genuine, lasting change can be shaped.

The Imperative for Action

The findings here point to an urgent truth: a standpoint approach is not an optional add-on or side project, but central to the effectiveness of programs and policies for justice-involved veterans. Veterans' standpoint is the connective tissue between a veteran's lived reality and a system's capacity to respond with relevance and respect. When trust, cultural competence, and clear pathways are embedded into interventions, the results extend far beyond improved individual outcomes; they reverberate through entire systems, making them stronger, more responsive, and more equitable. This is not a small shift; it is a reorientation that requires moving past fragmented service delivery toward a coordinated continuum of care. This continuum bridges the divides between criminal justice, healthcare, housing, employment, and community supports, ensuring that veterans are not left to navigate critical transitions alone. The goal is more than service provision; it is the creation of systems that actively honor the full humanity and dignity of those who have served.

A Shared Responsibility

The challenge, and the opportunity, belongs to all of us, including researchers, practitioners, policymakers, and communities alike. The veterans whose experiences are interwoven through these pages have lived through the consequences of systems that were not always built with them in mind, and in some cases, actively worked against their stability. They have navigated institutions that often failed to understand their needs, compounding the difficulties they already faced. These accounts are not endorsements of past choices, but reminders of the urgency to address the conditions that contribute to justice involvement in the first place. Meeting that urgency requires holding ourselves accountable for the policies we craft, the programs we fund, and the cultures we sustain. It means ensuring that every intervention and reform is worthy of their trust and responsive to the realities they face upon reentry. In doing so, we fulfill more than a policy goal or professional mandate; we take concrete steps toward building a more just, inclusive, and effective system. This is the enduring work the book calls for: not a finished blueprint, but a shared project to which every reader now has a stake.

References

Blue-Howells, J. H., Clark, S. C., van den Berk-Clark, C., & McGuire, J. F. (2013). The U.S. Department of Veterans Affairs Veterans Justice Programs and the sequential intercept model: Case examples in national dissemination of intervention for justice-involved veterans. *Psychological Services, 10*(1), 48–53. https://doi.org/10.1037/a0029652

Cecil, R. R., Robert, A. A., & Daniel, N. A. (2020). *Mastering modern psychological testing: Theory and methods* (2nd ed.). Springer.

Chinman, M., Shoai, R., & Cohen, A. (2010). Using organizational change strategies to guide peer support technician implementation in the Veterans Administration. *Psychiatric Rehabilitation Journal, 33*(4), 269–277. https://doi.org/10.2975/33.4.2010.269.277

Currier, J. M., McDermott, R. C., & McCormick, W. H. (2017). Mental health treatment-related stigma and professional help-seeking among student veterans. *Psychological Services, 14*(4), 531–542. https://doi.org/10.1037/ser0000129

Edwards, E. R., Fortuna, A., Holliday, R., Addison, H., & Tsai, J. (2025). Prevalence of mental health conditions, substance use disorders, suicidal ideation and attempts, and experiences of homelessness among veterans with criminal-legal involvement: A meta-analysis. *Clinical Psychology Review, 115,* 102533. https://doi.org/10.1016/j.cpr.2024.102533

Eichler, M. (2021). Equity in military and veteran research: Why it is essential to integrate an intersectional sex and gender lens. *Journal of Military, Veteran and Family Health, 7*(S1), e20210016. https://doi.org/10.3138/jmvfh-2021-0016

Elder, G. H., Jr. (1998). The life course as developmental theory. *Child Development, 69*(1), 1–12. https://doi.org/10.1111/j.1467-8624.1998.tb06128.x

Finlay, A. K., Smelson, D., Sawh, L., McGuire, J., Rosenthal, J., Blue-Howells, J., Timko, C., Binswanger, I., Frayne, S. M., Blodgett, J. C., Bowe, T., Clark, S. C., & Harris, A. H. S. (2016). U.S. Department of Veterans Affairs Veterans Justice Outreach Program. *Criminal Justice Policy Review, 27*(2), 203–222. https://doi.org/10.1177/0887403414562601

Glasgow, R. E., Harden, S. M., Gaglio, B., Rabin, B., Smith, M. L., Porter, G. C., Ory, M. G., & Estabrooks, P. A. (2019). RE-AIM planning and evaluation framework: Adapting to new science and practice with a 20-year review. *Frontiers in Public Health, 7*, 64. https://doi.org/10.3389/fpubh.2019.00064

Harding, S. (2004). *The feminist standpoint theory reader: Intellectual and political controversies*. Routledge.

Hartley, R. D., & Baldwin, J. M. (2019). Waging war on recidivism among justice-involved veterans: An impact evaluation of a large urban veterans treatment court. *Criminal Justice Policy Review, 30*(1), 52–78. https://doi.org/10.1177/0887403416650490

Heward, C., Li, W., Chun Tie, Y., & Waterworth, P. (2024). A scoping review of military culture, military identity, and mental health outcomes in military personnel. *Military Medicine, 189*(11–12), e2382–e2393. https://doi.org/10.1093/milmed/usae276

Hibler, D., Krause-Parello, C. A., Gliba, B., Morris, J., & Mullins, C. D. (2023). Joining forces with veterans: Veterans' and researchers' perspectives on veteran-centered engagement practices. *Journal of Community Engagement and Scholarship, 15*(2), Article 2. https://doi.org/10.54656/jces.v15i2.463

Hwong, A. R., Barry, L. C., Li, Y., & Byers, A. L. (2024). Comorbidities, healthcare use, and contact with healthcare transition services in older veterans after incarceration. *Journal of the American Geriatrics Society, 72*(6), 1847–1855. https://doi.org/10.1111/jgs.18885

Hyde, J., Byrne, T., Petrakis, B. A., Yakovchenko, V., Kim, B., Fincke, G., Bolton, R., Visher, C., Blue-Howells, J., Drainoni, M-L., & McInnes, D. K. (2022). Enhancing community integration after incarceration: Findings from a prospective study of an intensive peer support intervention for Veterans with historical comparison group. *Health & Justice, 10*(1), 33. https://doi.org/10.1186/s40352-022-00195-5

Joseph, J. S., Smith-MacDonald, L., Filice, M. C., & Smith, M. S. (2023). Reculturation: A new perspective on military-civilian transition stress. *Military Psychology, 35*(3), 193–203. https://doi.org/10.1080/08995605.2022.2094175

Kline, T. J. B. (2005). *Psychological testing: A practical approach to design and evaluation*. SAGE.

Knight, S. J., Haibach, J. P., Hamilton, A. B., Whittle, J., Ono, S. S., Butler, J., Flower, M., Ray, C. D., Pugh, M. J., & Zickmund, S. L. (2022). Veteran engagement in health services research: A conceptual model. *Journal of General Internal Medicine, 37*, 94–98. https://doi.org/10.1007/s11606-021-07309-z

Koenig, C. J., Maguen, S., Monroy, J. D., Mayott, L., & Seal, K. H. (2014). Facilitating culture- centered communication between healthcare providers and veterans transitioning from military deployment to civilian life. *Patient Education and Counseling, 95*(3), 414–420. https://doi.org/10.1016/j.pec.2014.03.016

Lancaster, S. L., & Hart, R. P. (2015). Military identity and psychological functioning: A pilot study. *Military Behavioral Health, 3*(1), 83–87. https://doi.org/10.1080/21635781.2014.995254

Meyer, E. G., & Wynn, G. H. (2018). The importance of US military cultural competence. In L. Roberts & C. Warner (Eds.), *Military and veteran mental health* (pp. 15–33). Springer. https://doi.org/10.1007/978-1-4939-7438-2_2

Noyes, J., Booth, A., Moore, G., Flemming, K., Tunçalp, Ö., & Shakibazadeh, E. (2019). Synthesising quantitative and qualitative evidence to inform guidelines on complex interventions: Clarifying the purposes, designs and outlining some methods. *BMJ Global Health, 4*(Suppl 1), e000893. https://doi.org/10.1136/bmjgh-2018-000893

Peppard, S. W., Burkard, J., Georges, J., & Dye, J. (2023). The lived experience of military women with chronic pain: A phenomenological study. *Military Medicine*. https://doi.org/10.1093/milmed/usac134

Sampson, R., & Laub, J. (1993). *Crime in the making: Pathways and turning points through life*. Harvard University Press.

Sampson, R. J., & Laub, J. H. (2010). A general age-graded theory of crime: Lessons learned and the future of life-course criminology. In A. Piquero & D. Weisburd (Eds.), *Handbook of quantitative criminology* (pp. 165–181). Springer.

Singh, K., Timko, C., Yu, M., Taylor, E., Blue-Howells, J., & Finlay, A. K. (2024). Scoping review of military veterans involved in the criminal legal system and their health and healthcare: 5-year update and map to the Veterans-Sequential Intercept Model. *Health & Justice, 12*(1), 18. https://doi.org/10.1186/s40352-024-00274-9

Smith, D. E. (1987). *The everyday world as problematic: A feminist sociology*. University of Toronto Press.

St. Cyr, K., Liu, J. J. W., Cramm, H., Nazarov, A., Hunt, R., Forchuk, C., Deda, E., & Richardson, J. D. (2022). "You can't un-ring the bell": A mixed methods approach to understanding veteran and family perspectives of recovery from military-related posttraumatic stress disorder. *BMC Psychiatry, 22*(37). https://doi.org/10.1186/s12888-021-03622-3

Tajfel, H., & Turner, J. C. (1979). An integrative theory of intergroup conflict. In W. G. Austin & S. Worchel (Eds.), *The social psychology of intergroup relations* (pp. 33–47). Brooks/Cole.

Tsai, J., Flatley, B., Kasprow, W. J., Clark, S., & Finlay, A. (2017). Diversion of veterans with criminal justice involvement to treatment courts: Participant characteristics and outcomes. *Psychiatric Services, 68*(4), 375–383. https://doi.org/10.1176/appi.ps.201600233

U.S. Department of Veterans Affairs. (2025a). Veterans Justice Outreach program. www.va.gov/HOMELESS/VJO.asp

U.S. Department of Veterans Affairs. (2025b). Health care for re-entry veterans services and resources. www.va.gov/homeless/reentry.asp

INDEX

Note: Page numbers in **bold** refers to Tables.

For Product Safety Concerns and Information please contact our EU representative GPSR@taylorandfrancis.com
Taylor & Francis Verlag GmbH, Kaufingerstraße 24, 80331 München, Germany

www.ingramcontent.com/pod-product-compliance
Ingram Content Group UK Ltd.
Pitfield, Milton Keynes, MK11 3LW, UK
UKHW022353190926
475702UK00015B/2267

* 9 7 8 1 0 3 2 8 6 3 0 4 7 *